D1328309

CHSP
HUNGARIAN STUDIES SERIES
NO. 4

EDITORS
Peter Pastor
Ivan Sanders

THE WAR CRIMES TRIAL OF HUNGARIAN PRIME MINISTER LÁSZLÓ BÁRDOSSY

Pál Pritz

Translated from the Hungarian
by *Thomas J. DeKornfeld* and
Helen D. Hiltabidle

Social Science Monographs, Boulder, Colorado

 Center for Hungarian Studies and Publications, Inc.
Wayne, New Jersey

Distributed by Columbia University Press, New York

2004

EAST EUROPEAN MONOGRAPHS
NO. DCLI

Originally published as *A Bárdossy-per*
© 2001 by Pál Pritz
© 2001 by Kossuth Kiadó

© 2004 by Pál Pritz
© 2004 by the Center for Hungarian Studies and
      Publications, Inc.
      47 Cecilia Drive, Wayne, New Jersey 07470–4649
      E-mail: pastorp@mail.montclair.edu

The printing of this book was made possible through a
grant from the Ministry of National Cultural Heritage,
National Cultural Fund of Hungary

NEMZETI KULTURÁLIS ÖRÖKSÉG
MINISZTÉRIUMA

The translation from the Hungarian original was supported
by a grant from the Hungarian Academy of Sciences

Library of Congress Control Number 2004112562
ISBN 0–88033–549–1

Printed in the United States of America

TABLE OF CONTENTS

THE LIFE AND TIMES OF
LÁSZLÓ BÁRDOSSY

THE DOCUMENTS

THE LIFE AND TIMES
OF LÁSZLÓ BÁRDOSSY

PROLOGUE

At the end of June 1945 Mátyás Rákosi went to Moscow for consultation, instructions and political discussions. While there, he lectured on the situation in Hungary at the Department of International Information (OMI) of the Central Committee of the Soviet Communist Party. The department head, Georgi Dimitrov, asked a number of questions. He queried his guest as to why no people's tribunals were established for the conviction of the so called fascists.

"The fascist leaders have all escaped," replied Rákosi. "Not a single fascist minister or secretary of state remained in Hungary....The most prominent fascists are in British or American captivity and they are in no hurry to extradite them." Dimitrov was not satisfied with this explanation and added that it was readily understandable that the British and the Americans were in no hurry but that it was incomprehensible why this was not the central theme of the Hungarian media and of Hungarian political discourse.

Rákosi did not accept the criticism.

I refer to this in every one of my speeches and the Communist Party publications constantly write about it. If we had some of the fascist leaders in our hands we would start a trial but all we have is Arrow Crossist small fry. Trying them would have no effect and all the leaders are gone. When I read,

he added,

that in Bulgaria every minister was captured I was envious and said how that country could be so very lucky. In Hungary they are all gone. We hope that the fascist leaders will be extradited and then we will arrange for the trials. This is extremely important since otherwise the people will forget what these men have done.[1]

The Hungarian political and military leaders captured in the West were finally returned to Hungary on October 3, 1945. *Szabad Nép*, the Communist Party newspaper informed its readership on October 16 that Dr. Ferenc Fenesi, the public prosecutor and Dr. Sándor Szalai, a journalist and lay prosecutor have prepared the indictment in the case of former Prime Minister László Bárdossy and that the trial had been scheduled for October 29.[2]

The death sentence was handed down on November 2. A few days later, the writer Gyula Illyés queried Lajos Zilahy, one of the most prominent Hungarian writers between the two World Wars, a member of the upper middle class and a former friend of Prime Ministers Gyula Gömbös and László Bárdossy. "What do you think about him now?" Zilahy replied, "Nothing, he is insane!"

According to Illyés's diary, he then added somewhat apologetically, "I have argued with him whole nights through. He pointed to the large tree in front of the house and said that this is the tree from which he would hang."

"Will he be hanged," asked Illyés. "When?"

"It would be best for him if it were done immediately," answered Zilahy and then added, "He will be extradited to the Americans and then he will again be returned. He may have to wait for his death for at least three months."[3]

As far as the extradition was concerned Zilahy was in error but as far as the hanging was concerned he was right. Bárdossy's fate had been decided while the fate of the other former Hungarian prime minister, Béla Imrédy, was still in doubt. In Imrédy's case Dezső Sulyok was the public prosecutor. When after the trial, and in complete privacy, Gyula Illyés asked him, "Is it death?" Sulyok answered, "Yes, but he will not be executed." "Why?," asked Illyés. "We must hand him over to the Americans," came the laconic answer.[4]

- - -

Who was László Bárdossy, how did they make him into a "fascist," why did he have to die more urgently than the real fascist Béla Imrédy, and how was the still controversial trial conducted? These are the questions that we will endeavor to answer objectively and calmly.

HIS CAREER

László Bárdossy was born in Szombathely on December 10, 1890, into a gentry-civil servant family. His father, Jenő Bárdossy, was a Ministerial Councilor and his mother was Gizella Zarka de Felsőőr. He completed his secondary education in Eperjes (Prešov) and Budapest and thus became familiar with some of the historic areas of Hungary. He studied law in Budapest, Berlin and Paris and, in addition to German and French, also learned English. His knowledge of languages and his very sharp mind soon raised him above his contemporaries. It is said that when he was taking an oral exam, his classmates passed the word, "Laci Bárdossy is being tested. Let us go and listen." His characteristic features were idealism, a highly moral perspective, a devotion to beauty and a strong preoccupation with esthetics. It is hardly an accident that the young graduate started his career in 1913 in the Ministry of Culture. It was in the ministry that he learned about the contemporary Hungarian governmental administration, its mentality and techniques.

He made very slow progress on the ministerial ladder. He started as an assistant clerk and in 1918 he was still only an assistant secretary. Hungarian history had progressed to the era of the counter revolution when he was promoted to the rank of ministerial secretary in 1921. This was still a low ranking and poorly paid position. Yet during these years he had been active and successful, having been for a period commissioner of education for Pest County.

The only truly positive feature of these years was national independence but even this was a dubious distinction for a crippled and internationally largely isolated country, whose societal developments were almost completely stifled. One of the requirements of the new situation was that an independent Ministry of Foreign Affairs had to be created. This work was begun by the liberal democratic revolution, in the fall of 1918, but the bulk of the work was really undertaken in 1921, after major political upheavals and principally in order to establish Hungarian diplomatic representations abroad.

The possibility of employing the officials of the former joint Austrian-Hungarian diplomatic service who were Hungarian citizens, was a given for the new ministry. There were so many of them that they could have filled every position in the new diplomatic service. Yet the contemporary Hungarian public opinion viewed these old Ballhaus Platz representatives with a jaundiced eye and already in 1918 there were strong voices advising against entrusting the management of the new Hungarian foreign policy affairs to this otherwise fully competent group of officials.

There was, therefore, a strong inclination among the leaders of the ministry to recruit competent, multilingual officials from other ministries. László Bárdossy was one of these. It helped him to get a position at the Dísz tér, where Hungarian foreign policy was conducted between the two wars, that he had been active in the preparations for the peace treaty.

Bárdossy made the following statement to the American officer who was interrogating him on September 9, 1945,

> The leading principles of Hungarian policies were established well before the World War II, and with the complete support of the vast majority of the Parliament and the population. In the light of these principles it was the evident moral and political obligation of every Hungarian government to make every effort and take every opportunity to recover the territories that were taken away at the end of World War I. This was a national obligation that was accepted and recognized by the entire Hungarian constitutional system. This obligation, stated openly and clearly, was assumed not only on behalf of the population of the crippled country but also on behalf of the Hungarians who were forced to live beyond the arbitrarily established boundaries.[5]

Bárdossy assumed his new position on February 18, 1922, and was assigned to the Press Division where he was appointed deputy chief. In 1926 he was promoted to ministerial chief of section and soon thereafter he became the chief of the Press Division. On March 1, 1930, he was sent to the Hungarian Legation in London as councilor, which meant that in the absence of the minister he was in charge of the legation.

It was not a particularly elevating experience to participate in the direction of Hungarian media policies in those days. The prestige of the country was at its lowest point vis-à-vis the rest of Europe and the well-known circumstances under which the counterrevolution came into being caused great displeasure abroad. This was further aggravated by hostile propaganda. The national point of view and social progress were mutually almost exclusive and this was another reason why Hungary was in such a very difficult situation in trying to battle the hostile propaganda of the Allied Powers and the even more pernicious propaganda of the Little Entente.

There were two reasons for these difficulties. Hungarian propaganda included many outdated elements and it was not appreciated that harping only on the Hungarian injuries was hardly sufficient to gain devoted supporters for the Hungarian revisionist goals. During this entire period the nation was unable to confront the true causes for the collapse of historic Hungary and it was not realized until the 1930s, and not even fully then, that the borders of pre-1918 Hungary could never again be reconstituted.

The second reason was the lack of adequate funds. The sums devoted to media propaganda were a fraction of the sums devoted for the same purpose by the Little Entente countries.

Bárdossy served at the London legation until the fall of 1934 and on October 24 he was appointed Hungarian minister in Bucharest. His expertise and diplomatic abilities were well recognized in the United Kingdom. This is shown by the following story. In 1933, 168 members of the British Parliament formed a group supporting the Hungarian revisionist goals and at the same time Count István Bethlen was on a lecture tour in Britain trying to gain popular support for Hungary. This triggered a response from the Little Entente countries and, on November 29, the ministers of Czechoslovakia, Romania and Yugoslavia went to Foreign Secretary Sir John Simon to protest. Through an indiscretion this became known and Bárdossy, who at that time was in charge of the Hungarian Legation, demanded an

explanation. The Foreign Office official who saw him gave an eva-
sive answer and his superiors were engaged in formulating the official response. The affair was put before the administrative head of the
Foreign Office and Permanent Deputy of the Foreign Secretary
Robert Vansittart, who could hardly be accused of being friendly
toward Hungary. Vansittart said, "Tell him [Bárdossy] as little as possible. He has a very good feel for things and is smart enough to ask
the right questions."[6]

PÁL TELEKI AND
LÁSZLÓ BÁRDOSSY

István Csáky died on January 28, 1941, and Bárdossy was appointed the very next day to succeed him as minister of foreign affairs. Pál Teleki was generally inclined to postpone things but when he was convinced about something, he could act rapidly and decisively. He had known László Bárdossy for a long time and knew that he was a sound Hungarian gentleman. He had heard much about his cultural proclivities and his brilliant mind. The years in London and Bárdossy's activities in Bucharest also counted heavily in his favor. Bárdossy's family relationship to the late Prime Minister Gyula Gömbös did not bother Teleki since he knew that Bárdossy did not harbor any tendencies toward political extremism. He had heard that Bárdossy was unhappy about the social conditions of the country and was talking about criminal culpability, but this also did not distress Teleki since he shared these same sentiments but also realized how hard it was to institute changes under such difficult circumstances.

Teleki had to reach a decision quickly since it was evident to him that the Germans were not at all indifferent about the person who served as Hungarian minister of foreign affairs and that in exchange for their dominant role in making territorial awards they wished to interfere increasingly into Hungarian domestic matters. He recalled with great regret that in November of 1940 he was forced under increasing German pressure to padlock the Polish Legation in Budapest.[7] The matter left a bad taste in his mouth particularly because he had hoped that the London diplomats would understand his reasons and realize that he had kept the legation open for fourteen months after the collapse of Poland. This is not what happened. The British minister in Budapest conveyed an expression of his government's displeasure on December

5, and spoke threateningly of the future of British-Hungarian relations.[8] Consequently, Teleki wished to produce a fait accompli and was therefore very pleased with the minister in Bucharest accepting the offer.

Hostile London

On February 7, 1941, Bárdossy received a report from György Barcza, the Hungarian minister in London, describing a conversation he had with Sir Anthony Eden, the British foreign secretary.[9] Bárdossy had disliked Barcza for a long time, considered him to be officious and read his reports with considerable reservations. He knew that, contrary to the majority of the British political elite, Eden was hostile toward Hungary and hence he was inclined to minimize the significance of Barcza's report. He did remember, however, Teleki's admonition and therefore he reread the report very carefully and in detail.

According to the report, the British foreign secretary viewed Great Britain's relationship with Hungary based on the conviction that Britain would defeat Germany. Eden conceded that Hungary was under very heavy pressure but immediately added that Hungary's position was compromised by its revisionist demands and indicated that these demands were a significant component in making the situation even more difficult. After the war, Britain would assess the previous condition of Hungary and would examine not only her accommodation with Germany but also her endeavors for independent initiative. Among the latter Eden included Hungary's joining the Anglophobe Tripartite Pact, the strongly pro-German tone of the Hungarian press and radio and the permission granted to Germany to transport troops across Hungary to Romania.[10]

Bárdossy became infuriated and decided not to respond to the Barcza report. He thought that if Barcza exaggerated, there was no need for an answer. If the report was accurate, there was also no need for an answer since the report reflected a hostile attitude toward Hungary that could not be overcome. Five days later, the minister cabled again reporting that Great Britain had severed diplomatic relations with Romania because of the large number of German troops stationed there.[11]

Bárdossy realized only too well that this action would cast a shadow over Hungary as well and immediately sent instructions to Barcza.[12] The envoy must emphasize that the transit of German troops was authorized by the Hungarian government on the urgent request of the non-belligerent Romania. Barcza was also to point out that for a long period of time the British government had not objected to the presence of German troops in Romania and Bárdossy considered this to be a covert criticism of the British action. The minister in London was also to state that the permit for the troop transit was given only to avoid much more serious and dangerous actions.[13]

- - -

During the ensuing weeks there was no easing of Hungarian-British tensions. The principal reason for this was that German troops became ever more strongly entrenched in Romania and this further strengthened Hitler's international position while, at the same time, weakening the British position.[14] This was at the heart of the issue and not the ups and downs of British-Romanian relations. They knew very well in London that German-Romanian relations were controlled from Berlin and that the Axis-arbitrated Second Vienna Award which divided Transylvania, was very unfavorable to Britain's former ally. Even though the current situation did not justify it, Britain was prepared to preserve its former attitude which favored Bucharest and opposed Budapest.

On March 12, Bárdossy sat at his desk and drafted detailed instructions for Barcza. Being very experienced in such matters, it was not difficult for him to express harsh words in a pleasant way.

"I have no doubts,"he wrote, "that Your Excellency will always find and skillfully use the arguments that we can employ against the strictures Britain has seen fit to make against Hungary's behavior. For the sake of precision, however, I will deal with the strictures in order."[15]

Concerning the stricture about permitting the transit of German troops, he recalled that on August 30, 1940, in Vienna, prior to the announcement of the Second Vienna Award, the Romanian government requested that Wehrmacht units be stationed in that country. How could any rational person expect, he asked heatedly and not unreasonably, that the Hungarian government would oppose the transit of the German troops and try to block it at the risk of the most serious consequences, at the same time when the British government did not consider it necessary to sever diplomatic relations with a Romania that had requested the presence of German troops?[16]

The change in the position of the British government was triggered by the changes in the conditions in the Balkans. Toward the end of October 1940, Mussolini attacked Greece. The dismal failure of this attack made it likely that Hitler would "resolve" the Greek problem. Because a suitably oriented Greece was critical for the British position in the Mediterranean, the German military presence in Romania became a serious concern.

It was easy for Bárdossy to point out that Greater Romania was largely indebted to Britain for its creation and continued existence. Romania enjoyed London's economic and political support for twenty-two years, frequently in opposition to Hungary and greatly to Hungary's detriment. It did not seem to disturb Britain that since 1937 Romania had established increasingly firm and friendly relations with the Third Reich. The removal of King Carol and the position of General Ion Antonescu were not the result of German armed action but, contrary to the view of certain London circles, the result of widely acclaimed Romanian domestic politics.[17]

If after all of this the intransigent British still claimed that in case of a British victory the new order of the Continent would be determined by the widest consideration of the demands of their faithful ally, Czechoslovakia and of their occupied friend, Romania, the British should not be surprised if in the face of such partiality Hungarian public opinion sought the support of its rightful demands from a different direction.[18]

Challenges and Contradictions of Symbiosis with the Germans

The challenges and contradictions of a symbiotic relationship with the Germans became apparent during these days in March 1941. The position of the Germans in the Balkans was greatly strengthened by Yugoslavia's joining the Tripartite Pact. The Hungarian-

Yugoslav friendship pact ratified the previous December was received favorably in Berlin since it was viewed as yet another link in the chain tying the Yugoslavs to the Third Reich. The fact the Hungarians initiated the pact to strengthen their position vis-à-vis the Germans seemed to have escaped the leaders of the Reich. The German-Yugoslav negotiations underwent several stages and the weakening of the threads to London, in addition to the improved likelihood of Hungarian territorial gains, caused much concern in some Yugoslav circles.

Rumors reached Budapest according to which Prince-Regent Paul made the integrity of the Yugoslav borders a condition for signing the pact. Paul also wanted an assurance from Hitler that no German soldier would be moved across Yugoslavia. Greece was not mentioned but it was obvious that a potential march across Yugoslavia could have no other target.[19]

On March 16 Bárdossy summoned Otto von Erdmannsdorff, the German minister in Budapest, and asked for an explanation with the irritation of an ally who saw his interest being endangered. With the pride of an equal he insisted that the granting of the above guaranty would adversely affect the Hungarian-German relationship and would also have a strongly deleterious effect on Hungarian public opinion.[20] In order for Berlin to see the effects of conciliation toward Yugoslavia on Budapest, Döme Sztójay, the Hungarian minister in Berlin was instructed to advise the Wilhelmstrasse that if Germany guaranteed the integrity of the Yugoslav borders, Bárdossy would not make his introductory visit to Hitler.[21]

While a strongly worded negative message was received from London, the Hungarian demarche produced a message from Berlin that indicated that the Hungarian interests were favorably considered. Barcza reported that Hungary would face the direst consequences if it permitted the transit of German soldiers toward a country regarded as an ally by Great Britain and particularly if Hungary participated actively in any military action.[22] Sztójay, on the other hand, could report that Berlin would guarantee the integrity of the Yugoslav borders only as far as Germany was concerned.[23]

Consequently, the Hungarian minister of foreign affairs could hold his head up high when he went on March 21 to Munich to meet with

Ribbentrop and Hitler. Bárdossy was well aware of the fact that the strings could not be tightened any further. At the given moment the adherence of Belgrade to the Tripartite Pact was the dominant feature and, as far as the Hungarians were concerned, it was an adequate proviso that Germany would not stand in the way of a territorial revision at some later date.

Even at this visit, however, Ribbentrop who was an expert at table-banging diplomacy used some threatening tones concerning the tense Hungarian-Romanian relations and the lack of national recognition granted to the Germans in Hungary.[24] In contrast, the Führer once again dazzled his guest with his well-proven ability to hoodwink his discussion partner. For this reason Bárdossy returned home with the illusion that Hungary could look forward to the further correction of the Transylvanian border.[25]

There was one extremely important point that was not directly a part of the negotiations. Hitler brought up the matter of the Soviet danger. Bárdossy, who was very sensitive to polished phrases, felt cold shivers running down his back when he heard Hitler say that if the Soviet danger became an actuality, Soviet Russia would cease to exist within few weeks thereafter.[26]

The Belgrade Coup

At dawn on March 27, 1940, Bárdossy was awakened by the telephone. The call came from the duty officer at the Ministry of Foreign Affairs. The official reported that the coup was performed by military officers, who asked Prince-Regent Paul to resign and placed young Peter II, educated in England, in his place. Prime Minister Draghiša Cvetković was replaced by Dušan Simović and the pro-German ministers were arrested.[27] Bárdossy left his home immediately and want to the Ministry of Foregn Affairs.

There additional information became available. He received details about the coup and the Hungarian information services provided him with reports about how the British Secret Service wove the threads leading to the change in regime.[28] During the day he had several discussions with Teleki who was desperately anxious and unhappy, particularly when he found out that there had been a telephone call from Sztójay announcing that the minister was flying to Budapest on Hitler's plane, carrying Hitler's message to Teleki and expecting to arrive at 5:00 P.M.

Sztójay, overawed by the historic moment arrived on time and first met with Bárdossy. The minister reported that he had been summoned to Hitler at 12:30 P.M. and that Hitler started the conversation by saying in a very hurried fashion that he knew that the Hungarians were dissatisfied with the results of their revisionist activities and that Hungary had territorial demands against Yugoslavia. He said that the time had come to realize them. He berated the Yugoslavs and said that if fate wanted to strike someone, it made that person stupid. He sent a message to Horthy, saying that Horthy should invade the Banat and take as much territory as he considered satisfactory. He, the Führer, would agree to all demands and naturally also endorsed Bulgaria's territorial demands in Macedonia.[29]

Following this discussion, Sztójay reported to the prime minister and then all three of them went to see the regent, by appointment.[30] Both Bárdossy and Teleki suspected that Horthy would be seriously affected by Hitler's message but did not expect enthusiasm lighting up his face and giving wings to his words.[31]

"Your Highness," said Teleki very unwillingly, "we are also aware of the magnitude of the opportunity offered to us. Yet, with an Eternal Friendship Pact signed barely a month ago, what can we do? What will Great Britain say? What will the world say? Your Highness, our national honor is at stake!" These last words were said very loudly by the prime minister who had a very difficult time in maintaining his temper.[32]

Horthy did not appreciate it if someone talked to him about honor. He therefore harked back to that part of Hitler's message which stated that in the future there would be no Yugoslavia and that the fate of Croatia would be determined jointly by the Croats and the Hungarians. He therefore concluded that since there was not going to be any Yugoslavia, the pact obviously was null and void.[33]

The not very smart Sztójay nodded diligently, but both Bárdossy and Teleki knew that the situation was much more complicated. London was unlikely to leave such a Hungarian action without reprisals. Their comments induced the regent to suggest that they should postpone a decision to the next day and then confer again with the military leaders in attendance.

A night's rest made the regent even more enthusiastic and the soldiers fanned the flames even higher. Both Teleki and Bárdossy repeated their arguments of the previous day and tried to use the threat of a Romanian and Soviet action to calm the excitement. Teleki also stated that the small Hungarian military force had to be preserved. Yet, it became evident during the very tense discussion that some compromise had to be reached.

They could reach agreement on the text of Horthy's message to Hitler. In this letter Horthy agreed that the territorial demands mentioned by the Führer were real and waited for satisfaction. He also expressed his pleasure in having joint military discussions and closed by saying that the changes in Belgrade could not have taken place without the Pan-Slav Soviet influence.[34]

The men drafting the letter were fully aware of the fact that the winds of change in Belgrade originated in London and not in Moscow and assumed that the German leadership was well aware of this fact. Because the great Hungarian political dilemma between Berlin's encouragement and London's firm opposition was a bottomless chasm, the mention of the Soviet's role in the events was an attempt to construct a bridge over the chasm. The bridge-building maneuver had to follow a script that would prove to be acceptable in London as well. Bárdossy acknowledged happily that he was in complete agreement with Teleki and they convinced the regent to send a reply to Berlin that was neither a negative nor an overtly positive one. This should gain them some breathing space to prepare a script acceptable to London.

Bárdossy knew that even the most daring construction was likely to fail and was also very dubious about being able to convince the new Belgrade leadership to assume a subservient attitude toward Berlin. It was in this spirit, attempting the impossible, that Bárdossy cabled to his minister in Belgrade, György Bakách-Bessenyey, on the next day.[35] Being conscious of the fact that he could not act openly, he instructed Bakách-Bessenyey to make a suggestion to Momčilo Ninčić, the new and former minister of foreign affairs, as though it originated with him [Bakách-Bessenyey]. He should advise the minister of foreign affairs that empty oratory would not keep the Germans from attacking the country. Solid proof would have to be offered that in a German-Greek war they would not turn against the former.

An Evening Conversation with Károly Rassay

The second endeavor of the minister of foreign affairs was a matter of domestic policy. He realized that the strength of the domestic opposition was not significant and that at the present time it could safely be ignored. He also realized that in a complex international situation conditions may change rapidly and that the presently insignificant forces could assume a leadership position. This induced him to have a conversation with Károly Rassay.

He knew that the anti-German parliamentary speeches of the liberal politician created considerable respect for him, but also that he had been active in the creation of the present regime, that he was the state secretary in the Ministry of Justice of the Károly Huszár government (November 24, 1919–March 15, 1920) and that even as an opposition politician he maintained a certain loyalty to the successive governments.[36] Knowing that he was a deeply committed Hungarian, Bárdossy hoped that Rassay might provide him with some ideas that could assist in escaping from the present dilemma or, at least, promise his support for the forthcoming action against Yugoslavia.

He asked Rassay to come and see him in the evening. During the day he studied the arriving bulletins, talked to his associates and dictated instructions. He was both excited and desperate and could not hide this from his guest. He knew that he had to open the conversation and that his words had to result in Rassay's cooperation. He spoke of the effect that the changes in Belgrade had in Berlin. He confidentially related that Sztójay flew home on Hitler's private plane. Even though he was silent about Hitler's offer, he could reasonably assume that by sharing the above information, his guest would realize that Hitler probably contemplated some military action and that there was a great likelihood for war. If that were to happen it would be catastrophic for Hungary since it could not rafrain from participating in the German military action. Bárdossy certainly emphasized the darkest side of the issue and not the possibly beneficial outcome.

These dramatic words made Rassay increasingly adversarial. "Your Excellency," he said, "in my opinion, breaking our solemn commitment to Yugoslavia, undertaken in the Eternal Friendship Pact, would result in a catastrophe for us, would make us a subject for universal contempt, would make our country a battlefield and would make our slender economy collapse under the burdens of war."[37]

– – –

In these stressful times there was no weekend rest at the Ministry of Foreign Affairs and both the minister and his staff worked on Sunday. It was then that Bárdossy replied to Barcza's query whether in the deteriorating Balkan situation Hungary would behave according to her commitment under the Eternal Friendship Pact.[38]

Our position will depend, he wrote, primarily on the behavior of the new Belgrade government.[39] If they provoke an armed conflict, nobody can expect that the Hungarian government could remain idle and watch while the Hungarian areas illegally taken away in 1918 become occupied by German or Romanian troops. Even Paragraph 2 of the Eternal Friendship Pact recognized the territorial demands of Hungary and the authority to protect the Hungarians living there. The behavior of the new Belgrade government canceled the December agreement. With these statements Bárdossy, without directly saying so, accepted the German point of view and aligned Hungarian foreign policy with Berlin.[40]

The Fateful Meeting of the Supreme Defense Council

In order to describe the Hungarian position, the Supreme Defense Council was called into session at 5:00 P.M. on April 1. The council was a governmental body under the chairmanship of the regent with the participation of the chief of the General Staff. It was staffed and administered by a general secretary. At this time the position was held by Antal Náray, a General Staff colonel.[41]

The session started under a cloud since Teleki and Bárdossy had found out the day before that the military leaders had exceeded their authority. What happened was that the German General Friedrich von Paulus had arrived on Sunday and within hours Chief of the General Staff Henrik Werth had reached an agreement with him concerning Hungarian military participation in the action. Accordingly, Werth wished to start general mobilization on April 1. The Germans fixed the start of war for the 12th and wanted the Hungarian troops to cross the border and start their attack on the 15th. Werth obviously viewed the entire affair as a technical problem and only worried about the time required for mobilization and for the crossing of the border.[42]

Teleki was incensed and even Bárdossy was made very angry by the gauntlet thrown into their face. Under duress, they agreed to the transit of German troops through Hungary but as far as Hungarian military participation was concerned they insisted that this decision had to be made by the Supreme Defense Council.

After Miklós Horthy's opening statement it was Bárdossy's task to explain the international implications of the proposed action. His freedom of action was severely curtailed by the fact that the regent had announced Hungarian participation as an accomplished fact and had designated the agenda of this meeting to be restricted to a discussion of the time of attack, its goals, the extent of the forces committed and their behavior.[43]

After the statement from the highest authority, Bárdossy started his speech by saying that every opportunity for the liberation of their Hungarian brethren under foreign rule had to be grasped firmly. Yet, the Eternal Friendship Pact made it impossible to act as long as Yugoslavia existed. By this statement he negated the comments that he had sent to Barcza in London. He did not use the British as an argument and did not refer to any international issue but limited himself to a statement about Hungary's historic responsibilities. With this broad perspective he opened the discussion to a more measured and circumspect atmosphere.

He clarified his ideas about the date of engagement and designated the goal of the action as the retrieval of the territory that had been Hungary's for a millennium. He believed that such a step was defensible before the world. In contrast, however, he emphasized that if Hungarian troops invaded other Yugoslav areas, Hungary would be guilty of violating political ethics and might become involved in military activities greatly contrary to national interests.

Looking first at Horthy and then at Minister of Defense Károly Bartha and finally at Werth, he spoke of the questionable outcome of the World War and stated that in case of a British-American victory, Hungary would not only lose the newly acquired territories but might be confronted with a situation worse even than Trianon. In conclusion he alluded very guardedly but unmistakably to the interest of the Soviet Union in the Balkans.[44]

These reasoned sentences induced Minister of Interior Ferenc Keresztes-Fischer, Minister of Industry József Varga, Minister of Supplies Dezső Laky, Minister of Justice László Radocsay and Minister of Agriculture Daniel Bánffy to voice their own reservations [45] while   Minister of Finances Reményi-Schneller and the highly respected Minister of Education and Religious Affairs Bálint Hóman urged alignment with Germany.[46] Werth attacked Bárdossy violently and argued that the enemy had to be pursued until it was destroyed.

The discussion was closed by the prime minister. He once again stated his ideas about the inexhaustible strength of the Anglo-Saxon world and about the conditions under which Hungary might take action. Finally he objected to the size of the forces to be used claiming that for a simple task of occupation smaller forces would be more than sufficient.[47]

In closing the four-hour discussion, the regent decided on a limited action to achieve the Hungarian goals. He instructed the chief of the General Staff and the prime minister to agree on the number of troops to be involved and to submit the agreement to him.[48]

A Dramatic Cable from London

On the afternoon of the following day, April 2, Prime Minister Teleki was informed that the German troops preparing to attack Yugoslavia crossed the German-Hungarian frontier on their way south and that their commanders had already arrived in Budapest.[49] He became so distressed that he decided to go to the Dísz tér to discuss the not unexpected but nevertheless new situation with his minister of foreign affairs.

"It is beginning," Teleki said when he entered Bárdossy's office. Bárdossy knew what he meant since the news had already reached the ministry.

"Barcza's cable from London has just arrived," Bárdossy answered and immediately proceeded to destroy his envoy's credibility. "He exaggerates and puts his own words into the mouth of the British to keep us from acting."

Teleki remained standing and only held out his hand for the decoded cable which Bárdossy, also without saying a word, handed over to him. In the lapidary style typical of coded cables, Minister Barcza stated that if the Germans attacked Yugoslavia and the Yugoslavs resisted, as could be expected, they would immediately become the allies of Great Britain. In this case the response here to any change in the Hungarian-Yugoslav relationship would be as follows:

> 1. If the Hungarian government permits or assists German troops to enter the country and use it as a base of operations against Yugoslavia, we must expect that Great Britain will sever its diplomatic relations with all the dire consequences of such an action.[50]
> 2. If the Hungarians were to join in the action, on whatever pretext, e.g. protection of Hungarians in Yugoslavia, an immediate declaration of war by Great Britain and a possible later declaration by Turkey and the Soviet Union must be anticipated. In such a case our behavior would be considered inimical to the Allies and, following an Allied victory, we would also be charged with violating the Eternal Friendship Pact. This pact here was interpreted to mean that for the time being we had relinquished our territorial demands.[51]

Teleki had read the cable in a quiet monotone, hoping that perhaps this would lessen his ever more severe distress. When finished he only said one thing and this seemed to be addressed to a Higher Power, "I have done everything I could. I can do no more." He then added in a slightly different tone, "I am leaving." It was unclear whether he addressed those present or perhaps his God.

Bárdossy only nodded his head and seemed to be frozen to his seat. His departing guest was ushered out by the chief of the Press Office.

Pál Teleki's Tragedy

The following morning, while at breakfast, the minister of foreign affairs received the not entirely unexpected news that the prime minister had committed suicide during the night.

Everybody realized that under the prevailing situation the post of the head of government could not be left vacant even for a few hours. Horthy immediately started the negotiations and summoned his advisers, his trusted friend Count István Bethlen, the highly regarded minister of the interior, Ferenc Keresztes-Fischer, and the personally disliked but politically very astute former minister of foreign affairs, Kálmán Kánya. All three recommended Bárdossy for the position. In these deliberations one of the principal considerations was the probable Berlin reaction. The person to be selected had to be neutral and not committed to either side. At this time László Bárdossy was still such an individual.[52]

It was also in his favor that he had no political party at his back and, in fact, was not a politician. A man was needed who may have been deeply shocked by Teleki's act but who was willing to proceed according to the principles that had been worked out earlier, actually to a large extent by the late prime minister. A man was needed who was willing to implement the wishes of official Hungary. Bárdossy was willing to accept this role. He was promptly summoned to a regental audience and the audience itself was over promptly. Straight questions were given a straight answer.

The eulogy at the bier of the late prime minister was delivered by the new prime minister.

The First Days as Prime Minister

Somewhat earlier than anticipated, the German troops crossed the German-Yugoslav border on April 6 and the Hungarian-

Yugoslav border on April 7, sweeping all resistance away in their occupation of the country. The Yugoslav air force, supported by British planes, attacked Szeged, Pécs and Villány on the 7th and bombed the air fields used by the Germans. One Yugoslav plane was forced down and six British planes were shot down.[53] Bárdossy that same evening instructed Barcza to file a protest in the strongest terms, but did not proceed further waiting for any news from Zagreb.[54]

London, however, offended by the events, did take action even before the Hungarian protest. While the cable from Budapest was still being decoded, Barcza was summoned to the Foreign Office and informed that diplomatic relations had been severed.[55]

On April 10, the Hungarian consul in Zagreb, László Bartók, telephoned saying that Eugen Kvaternik, the Croatian Ustaša leader had declared the independence of Croatia.[56] This was the signal for the Hungarian troops to start moving. Prime Minister and Minister of Foreign Affairs Bárdossy advised the regent to inform the country about the sequence of events in his proclamation. Bárdossy drafted the proclamation and Horthy accepted it without any amendments.[57] Bárdossy also considered it important that he not be held solely responsible for every consequence of the Hungarian action in case of a major change in the war. In order to document a joint responsibility he summoned the Foreign Affairs Committee of Parliament, under the chairmanship of Kálmán Kánya for 5:30 P.M. on the 11th.[58] In his presentation he emphasized that the goal of the previous administration was the preservation of peace in the Balkans and that this was the reason for the pact with Yugoslavia. He did not deny that the pact was an integral part of the friendly cooperation with the Axis Powers and of the political system based on this cooperation. It was the coup in Belgrade that upset all these arrangements. According to him the Eternal Friendship Pact was cancelled by the bombing raids against a number of targets in southern Hungary and the Hungarian government fulfilled its primary obligation when it responded by occupying the Délvidék (Vojvodina) an area which was part of pre-Trianon Hungary. Bárdossy did not refer to his cable to Barcza on March 30, in which he alleged that the pact was nullified by the Belgrade coup.

The first one to respond to the presentation was Count István Bethlen, the grand old man of Hungarian politics. Bethlen opened by saying that he supported the actions of the government fully and without reservations. He claimed, "that under the prevailing conditions no other action was possible and that our national honor and millennial historic mission would have been sullied if, after the disintegration of Yugoslavia, we had not done our duty toward our ancient patrimony and our Hungarian brothers and sisters living there. However," and here his voice became very stern, "the government has an obligation toward the country to see that the military take not one step beyond the historic territory that had belonged to the Crown of St. Stephen. We must accept the fact," he said in a resigned voice,

that the Serbs, the British, and perhaps other countries will accuse us of a grave breach of promise. We must be clear that we will probably be unable to convince them of our rectitude. It is therefore even more important that the borders be maintained precisely to emphasize that we are not at war with Serbia or with any other country. In this way we might perhaps find some of the more objective foreign countries to be on our side.

- - -

Since the Germans were carrying most of the burden, the occupation of the Délvidék was accomplished easily and rapidly. Bácska (Bačka), the Baranya (Baranja) triangle, the Muraköz (Medjumurje) and the Muravidék (Murje River region), a total of 11,475 square kilometer, with more than one million inhabitants were returned to Hungary. Of the population 39% were Hungarian according to the Hungarian census but only 30% according to the Yugoslav figures.

THE FATAL STEP
OF ATTACKING
THE SOVIET UNION

Henrik Werth's First Attack

On May 6, 1941, the Prime Minister and Minister of Foreign Affairs Bárdossy had dealt with the routine matters of the day when a special messenger delivered a memorandum from Henrik Werth, the chief of the General Staff.[59] The memorandum exceeded his worst expectations. He turned beet-red and ashy pale in turn as he read the document before throwing it on the table.

The general wrote that Moscow was engaged in a double-dealing policy vis-à-vis Berlin. This would force Germany, now that the war in the Balkans was finished, to conclusively regularize its relationship with the Soviet Union once and for all.[60] In his politically ornamental language Werth went on to say that this "regularization" may be done with armed forces. If it should come to an open conflict, the participation of Finland, Hungary and Romania would become inevitable.

Bárdossy was fuming, as he saw in the memorandum an attempt by Werth to set a policy for Hungary. Bárdossy saw him blinded by devotion to Germany, which made him write that the outcome of a German-Russian war is not in doubt since a German victory is certain. For Bárdossy the memorandum was political blackmail pure and simple.

The conclusion of the memorandum in which Werth asked for a definite and unmistakable clarification of Hungary's political stance vis-à-vis a German-Russian armed conflict, was courteous but as far as its contents were concerned precisely as infuriating as the rest of the memorandum.[61] As always, its views were narrow-minded. Only a very obtuse individual could assume that in politics anything could ever be "conclusively regularized."

Bárdossy drew the obvious conclusion. There was no question but that a German-Soviet war was imminent. The conclusion of the memorandum made that clear. As far as the more distant future was concerned, the only way to prevent Hungary from ever confronting the Soviet Union in isolation or having to defend its borders by itself, was by siding without any reservation with Germany in the evolution of the forthcoming German-Soviet relations.

At first, Bárdossy was ready to respond strongly but then he reconsidered. Consequently, the answer was drafted on May 12.[62] The letter set out to demonstrate Werth's political dilettantism, calmly but with unmistakable force. Thus, right at the beginning of the letter, Bárdossy advised the general that the requested political and military agreement concerning commitments and support was totally unimaginable in view of the enormous difference in power between the two countries.

Cooperation against the Soviet Union, urged by the general, was declined by Bárdossy with the somewhat dubious argument that in the past Germany kept all her political and military plans in deepest secrecy and would not welcome any Hungarian offers. In fact in August 1938, in Kiel, Hitler, hoping for active cooperation, shared with Horthy the German plans for the destruction of Czechoslovakia.[63]

Hitler's Diabolic Hungarian Policy

On April 30, 1941, Hitler designated June 22 as the day to begin the attack against the Soviet Union and Bárdossy assumed that Werth's memorandum was based on information he had obtained from the German General Staff. The plan of the attack, Operation Barbarossa, was signed by Hitler on December 18, 1940. It did not include any request for Hungary to participate in the action.[64] This could have meant only that the Führer considered Hungary's dependence on Germany to be so strong that the Hungarians would become involved in the conflict without the need to hold out any further territorial concessions.

The German military leadership was aware, however, of the enormous risks of the armed engagement and therefore it wished to strengthen its relationship with the Hungarian military and wanted Werth to motivate the Hungarian political leadership. General Kurt Himer, who served as a liaison between the German High Command and Hungary in preparing the action against Yugoslavia, was still in Budapest and was negotiating during the last days of May about Hungarian cooperation in the aggression against the Soviet Union.[65] Even though he admitted that he had no authority from Berlin to do so he nevertheless advised that the Hungarian forces be mobilized.

As a result of this advice, Werth submitted additional memoranda to coerce the prime minister to take action. In the first one he indicated that the Germans did indeed wished to assign a role to Hungary in the war against the Soviets and in the second one he impudently insisted that that the Hungarian government make an offer of participation in the action against Moscow.[66]

- - -

The military pressure on Bárdossy was further increased by the diplomatic bullying by his minister in Berlin. He predicted on May 24 that the German attack would begin toward the middle of June.[67] Sztójay knew that Hitler would not ask Hungary for military participation and therefore he kept harassing Bárdossy with reports that the Romanians would have a major role in the attack and that consequently they would be given Bessarabia and that as compensation for their "contribution" they would endeavor to get a reversal of the Second Vienna Award. In order to avoid this predicament, Sztójay urged that Berlin be offered active cooperation.

Between June 10 and June 14, Ernst Freiherr von Weizsäcker, the German undersecretary of state for foreign affairs, was negotiating in Budapest and denied both to the regent and also to the prime minister-minister of foreign affairs that a German attack against the Soviet Union was imminent.[68] Weizsäcker was not a Nazi and was sincerely concerned for his country in view of Hitler's insane ambitions.[69] Both Horthy and Bárdossy were well aware of this. Consequently, Bárdossy understood that the denial of any imminent action was very questionable but also felt that Weizsäcker's statement might make his [Bárdossy's] burden somewhat lighter. It was for this reason that he advised Sztójay on June 14 as follows:

I have mentioned the probability of a German-Russian conflict three times to Baron Weizsäcker. He emphasized each time that the rumors about the German government's decision to go to war had no foundation in fact, at least at the present time. According to him anybody who claimed that the conflict would begin within a specified period of time, knows more than the Führer.[70]

In view of this, it would have been impossible for us to make an offer. I am convinced, he continued, that it is completely impossible to assume that if the Reich government agreed to Romania's military participation against the Russians it would change the Vienna award and give us additional territory in Southern Transylvania even if we were to participate in the war against the Soviets.

There is no doubt that in Bárdossy's mind the possibility of Hungary participating in the war against the Soviets was one of the options as early as June 14. He gave credence to the rumors about the impending attack and, under the pressures weighing on him, was inclined to feel that Hungarian participation was inevitable. He realized that in order to keep Northern Transylvania, the expected Romanian merits would have to be counterbalanced. How to participate was not yet clear to him but he did not believe that Hungary should make an offer. In conclusion he wrote,

I do not believe that it is necessary to acquire further merit in Hitler's eyes. The Führer has repeatedly stated to Your Excellency how much he appreciated everything we have done for the Reich by allowing the German troop transit through Hungary and that in the action against Yugoslavia we were well ahead of Bulgaria, which also had a direct interest in the affair.[71]

Bárdossy Takes Action against Werth

Bárdossy felt that he could strengthen his position, give himself more elbow room and decrease the pressure brought on him by Werth if he were to summon the Council of Ministers for an emergency session that day, June 14, to discuss the contents of the latest memorandum.[72]

To inform the council and, hopefully, to turn their thoughts against Werth, he opened the session by reading the entire Werth memorandum.[73] He was quite aware of the fact that his ministerial colleagues were not well informed about military matters but that they were quite aware of the weakness and small size of the Hungarian military establishment.

For this reason he emphasized that the author of the memorandum wished to mobilize about one half of the armed forces. He knew that his words would echo the words they all had heard frequently from Teleki. Particularly Teleki's memorable conviction that the outcome of the war was in doubt and that therefore, in order to avoid a repetition of the 1918–1919 events, preservation of the Hungarian armed forces was a fundamental national necessity.

He felt that he had the confidence of the group and therefore he formulated his arguments against Werth accordingly. Hungary had demonstrated repeatedly, he said, that it stood wholeheartedly on the side of the Axis Powers and that the Führer and chancellor had repeatedly stated how much he appreciated the permission for the German troops to cross Hungary and Hungary's participation in the action against Yugoslavia. Therefore, he emphasized, there was no need for further demonstration of pro-Axis policies by participating in a possible German-Russian conflict.[74]

"Furthermore," he added rather sharply, "in spite of repeated inquiries by the Hungarian government, Berlin has given no information whatever concerning any change in German-Russian relations or about the possibility of an armed conflict."

Under such conditions it was a logical conclusion that the Germans were not expecting any active cooperation on Hungary's part. Any large scale Hungarian military activity was clearly not desirable since these could not remain hidden and might prematurely disclose to Moscow Berlin's potential intentions. Such activity would be contrary to the Reich's interests and might also trigger some military action by Russia against Hungary.[75]

The prime minister also had a good answer to the Romanian argument. He said that since Germany guaranteed Romania's territorial integrity by the Second Vienna Award, it was extremely unlikely that it would deprive Romania of Southern Transylvania while expecting Romania to cooperate in any armed action against Moscow.

Bárdossy was confident that he could ask for a vote on the issue. Before doing so, however, he maliciously highlighted the glaring inconsistency in the general's memorandum. Werth went out on an absurd limb when in the same document he spoke of the full month required for the Hungarian army to become ready and at the same time stated that the German victory would be so rapid that the Hungarian soldiers would certainly be home before the harvest. He wrote this just about two weeks before the Feast of St. Peter and St. Paul, the traditional beginning of the Hungarian harvest.[76]

Bárdossy probably knew deep down that he should have stopped earlier and not allow free rein to his dislike of Werth and also that his words would surely be reported to the general, but he went ahead anyway. The government unanimously rejected the idea of any unrequested Hungarian offer.[77]

On the Eve of the Attack against the Soviet Union

On instructions from Foreign Minister Joachim von Ribbentrop, the German minister requested an appointment with Bárdossy on June 16, 1941. Under the guise of the customary mendacious Nazi phraseology Otto von Erdmannsdorff spoke of the Soviet troop concentrations along the German border which might force the German government to make certain demands at the beginning of July.[78]

Bárdossy immediately realized that the war could begin early in July. He barely listened to the oratory of the German minister about the doubtful outcome of the negotiations and about the German government's request that the Hungarian government take the necessary steps to strengthen its borders with the Soviet Union. When Erdmannsdorff asked that his comments be kept completely confidential Bárdossy nodded his head and saw his visitor to the door.

In those days Werth was a frequent visitor in the Sándor Palace, which housed the office of the prime minister. On June 19, Franz Halder, the chief of the German General Staff, conferred in Budapest with Werth who then immediately went to inform the prime minister. Bárdossy was shocked to find out that the attack was not planned for July but would be initiated within days. He was relieved to learn, however, that the Germans not only abstained from asking for active participation in the aggression but did not even ask for any increased military preparations.[79]

Werth could not accept this state of affairs and became increasingly insistent with the prime minister who, according to Werth was "incapable of taking any action." Werth was firmly convinced of a German victory and saw that the Führer assigned a role in this to both the Finns and the Romanians. He was desperate for Hungary to have a role to play as well. He also decided to bring increased pressure on the Sándor Palace. On Saturday, June 21, he sent a confidential report to Bárdossy advising the prime minister that the war would begin within forty-eight hours. German circles were surprised, said the report, that the Hungarians seemed to be totally disinterested and that no steps were taken to seriously strengthen the border or activate the air defenses even though Russian air and ground counter attacks could be anticipated.[80]

Visits by the German Minister

On Sunday morning, June 22, the household in the Virágárok utca was still asleep when the telephone started shrilling heartlessly. Erdmannsdorff was at the other end of the line and asked Bárdossy if he could see him immediately.

Bárdossy realized immediately that the minister would announce the war and wondered if he would bring any requests. He did not. Hitler saw no reason to change his earlier position. Bárdossy, indicating understanding and satisfaction, acknowledged the message[81] but even while doing so probably wondered what the military clique was planning and what Horthy's reaction was going to be.

Erdmannsdorff had a much warmer reception when he visited Horthy later that morning and delivered a letter from the Führer. "Believe me, minister," began the regent,

I have been waiting for this day for twenty-two years. Now I am happy. Mankind will be grateful to the Führer centuries hence for this act that will bring back the peace. Britain and the United States will have to realize that Germany is unbeatable since its food supply and military raw materials will be amply supplied by occupied Russia.[82]

Horthy did consider that the maritime powers could not be defeated and even in his greatest enthusiasm he could not believe that Germany could defeat Great Britain and the United States. It was his strong anti-Bolshevik feelings that made it impossible for him to imagine that the German aggression would line up the Anglo-Saxon world on the side of Moscow. Yet, this is precisely what happened and it was this that determined the fate of Hungary.

Bárdossy saw clearly that the Führer would not abandon his sphinx-like mysteriousness but he also realized that Berlin would expect Budapest to demonstrate its solidarity with the Axis in the new situation. One such step would be severing diplomatic relations with Russia, he thought, but this would not be in the best interests of Hungary. Hungarian information gathering services have been functioning well and perhaps Ribbentrop would agree that in this way useful information could be obtained for Germany. Bárdossy was clearly grasping at straws. Monday afternoon he discussed this with a small group in the Ministry of Foreign Affairs and the group agreed with his ideas, as he had expected. Antal Ullein-Reviczky was present at this discussion and in his characteristic impetuosity and ignoring the need for discretion in matters of state, informed the German News Agency about the discussion.[83] It only took a few minutes before Erdmannsdorff had the report on his desk. He viewed this as yet another one of Hungary's "ungrateful" acts and immediately telephoned the prime minister asking for an explanation in a very irritated voice.

Severing Diplomatic Relations with Moscow

It was after these preliminaries that the Council of Ministers met on June 23. Bárdossy knew from his predecessors, Kánya, Csáky and Teleki, that the government was not particularly interested in matters of foreign policy. Such matters were of great interest only very rarely and discussion of them was primarily a matter of information exchange. He was aware, however, that the momentous events of the previous day could be assumed to be of interest to his ministerial colleagues or that, at least, he thought cynically, they may have some feelings about them.

In general, he perceived that the members of the government were influenced only by Hitler's great victories and the hope of territorial gains. They were united in their hostility toward the Soviet Union and the memory of Béla Kun's Hungarian Soviet regime and its terror squad, the Lenin Boys, still loomed as a nightmare although these lasted for only three months in 1919. His colleagues saw a direct link between the Hungarian Soviet Republic and the Moscow system. Even those who viewed the actions of the Wehrmacht with apprehension were awed by the phenomenal successes in France and had no doubt that the Führer would smash the clay-footed ogre of the Soviet Union into smithereens within a few weeks thereby ridding the world of the Communist-Bolshevik menace.

He was not mistaken. The Council of Ministers accepted the information provided and agreed to the proposal concerning the suspension of Hungarian-Soviet diplomatic relations. They were reassured by the words of Károly Bartha, the minister of defense, who told them that the campaign would be completed in six weeks and were very doubtful about Ferenc Keresztes-Fischer's cautionary remarks about the hazards of an uncertain future.[84] After the session the decision was conveyed to the German minister with the request that it be forwarded to Berlin.

The pressure from the military was increasing steadily. For them six weeks was all there was. They believed that the entire future would be decided during this time span and this was the motivating force behind all of their activities.

On the very day the aggression began, Kurt Himer was granted permission to begin discussions with the Hungarian General Staff.[85] When Himer reported that the Werth group was bitter because the German political leadership would not allow Hungarian participation, Alfred Jodl, the chief of the Wehrmacht's Operational Staff, denied that they did not want Hungary's eventual participation.

"We will accept any Hungarian assistance at any time," he said, "and we will gratefully accept anything they may offer, but we are not going to make any demands."[86]

Looking at this statement dispassionately it is apparent that Jodl, in fact, repeated Hitler's point of view but dressed it up to make it more agreeable for the Hungarians. Werth, Bartha and company only heard the encouragement. It was obvious from a telephone discussion between Franz Halder and Jodl that the German point of view had not changed one iota. This conversation took place at the same time when Bárdossy was still considering the option of keeping the legation in Moscow.

He thought, with ruthless cynicism, that the matter hinged on whether the Hungarian military leadership could mobilize the political organs of government in order to make them volunteer their participation.[87] At the moment they could not. Werth notified the prime minister on June 23 that the German military position in this matter was clear. The same day Werth and the minister of defense went to see the regent who was at his estate in Kenderes, but could accomplish nothing. The soldiers waited for Hitler to take a position but since the Führer preserved his silence the Hungarian political leadership was able, for the time being, to restrain the military.[88]

- - -

This was the political line that should have been followed and the blind faith of the Hungarian military in a rapid German victory should have been exploited. Only a short waiting period was needed during which the machinery of government could have been strengthened and concentrated in a few hands. It was evident that the German strategy had to assume a victorious Blitzkrieg. If the aggression was not successful, like a lightening strike, a situation would develop from which the Germans could no longer emerge victorious. If they were not victorious, than all Hungarian forces would have to be concentrated on trying to maintain the greatest distance between the two countries.

Bárdossy was constitutionally incapable of such steadfastness. What were needed was character, serenity, self-assurance and strength. Qualities that characterized Miklós Kállay.

Even beyond this, what was really needed was statesmanship. Unfortunately there was none. It was bad for the country and it was bad for Bárdossy that on April 3 he was raised to be head of government. His nervous system was not up to withstand the leaden pressure of these fateful hours. He did not realize that these days represented the maximal need for such clarity. The aggression of June 22 did clarify that German-Soviet relations had been based on the lies of both parties. To see clearly one had to wait only a very short time, namely for the reaction from London and Washington.

The June 23 action also clarified Hungarian-German and Hungarian-Soviet relations. Moscow actually expected steps much worse than the simple severance of diplomatic relations. This is as far as it should have gone. Oh, if one only could have stopped here....

The Bombing of Kassa and the Regent's Decision

On Thursday, June 26, at 12:10 P.M. three Soviet fighter planes fired machine guns at an express train on its way to Budapest between Tiszaborkút and Rahó.[89] Exactly one hour later planes, unidentified to this day, dropped twenty-nine bombs on Kassa (Košice).

Around 2:00P.M. Henrik Werth, bypassing László Bárdossy, reported the above to the regent. Without any investigation, Werth claimed that the air raid was a Soviet attack.[90] Miklós Horthy valued Werth's technical expertise very highly and it was difficult for him to back the political leadership in their red-hot battles with his highly esteemed general and his clique. The bombing infuriated him and he allowed his emotions free reign. He decided! Without a moment's hesitation he ordered Werth to prepare a retaliatory blow.

"Is Your Highness declaring a state of war?" Asked the chief of the General Staf.

"Yes!" Was the curt answer.

Werth knew very well that they had acted unconstitutionally since they did not seek the government's approval for this action. He did not mind and consoled himself with the thought that history always justified the victors. Werth was sick and tired of having been lectured and restrained repeatedly when he was convinced that it was he alone who represented the best interests of the country.

The prime minister was summoned by the regent at 3:00 P.M. and was informed of the events assuming that he would accept the role assigned to him. He accepted. This was Bárdossy's greatest mistake. If we put the historic consequences, the road that led to the tragedy of the country and the death of tens of thousands of troops and civilians into the balance, it was Bárdossy's fault. The role he accepted was an important one but it was not the leading role. The leading role was that of Regent Miklós Horthy's, who later denied having had any part in the action.[91]

Miklós Horthy was a child of the nineteenth century. Of the century when human relationships were elevated to a high pedestal and when a statement had an unquestioned and unquestionable value. A word of honor could make the difference between life and death. This was the world in which the regent grew up. Yet for his erroneous decision he did not accept his historic responsibility. He depicted his prime minister in a misleading fashion, even though Bárdossy, even when faced by death, tried to exonerate him. Horthy was able to avoid being taken to account.

- - -

"I could not hold my head up," he told Bárdossy who was crushed by the weight of the moment, "if I would allow this infamous attack to go unpunished."[92]

He spoke in the first person and considered the decision to be his alone. He claimed it at that moment, although later he attributed its odium, in an ignoble fashion, to his prime minister. Bárdossy was deeply offended. The regent had expropriated the prime minister's prerogative of having the government determine the position to be taken.[93]

While he was listening to Miklós Horthy his mind was in turmoil. Should his actions be governed by his convictions or by his offended sensibilities? Should he resign or should he take the responsibility for the declaration of war when he had no part in the decision-making process. He chose the latter. It was the wrong decision albeit made in good faith.

We have no good answer as to what would have happened if on June 26 at the regental audience he would have tendered his resignation rather than hurrying off to call the Council of Ministers into session. We do know, however, that later, in March 1942, in a situation even more difficult than the June 1941 one, his successor, Miklós Kállay refused to do the Germans' bidding. Even Bárdossy would have never called Miklós Kállay a Germanophile. On the contrary, Bárdossy criticized Kállay since the latter's anti-German policies, in Bárdossy's views, endangered the country's interests.

We also know with complete certainty what the inheritance of the Bárdossy government turned out to be. Instead of the success of taking minimal steps it was a state of war with the three major world powers. It was not blind fate but the entry into the war against the Soviet Union that started the country on the slippery slope that led to a declaration of war against the two other world powers.

- - -

This was the point at which the balance had to be drawn, but the story continues. On Horthy's unspoken question, Bárdossy after a lengthy pause announced that he would return to the Sándor Palace and summon the Council of Ministers into session.

The behavior of the body caused no surprise. The minister of the interior again and now with even greater emphasis cautioned against the hazards of this leap into the dark. His words had no echo. The council took a position in agreement with the regent's proposal including the decision to engage in hostilities with the fewest forces possible.[94] This was in fact what happened, but the outcome was quite different from the expectations.

László Bárdossy's Action and His Great Responsibility

The next morning the prime minister asked to address the lower house of Parliament.

Honored House, I must make a very brief announcement. The president of the lower house has used the appropriate terms to describe the inexcusable attack of the Soviet Union, completely contrary to the Law of Nations. The royal Hungarian government states that consequent to the attack a state of war exists between Hungary and the Soviet Union.[95]

The strange and brief statement was received by the house with enthusiastic approval. This was the beginning of one of the most important and in its consequences the most dramatic of the events in twentieth century Hungarian history.

The government did not insist that the regent seek its opinion and the house chose to ignore the rights granted to it by the constitution of the country.[96] These rights included the undisputed authority of the house in agreeing to or denying the employment of Hungarian military units beyond the borders of the country. Actually, even before the house had been informed, Hungarian planes had bombed Russian cities and a few hours later ground troops had also crossed the Hungarian-Russian frontier.

Before the People's Court Bárdossy said later that the reason he did not ask for a vote by the house was that he was not aware of the steps that should have been taken legally. "I am fully aware," he said with brutal honesty, "that I should have known the law. I was under the impression that speed was essential and it was for this reason that I made the announcement."[97]

We have seen that there was no immediate reason that would have justified such irresponsible haste. Even the erstwhile regent stated in his memoirs in 1945 that he recalled no direct German pressure and that the German pressure was only "atmospheric."[98]

We can accept this explanation to be correct and objective. It is not very difficult to see that under only atmospheric pressure it would have been possible and essential to find the minimal way to stick to the rules of the game, to weigh the situation soberly and dispassionately and to find a better solution to preserve the national interest.

Bárdossy claimed that if they had not acted immediately there would have been a German occupation and that this would have been suicidal. Suicide was not an option in exchange for a somewhat doubtful resurrection. Let us hear what he had to say:

The court may laugh but I was not aware of these constitutional legal requirements. I was only familiar with those constitutional rules that were in effect when I was studying law. The regulations pertaining to the use of troops beyond the borders and to the declaration of war were introduced in the 1920s when I was no longer concerned with constitutional issues. I was limited to my own area of expertise. Thus it completely dropped out of my memory.[99]

The Minister of Justice did not warn me. I must accept full responsibility for what happened.[100]

Indeed! A head of government or any other leader is always ignorant of many things. It is patently impossible to know everything. This is precisely why the governmental structure, its precise division of responsibilities and its hierarchy were devised and refined over long periods of time so that this issue should not become a major problem. It was the machinery of government that had to fulfill its responsibilities to the nation and to the people. The fact that Bárdossy assumed the full responsibility and did not wish to saddle the minister of justice, also referred to as the keeper of the seal, with any of the responsibility, throws a bright light on his character and noble human traits.

From a broader perspective, however, this is not the issue. It is more significant that as a person Bárdossy was not circumspect and did not instruct his subordinates to advise him on the precise legal requirements pertaining to the situation. From the perspective of the quarter-century-long system, hallmarked as the Horthy era, the essential point is that the officials and not only Bárdossy, who undoubtedly carried the heaviest load of responsibility, failed to recognize the terrible dangers that lurked behind the irresponsibly hasty decision.

Most of these officials had no foreign policy experience and could not distinguish between ideological perspectives and political ones. It was not a question of the nature of the Soviet system and whether the views about it were justified or not. This criticism is largely correct and it makes no difference that those who denigrated Stalin's rule most vigorously frequently themselves did little for the common good.

While he never trumpeted his views when in power, Bárdossy did state before the court, and surely not to gain favor, that in Hungary there was never any real Parliamentarism (sic).[101] Yet in his maiden speech as prime minister he urged social justice, a moderate land reform, modernization of governmental administration, health care and improved social policies.[102]

- - -

The prime minister did ask for parliamentary approval on July 24 and obtained it on October 23.[103] The deputies obviously did not debate for months about the correct move. This delayed action also demonstrates to what extent Hungary's entry into the war was not the hasty, thoughtless decision of one man but was a collective decision.

IN THE MAELSTROM
OF THE WORLD WAR

The Hungarian armed forces started the fight with 45,000 men under the command of General Ferenc Szombathelyi. They reached the Dniester River in a few days but only the so-called Rapid Deployment Force proceeded further. This division advanced a total of about 1,000 kilometers but had suffered such heavy casualties that on December 4 it was sent home, with German approval.

In view of the huge territorial gains and captivated by the screaming propaganda even those began to believe in a German victory who were greatly opposed to the whole world becoming Nazi. There were very few who realized that the bulk of the Red Army kept slipping away from the threatening German forces and that there were no decisive battles being fought.

Even the military circles ignored the deterioration of the Hungarian fighting forces and did not appreciate the truth of the well-known maxim about the risks of assigning troops to the front that had no heavy weapons, barely had any artillery and were without effective anti-tank or anti-aircraft guns. The senior military leaders were completely blind. They saw the examples of Finland and of Romania and would have gladly thrown the entire Hungarian army into the battle. Still in 1941, the Romanians sent two more armies to the front and suffered enormous losses.

Entry into the war against the Soviet Union did not improve the bad relations between Bárdossy and the military clique.

Further Fights with Werth and Victory over Werth

Werth never forgave the prime minister and minister of foreign affairs that, as he put it, in spite of Hungary's traditional anti-

Soviet stand, Bárdossy held back and that only after the bombing of Kassa was he willing to enter the war. Since Werth considered this very detrimental to Hungary's best political interests he wrote three memoranda during the summer in order to change Bárdossy's lukewarm attitude. In order to increase the pressure Werth did not only send the memoranda to Horthy but made a number of copies so that a larger audience should see the existing difference of opinion.

After the first memorandum, Bárdossy swallowed his anger and did nothing.[104] After the second one, he went to the head of state. He visited Horthy in Gödöllő and asked that the chief of the General Staff be relieved from his duties. Horthy even now refused to side with his prime minister. He explained that Werth was his best educated general who was respected even by the Germans who regularly asked for his opinion. Horthy advised the prime minister to leave the memorandum without a written answer.[105]

Bárdossy again swallowed his bile but now he summoned Werth and told him emphatically that these criticisms were unacceptable behavior. Bárdossy also indicated very courteously that he was willing to discuss and clarify any differences of opinion that may arise.[106] Both knew that there really was nothing to clarify. The two views were in open conflict and one of them had to give way.

The general was so confident of his position that on August 19 he sent an even stronger memorandum to the Sándor Palace in which he made further accusations. He claimed that it was the slender Hungarian participation that was responsible for the very severe German losses in the Lemberg (Lwow) battle and therefore for the slow down of the entire campaign.[107] According to Werth, the implications and importance of the above would be fully appreciated only after the end of the war and it would be then that the Germans would hold the Hungarians accountable.

Bárdossy was taken aback by the language of the memorandum. In it, the chief of the Hungarian General Staff accused the prime minister in the name of the German army. As though any decision of the Hungarian government could have contributed to the serious losses suffered by the German armed forces. He wished to stop Werth's insubordination. For this reason he decided to see the regent and have him choose between Werth and Bárdossy.

He wanted to make sure, however, that he would not lose the game and did not want the regent to decide on the basis of his instincts and preferences. He carefully studied the memorandum, thought about it at length and only then drafted his answer, addressed to Werth but really meant for Horthy.

- - -

In drafting the response he was very careful that its tone be pleasing to the head of state. It was with the "deepest respect" that he asked for permission to submit his response, used the expression with deep respect repeatedly in the text and concluded with "deferential respect."[108] He knew very well from past experiences that the regent was more favorably inclined toward his chief of the General Staff and therefore he used two possible alternatives in determining the size of the Hungarian forces fighting on the German side.

He knew that it would be inadvisable to try to justify the appropriateness of the modesty of the Hungarian commitment and he therefore indicated that the forces involved were an appreciable percentage of the total strength of the country. The well-armed and expensively supplied Rapid Deployment Force and the Army Air Force were the most important components of the Hungarian army and the most useful ones in modern warfare.[109]

His second argument consisted of showing that Werth's and Bartha's prognoses were wrong. He recalled that both thought that the Hungarian forces would be needed for only a very short time and it was for this reason that Werth had recommended on June 26 that only the Rapid Deployment Force be used in the campaign against the Soviets. Bárdossy was aware that in questioning Werth's highly respected military strategic ability he could turn the regent against himself. It was for this reason that he wrote that even the greatest expertise could not always foresee how a war was going to turn out.[110] He used this great tact to strengthen his own position and stated that the mistake was the government's responsibility and that not even a shred of it could be laid at Werth's doorstep. It was a clever move to involve the government and thus suggest that his opinion was actually a component of the opinions of a number of people.[111]

He then went to the attack and wrote that he had to protest that the chief of the General Staff, who had his say earlier, now accused the government of "omissions" and of having caused Hungary irremediable damage with its decisions.

The heaviest blow that Bárdossy delivered against his opponent concerned the smashing of the latter's ideas of the future, particularly as far as a population expulsion was concerned. Werth, during the discussions of increased military participation, wished also to discuss the recapture of the historic borders of the country, the expulsion of the Romanians, Slavs and Jews from these areas and also a share in Soviet supplies of raw materials.

Bárdossy indicated that the expulsion of the Romanians and Slavs from Hungarian territory would involve approximately eight million people. Within the borders of historic Hungary, other than in Croatia-Slavonia, there was an area of about 100,000 square kilometers. inhabited exclusively or to a greater extent by Slavs and Romanians. After expulsion such an area would be essentially uninhabited. In addition, an area of about 50,000 square kilometers would have its population severely depleted.[112]

Depopulating such an enormous area would significantly reduce the national assets. It seems likely that the expelled population would take its animals and other assets with them, as had happened in other population exchanges. The agricultural and industrial paralysis of the evacuated areas would adversely affect all other parts of the country. The remaining population, about eleven million Hungarians and two million Germans could not possibly replenish the vacated areas. It would take about 114 years to get the population of the country back to the present twenty-two million people assuming that the current growth rate would continue. There were scattered Hungarians living outside of the Carpathian Basin but their repatriation would be highly problematic.[113]

If the enormously complex expulsion would be implemented even the most vivid imagination could barely envisage the disastrous effects it would have on the life of the entire region. It would also be impossible, he concluded, that the Axis Powers would assume responsibility for the expulsions that were not even in the best interests of the country.

He reread the message and liked what he read. He felt that it was impossible for him not come out ahead in the fight and it was in this spirit that he concluded by giving the regent a choice. He wrote, "Since the chief of the General Staff claims the right to judge the decisions and actions of the Hungarian government and to make demands regarding his activities in the future, I must state with great respect, that I do not see that my cooperation with the chief of the General Staff is at all assured.[114]

The failure of the German Blitzkrieg made the regent irritable vis-à-vis Werth's political ambitions and made him receptive to the ideas in the Bárdossy letter. The general realized that he was in a vacuum and therefore on September 5, for reasons of health, tendered his resignation.[115] Horthy had no objection and on the very next day appointed General Szombathelyi to replace him.[116] On September 7 László Bárdossy, prime minister and minister of foreign affairs, accompanied by the new chief of the General Staff left to visit Hitler at the Führer's headquarters.[117]

- - -

The Molotov-Ribbentrop Pact of August 23, 1939, pushed the five-year Anti-Comintern Pact between Germany and Japan, of November 25, 1936, into oblivion. After the attack on the Soviet Union, however, the Anti-Comintern Pact, joined by Italy in 1936 and by Hungary on February 24, 1939, became once again a major propaganda weapon. The pact, expiring in November 1941, was extended for another five years. At the signing, Hungary was represented by László Bárdossy.

The State of War with Great Britain

Iosif Vissarionovich Stalin did not think much of Hungary, this bean-shaped little country in the Carpathian Basin that in his eyes did not amount to a hill of beans. He thought with dislike of the Hungarian leadership that declined his offer of cooperation against Romania. And he was particularly annoyed that the gesture made by Commissar of Foreign Affairs Viacheslav Mikhailovich Molotov to the Hungarian minister on June 23 was silently ignored by Budapest. The Soviet official declared that the USSR had no territorial claims against Hungary, and supported its revisionist stance against Romanaia. Admittedly the gesture was made at a time of profound crisis but nevertheless an offer from a major power to a small country should have received some acknowledgment.[118]

When in October Stalin urged his ally Winston Churchill to have Great Britain declare war on Germany's allies, he included Hungary with Finland and Romania ignoring the substantially different conditions in the three countries. London initially refused to consider this request and nothing was said. When an answer could no longer be avoided, on November 4, Churchill argued on behalf of all three countries. He claimed that in all three countries a considerable portion of public opinion was opposed to the course taken and that a declaration of war would place these people into an awkward position. Further that such an act would make it seem to the rest of the world that these countries were Hitler's allies rather than his satellites and that, in fact, Germany was at the head of major coalition. The arguments did not sway Moscow and Churchill eventually yielded.[119]

In Budapest the British Legation had been closed since April and British interests were represented by the United States Minister Herbert Pell. Bárdossy barely shook off the dust of his trip to Germany when on November 29 Pell, a friend he had not seen for some time, asked to see him. Bárdossy was astonished by the ultimatum in the form of a note.

The note stated that Hungary was abetting and substantially assisting the Third Reich's aggressive engagements. Therefore, unless Hungary ceased any military action by December 5, His Majesty's Government would declare a state of war. "Mr. Minister," Bárdossy tried to collect his thoughts,

> There is no Hungarian soldier at the front. Our soldiers are strictly in the communication zone. Today is the 29th of November. It is physically impossible to bring them all home by December 5. I assure you that my government has no intention of sending any additional soldiers to the Soviet Union.[120] I would like to hope that His Majesty's government that has repeatedly demonstrated its understanding of our difficult position will not make this position even more difficult.

The American minister sensed the bitterness behind this statement and was sympathetic toward the people of the host country. He offered to serve as an intermediary and asked Bárdossy to put his arguments into writing.

The former Hungarian diplomat now prime minister, however, did not trust the British and his words had been crafted by diplomacy and not by sincerity. He was deeply offended by a number of things the British had done, for instance, that in April Churchill did not distinguish between Germany and Hungary and ignored the fact that Budapest was trying to do the right thing by the Hungarians in the Délvidék.

He also was very much, perhaps too much, aware of the fact that Berlin was considerably closer to Budapest than London. He was afraid of the Germans and apprehensive about putting his arguments on paper. Hence, he only emphasized to Pell that Hungary was waging a defensive war against the Soviet Union.[121]

This was not a good answer since it did not correspond to the facts. Bárdossy should have known that there were quite a few people in the Foreign Office who viewed the issues of this region from the pro-Soviet and anti-Hungarian perspective of Edvard Beneš and not on the basis of legitimate Hungarian complaints.

It was a mistake to give these influential officials further ammunition. What he should have written about was the impossibility of meeting the demands and of the good intentions of the country that would hopefully bear fruit in the future.

- - -

On December 5 the London ultimatum expired. During the past few days Bárdossy vacillated between sober reasoning and emotion-driven irritation. It can be mentioned as a sign of his more sober reasoning that at a dinner given to the visiting governor-general of occupied Poland, Hans Frank, on December 1, he spoke of Hungary not having any territorial demands beyond the historic borders of the country and thus nullified Szombathelyi's September request in Germany that Hungary wished to participate in the readjustment of the Hungarian-Polish border.[122] As the days passed, however, emotions took over ever more strongly. Emotions that never give good advice suggested to him that the British action was not only unjust but offensive.

In a circular to the Hungarian legations he wrote that the government would acknowledge the British government's communication without further comment and that Hungarian behavior would not be determined by the wishes of the British government. The entire Hungarian nation was deeply shocked and offended by the British decision that simply meant that Great Britain wished to assist the Soviet Union by terrorizing and sacrificing Hungary.[123]

It was unnecessary to involve the nation in this matter. Bárdossy himself admitted at the time of his trial that the nation would have much preferred not to become involved in the war against the Soviet Union.[124] We must also repeat that Great Britain's ultimatum was in response to its ally's not unreasonable demand and was made under some duress. The nation was busy with its daily life. Its principal objective was to survive the whole sorry affair. It was not Great Britain that terrorized Hungary but its own rulers. They were the ones who brought on the war. It would have been better to think about the reasons that made Great Britain line up on the side of the Soviets. It would have been better if, instead of the evident extreme touchiness and the related and unjustified arrogance, he would have calmly accepted the fact that London was fulfilling its obligations to its ally.

He assumed the entire odium for the rejection of the ultimatum. He saw no way out and since he could not conceive that anyone else could find such a way and also that any opposition would be a pointless, time-wasting and nerve-wracking importunity, he acted strictly on his own and did not consult the government or the leading opposition deputies. He was too proud a man to seek ways to share the responsibility and he was particularly anxious not to consult the head of state.

On December 5 he simply announced to the house that as of that evening Hungary was presumably in a state of war with Great Britain. He was neither surprised nor particularly pleased when the honorable house greeted the announcement with a shout of "hurrah" by a large majority and, without dissent, lined up on the side of Germany. The deputies rose and instead of thinking about and questioning it, started singing the national anthem. Some of them reached for their handkerchief and wiped tears from their eyes.[125]

The following evening he received from Pell the anticipated British memorandum. Accordingly, one minute after midnight saw the beginning of the state of war between Great Britain and Hungary. One day later London's allies, Australia, South Africa, Canada and New Zealand also declared war on Hungary.[126]

Going to War with the United States of America

Two days later, on December 7, 1941, the Japanese navy launched an unprovoked, devastating attack against the United States naval and army base at Pearl Harbor. Historians argue to this day about Hitler's motivations but the fact remains that on December 11, Germany, with Italy, declared a state of war to exist between them and the United States of America.[127]

The Führer announced his decision in a great speech in the Reichstag. In his speech he stated again and again that the United States had repeatedly provoked Germany. He emphasized this because the Tripartite Pact was technically a defensive pact and the signatories had to render assistance only if another signatory was attacked. Hitler, therefore, wished to prove that his empire had been the victim of aggression and therefore he wanted to involve all of his allies in the war against the United States. Hitler's step was insane but had its own logical basis. It made the fight global and the options were victory or death. There was no longer any room for the tactics that followed the entry into the war against the Soviet Union and which were described above.

Sztójay's cable was placed before Bárdossy immediately and in it the minister advised that Baron Weizsäcker hoped that the Hungarian government would draw the obvious conclusions in the spirit of the Tripartite Pact.[128] Bárdossy knew that this time he could not act on his own, but he also wished to avoid a multilateral and protracted discussion of the Hungarian position.

He immediately summoned the Council of Ministers into session.[129] At the meeting he strongly emphasized that according to the speech of the Führer the state of war was the result of the aggressive actions by the United States. He mentioned two possibilities: the suspension of diplomatic relations and the declaration of war. Unable to curtail his impatient personality, he demanded that the council reach a decision that same day. Even his train of thought was brought into disarray by the burdens of the situation. On the surface his words made sense but underneath his thoughts were clearly in turmoil.

He said that it was patently impossible to provide any assistance in the fight against the United States. Therefore it was not necessary to declare war.[130] The question was whether the German government would be satisfied with a severance of diplomatic relations and whether this would satisfy Hungary's obligations under the Tripartite Pact?

"Gentlemen," he said, rejecting the option of severing diplomatic relations, "I believe it is desirable that we do not wait for Berlin to state its wishes. Weizsäcker's message is clear. I recommend that we declare our solidarity with the Axis Powers."[131]

He did not mention a state of war, he only spoke of solidarity. Carrying this concept to absurdity, it might even have allowed for a continuation of diplomatic relations.

Ferenc Keresztes-Fischer was the first one to speak and, according to his well-known views, spoke very conservatively. He addressed the concrete hazards lurking behind a declaration of war. In this way he criticized the head of government who had already ruled out any possible military action against the United States. He raised the alarming possibility that in order to maintain order Hungarian troops might have to be sent to Serbia.

Bárdossy, who was not familiar with the contents of the agreement between Germany, Italy and Japan, signed that day, emphasized that this agreement could not have deleterious effects on Hungary. It could not be asked to march into Serbia on the basis of the Tripartite Pact and the geographic location of the country obviously excluded any possibility of armed action against the United States. Minister of Defense Károly Bartha was ambivalent. He emphasized the potential advantage over neighboring countries by a prompt declaration of war but he also wondered if the declaration may not be considered to be "grotesque" in view of the enormous disparity in power between Hungary and the United States. Ferenc Keresztes-Fischer made no bones about it: Japan was the aggressor.[132]

At this point Bárdossy closed the discussion. He made the group unanimously accept a declaration which contained the unqualified solidarity with the Axis Powers and the severance of diplomatic relations with the United States. He asked for a free hand in case he had to go further. He received unanimous approval to declare the existence of a state of war if this should prove necessary.[133]

It was along these lines that he informed the regent who was being treated in the Szieszta Sanatorium. The roles had been reversed. On June 26 the head of state decided and Bárdossy accepted it. Now, in essence, the prime minister decided and the head of state did the accepting.[134]

Bárdossy buried his head into the sand. He did not wish to, because he did not dare to, confront the expected German indignation. It was simpler to call Herbert Pell who was very relieved that the prime minister did not declare war. The Germans, however, were naturally not satisfied with such a luke-warm form of solidarity.

- - -

On the basis of the Tripartite Pact of September 27, 1941, and on the basis of having become a signatory to this agreement on November 20, 1941, as well as on the basis of the principles of solidarity agreed to on December 11, 1941, Hungary considered that the state of war existing between Germany, Italy, Japan and the United States of America equally applied to and was in existence for Hungary as well.[135]

This is where Bárdossy had come to. And this is where he had led Hungary to. It was not done out of evil intent and not even entirely in free will. Yet, his policy cannot be excused, it can be understood, but he cannot be exonerated.

Evidently the conditions were weighty and increasingly suffocating. Yet, these conditions were not the result of blind fate, but of many bad decisions for which the prime minister was principally responsible. It was not necessary to proceed at such a rapid rate to a point where it became increasingly difficult to do anything beneficial for Hungary or to distance her from Hitler's will. The prime minister again raised the ogre of a German occupation. There is no valid answer as to what would have happened if there had been no declaration of war against the United States. We do know, however, that to this day there is no documentary evidence that Hitler ever considered the possibility of occupying Hungary earlier than September 1943.

The naively conspiratorial Hungarian attempts toward a separate peace were well known to the Germans. As far as the Nazis were concerned this was the greatest sin and yet it did not result in an occupation. Prime Minister Kállay rapidly became a persona non grata in Hitler's eyes and in March 1943 he demanded that Horthy dismiss him. The regent refused to do so and the retribution was limited to Berlin's instructions to the German Minister Dietrich von Jagow to avoid the prime minister. In September 1943 it was not the Hungarian policy, but the changes in Italy that motivated Hitler's plans for occupation.

- - -

At his trial before the People's Court Bárdossy was also indicted for his policies of 1944.

During the appeal hearings, in his speech delivered as his closing statement, he made a shocking point: In order to protect Hungarian lives and Hungarian assets and to minimize and control destruction, a political and military unit should have been created that by its weight could have forced the German army to evacuate the country rapidly and that during the retreat the national treasures be protected as much as possible.[136]

He not only castigated the October 15, 1944, attempt to leave the war with harsh words but also indicated what should have been done: By utilizing the nation's political and military strength (army and legislature) the German army should have been forced to respect Hungarian assets and to control its vengeful and hateful excesses.[137]

We can ask very quietly that if we applied this yardstick to the foreign policy of the Bárdossy government what conclusions could we draw? It seems almost unnecessary to try to answer this but we may calmly and hopefully objectively conclude that in 1941 there was much greater political elbowroom than in 1944. Not only because after March 19, 1944, Hungary was an occupied country but also because there was much more freedom of action even in domestic policies. Bárdossy gave no evidence whatever that he attempted to consolidate the national forces. There is no evidence that as prime minister and minister of foreign affairs, when he could have done the most, he did anything at all along the lines suggested by his statement of 1945.

The Isolation of László Bárdossy

Much to the surprise of public political opinion, the daily newspaper of the Hungarian Social Democratic Party, *Népszava*, on Christmas Day 1941, announced the formation of the National United

Front to stand against the increasingly one-sided, pro-German official policy. The idea originated with the Communist Gyula Kállai who worked in the editorial office of the paper. His party had been outlawed and was ineffective but had been seeking for years an opportunity for a more successful political activity. Now that the country was ever more heavily in the shadow of the Third Reich the Communists wished to concentrate their organizational skills in fostering the idea of national independence.

In the Christmas issue the various stages of the Hungarian independence issue were discussed by Communist and Socialist intellectuals as well as by the young village-sociologist writers who once again described the revolting poverty and squalor of the Hungarian villages. The group advocating national unity also, and most surprisingly, included the conservative Gyula Szekfű and the nationalist Endre Bajcsy-Zsilinszky.

Szekfű's article was set on the front page. It was the work of one of the most prominent historians whose famous work *Három Nemzedék* [Three Generations], written in 1920, served as the ideological basis for the counterrevolution. Even though during the past two decades he was increasingly critical of the system, in 1941 he was still very much a member of its inner circle.

Endre Bajcsy-Zsilinszky was also one of the organizers. Even though he had increasing difficulties with the sordid reality negating the captivating slogans, he was still fighting his battles for a better country from within the protected bastion of the establishment.

It was this circle that organized the Történelmi Emlékbizottság [Historical Commemorative Committee] in January 1942. This committee invited society to gather and preserve the data and documents attesting to Hungary's millennial battle for independence. There was no doubt that they were addressing both the past and the future.

This was well known to the Minister of the Interior Ferenc Keresztes-Fischer. While he was always in the minority in the government with his admonitions, he thought that by supporting this committee he might find an expression for his deepest convictions. The highly influential minister, however, had other tools as well.

As early as the fall of 1941 he visited Miklós Kállay at his country estate. Kállay had been the minister of agriculture in the Gömbös government from 1932 to 1935. Since 1937 he was active as the president of the National Irrigation Administration.

Keresztes-Fischer indicated to his host that he should get ready for a greater task.[138] Lipót Baranyai, the president of the Hungarian National Bank and Ferenc Chorin a leading figure of Hungarian industry and banking, soon thereafter spoke even more clearly. Subsequent visitors included the chairman and two vice chairmen of the governing party. They were unanimous that Bárdossy was leading the country into perdition. He had to be replaced and it was Miklós Kállay who had to take his place.[139]

- - -

The regent and his entourage were not quite ready for a change. Miklós Kállay was going to get a dreadful inheritance anyway, let the present prime minister take care of two issues. Let him try to hold Ribbentrop's demands to a minimum and let him move through Parliament an act establishing the position of deputy-regent.

On New Year's Day Hitler addressed a letter to Horthy in which he asked for additional Hungarian troops for the major offensive beginning in the spring.[140] There was no doubt in Budapest what the purpose of Ribbentrop's visit was going to be.

Ribbentrop managed to be bombastic, underhanded and rude all at the same time. He was spouting tirades about the certainty of the forthcoming German victory, about the destruction of communism in 1942. He then rapidly progressed to a demand that the entire Hungarian army be sent to the Soviet Union. When he saw the consternation on Bárdossy's face he immediately became threatening. He talked of the fair and passionate nature of Hitler and, trying to frighten his reluctant host, indicated that it was possible that under such circumstances the Führer might choose to forego Hungarian assistance.[141] He added, however, that such a decision would make the worst possible impression on German public opinion, the Nazy Party and the government. Then, seeing that Bárdossy was looking for a compromise and knowing that he had been bluffing when he asked for the entire army, Ribbentrop again changed tactics and suggested that the magnitude of Hungarian sacrifices may be proportional to the future satisfaction of Hungary's territorial claims.

During the negotiations these seemingly friendly segments were the most dangerous ones because under German leadership a new Little Entente was being formed whose members were making far greater sacrifices on the altar of Nazi victories than Hungary. It would thus be totally unrealistic to expect any additional territorial changes.

Ribbentrop's demands were not limited to soldiers. He again brought up the issue of crude oil shipments. Of the 40,000 tons demanded in November as a supplement to the annual quota, Bárdossy only authorized 6,000 tons.[142] Now the Germans demanded an additional 60–80,000 tons. They also asked for 20,000 young German-Hungarians to be inducted into the Waffen-SS. There had been trouble earlier with a segment of the German population in Hungary. Therefore this request was considered favorably with conditions that would simplify some of the existing problems. Agreement was conditional on only those young men being inducted who were ethnic German nationals and who were members of the Volksbund. In any case written permission from the parents was to be required [In Hungary at that time majority was not reached until the twenty-fourth birthday].

Berlin had to agree to give these young men German citizenship since induction into the German army meant the loss of their Hungarian citizenship. And, in spite of Ribbentrop repeated hectoring, Bárdossy refused to take the responsibility alone or only with the spinelessly pro-German minister of defense in this most important issue. Even a partial compliance with the German demands would have meant the collapse of Bárdossy's minimalist program.

He also had no doubts about the message contained in the Christmas issue of *Népszava*. He discussed the matter repeatedly with the government and insisted that Horthy also be present.[143]

Finally, on the last day of the visit, on January 10, Horthy and Bárdossy together delivered the answer to Ribbentrop, much to the latter's relief. While Hungary could not release its entire army for the eastern campaign it was willing to go to the absolute acceptable limits and participate in the campaign with much larger forces than so far.[144]

Wilhelm Keitel, the chief of the German Military High Command (Oberkommando der Wehrmacht), arrived in Budapest on January 20, 1942, to settle the details of the agreement. The situation at the front and the frequent German visitors strongly suggested to a number of

Hungarians that Hungary was likely to participate in the war to a greater extent that heretofore. It was against this possibility that Endre Bajcsy-Zsilinszky raised his voice with his customary impetuosity. On January 19, he wrote a very long letter to the prime minister.[145]

- - -

Bárdossy presented his reply at the January 19 session of the Foreign Affairs Committee of the lower house. He stated firmly that Hungary's place was on the side of the Axis Powers and that the Second Hungarian Army was being dispatched to the front.

Endre Bajcsy-Zsilinszky was a member of the committee and could see that his long letter had been a call into the wilderness. Being furiously angry he declared that the agreement with the Germans was unconstitutional and he also condemned the Újvidék (Novi Sad) massacre of Serbs and Jews by Hungarian troops in the strongest possible terms.

Bárdossy responded harshly and his words were made even more hateful by the vociferous approval of the fascist Imrédyst and Arrow Crossist deputies.[146] From this time on Endre Bajcsy-Zsilinszky not only had nothing good to say about Bárdossy but considered him as one of the most despicable figures in Hungarian history.

The Last Weeks in the Sándor Palace

Contrary to the indictment before the People's Court, the verdict concluded that Bárdossy was not in a position to prevent the Zsablya (Žabalj) and Újvidék atrocities committed at the beginning of 1942. Bárdossy had ordered an investigation by the proper authorities and had urged its completion. He was not in a position to prevent the suppression of the report and the final quashing of the indictment took place months after his resignation. Consequently he was found innocent of this accusation.[147]

On the third day of the trial, the presiding judge, in order to show the guilt of the accused, inaccurately and omitting most of the sentences favorable to Bárdossy, read Bajcsy-Zsilinszky's letter of January 1942.[148]

Bárdossy evidently did not remember the letter but was extremely annoyed that the court brought Bajcsy-Zsilinszky up as an accuser when Bajcsy-Zsilinszky also represented an intransigent revisionist point of view. In addition the judge asked him if he had been present at the session of the Arrow Crossist Parliament that suspended Bajcsy-Zsilinszky's parliamentary immunity. Bárdossy answered that he did not remember but then, breaking his self-imposed serenity, he stated forcefully, "The deputy liked to send me letters. I wonder why he did not make his 'nation-saving' statements before the house? Why did he bombard the prime minister with these missives when the prime minister was accountable to the house?"[149]

Bajcsy-Zsilinszky had been hanged barely ten months earlier, on Christmas Day 1944, on the orders of the war puppet Arrow Cross government. His crime was his opposition to the trend that placed Hungary on the side of Germany and caused the tragedy of the country. One of the most prominent supporters of this trend had been László Bárdossy.

The accused Bárdossy was correct in stating that as far as demanding territorial revision was concerned there was no difference between them. He could also have said that in the political program of the martyr there had been serious internal contradictions. Yet, to speak in these terms of the man who on numerous occasions proved his courage, who a number of times completely alone stood up against the wildly hostile house, who was the only major figure to try to defend Hungary with arms against the March 19, 1944, German occupation of Hungary and who was not reluctant to sacrifice his most precious possession, his life, for his patriotic convictions, was a most despicable act.

- - -

During the dramatic year of 1941, the seventy-three-year old Horthy was frequently ailing and some believed that he was suffering from some fatal illness. It was reasonable to assume that on his death in office an extremist, pleasing to Hitler, would take his place.

The circle around the regent believed that one way of mitigating the situation would be to appoint Horthy's oldest son, István, as deputy regent. He was known for having made a series of much stronger anti-

Nazi statements than his father. As president of MÁV (Hungarian National Railroads) he had demonstrated his social sensitivity.

Toward the end of November, Horthy asked Bárdossy to initiate the required steps. His letter indicated that he wanted an act that gave his son the right of succession, i.e. that his son could follow him in the regental position.[150]

The Arrow Crossists and the Imrédysts opposed István's appointment as deputy regent and there were others who were against any formal act of succession. Hence the legislative proposal omitted this latter point. There was much debate about the entire legislation, however on February 19, 1942, the lower house, unanimously and by acclamation, elected István Horthy deputy regent.[151]

THE FALL

On March 4, 1942, the head of state informed his prime minister that he no longer trusted him and asked for his resignation. Bárdossy was deeply offended but still, that same day submitted his resignation citing his state of health as the reason. In order to make the reason for the abdication more credible he had himself admitted to the Szieszta Sanatorium. The quiet surroundings and the stress-free environment in fact were beneficial for him. It was also a suitable environment for him to ponder the reasons for his dismissal. He saw very clearly that the reasons were related to his foreign policies and not to the domestic ones.

He could accomplish practically nothing of his domestic program and hence this could hardly be the reason for discontent. A major negative domestic issue was the enactment of the third anti-Semitic legislation but he did not think that he was being blamed for it. The anti-Semitism widely held by the gentile middle-class was shared by Bárdossy but his comportment with the Jewish population was dictated largely by the foreign and domestic political environment of the country. It was for this reason that he submitted the third anti-Semitic law (Act XV, 1941) to Parliament. It contained the requirement of premarital physical examination and forbade marriage between Jew and gentile. The act also declared that a sexual act between Jew and gentile was criminal miscegenation and thus punishable.

He knew, however, that he could not be held accountable for the Kamenets-Podolski massacre. In this area, at the end of August, 1941 about 10,000 Jews expelled from Hungary had been murdered. The reason behind the expulsion was the decision that Jews who fled to Hungary from neighboring countries and held no Hungarian citizenship had to be "repatriated" to Galicia. The attack against the Soviet Union made this possible. It did not mean, however, that the Hungarian leadership, including Bárdossy knew that the expulsion would lead to the massacre of the Jews. When one of them, escaping back to Hungary, reported the shocking story to Keresztes-Fischer, the minister of the interior immediately halted further deportations and Bárdossy did not reverse the decision of the minister.[152] Bárdossy, therefore, concluded that it was his pro-German policy which led to his condemnation.

Debate With Miklós Kállay

Bárdossy was relieved from his duties on March 7. Two days later Miklós Kállay became the new prime minister who in order to allay Berlin's suspicions, took over the entire former cabinet.

For the same reason, and knowing that it would be refused, he offered the post of minister of foreign affairs to Bárdossy. He went to see his predecessor at the sanatorium and it was here that he received the very welcome rejection of the offer. This was the last time that they ever met and this meeting was a deeply agitated one.

The fallen head of government spoke passionately. "You will lead the country into a catastrophe," he said.

Everybody knows that you are anti-German and pro-British and that you are not an anti-Semite. You will run after the British, but you will never catch them. Bethlen tried it and failed and so will you. They are obligated to our enemies, the Russians and the Little Entente and will never abandon them.[153] You will lose the friendship of the Germans and Hungary will be left alone. If the Germans lose the war, we will also be considered a loser and there is nothing you can do about it. This was decided after World War I and at Trianon.[154]

It was his profound resentment that made the words so offensive although their content accurately reflected the slanted perspective that was the reason for the former prime minister's many hasty decisions and which in future years made him increasingly rigid. He was unwilling to realize that it was he who led the country toward a catastrophe and that it was under his prime ministership that the country had made the most rapid strides toward the catastrophe already looming on the horizon.

It is true that in the Délvidék issue and in the Soviet war he did precisely what he was expected to do, but the state of war with Great Britain and with the United States was largely his personal accomplishment. When he mentally reviewed the course of events he was correct in feeling that over time the country's position became increasingly difficult and that his freedom of action became more limited. Yet, instead of facing up to his responsibilities, he kept harping on the minutia with which he tried to avoid taking the fateful steps.

He viewed the British political obligations essentially correctly, but he refused to acknowledge that it was Hungary's acceptance of the territorial revisions from the hands of Germany that lay at the root of the deterioration of British-Hungarian relations. But when he now said that the British would "never" change he forgot that the British criticism of the breach of the Hungarian-Yugoslav Eternal Friendship Pact was truly applicable to this situation.

The adherence to the point of view after 1941, that the only way was the German way, was a rejection of any policy that sought to distance itself from Germany. Such a policy had only a very narrow path to tread but there was such a path and perhaps it could have been broadened. But only with a policy better than his.

Fráter (Brother) György, Alias László Bárdossy

He made no self-assessment but he was very anxious to justify his failed policies among the widest possible circle. For several months he stayed away from public affairs and spent much time at his home in the Virágárok utca. On occasion he took the bus, went downtown and spent hours at the University Library. He studied original documents and made notes from old books. He visited the East European institute, named after Pál Teleki and there consulted historians.

The following year he published a book entitled *Magyar politika a mohácsi vész után*. The central figure of the book was Fráter (Brother) György (Cardinal George Martinuzzi) and he used the cardinal as a reflection of himself. By examining the failure of the cardinal's policies he was arguing for the understanding and acceptance of his own policies as prime minister and minister of foreign affairs. He had accepted the war against the Soviet Union and the state of war with Great Britain and the United States to protect the country from German occupation— the worst possible event. He could therefore write about Fráter György with great understanding that the foundation of his policies was to keep both the two great opposed forces out of the country and not to alternate between them, allowing now the one and then the other to have a role in and an influence on the life of the country.[155]

When reading the book, Endre Bajcsy-Zsilinszky, who still considered Bárdossy a statesman at the beginning of 1942, became infuriated. This man, he wrote in one his letters, one of the greatest malefactors in Hungarian history, has the unmitigated gall to distort the events of past times and has used them to exonerate himself and instruct others how a real politician and major statesman ought to behave.[156]

Presumably Bajcsy-Zsilinszky exaggerated as much in this instance as he had earlier in his letter of January 19, 1942, albeit in the opposite direction. Yet in this instance he was closer to the truth since Bárdossy clearly made a mistake when he tried to explain the motivations of his actions by the career of Fráter György. Even though there were some similarities between the situations in the sixteenth and twentieth centuries, the situation after Mohács was quite different. At that time the independence of the Kingdom of Hungary was threatened by two much larger forces, while in 1941 the German danger was real but the Soviet danger, in the Stalin configuration, was not a realistic concern.

It was Bárdossy's entering the war that tempted fate. The statesmanship of Cardinal Martinuzzi consisted of getting the best possible conditions for Hungary after the country was already torn into three parts. Bárdossy, attempting to avert the threatening German peril by inept and unstatesman-like policies, let the Soviet danger loose on the country. It may be improper to suggest, however, that after the Second World War all the countries in this region shared the same fate. There is little benefit in the what if discussions but it is sufficient to point out that the goodwill of the three major world powers would have been a vastly different matter than what resulted from entering the war. At the very least, Hungary would have entered the Soviet sphere of influence under much more favorable conditions and circumstances.

The Last Years

In 1943 he accepted the presidency of the anti-Semitic Egyesült Keresztény Nemzeti Liga [United Christian National League] and in May 1944 he became the parliamentary representative of his native city, Szombathely. He made forceful speeches on the need to continue in the war, worked hard to unite the extreme right-wing parties and participated in the Nemzeti Szövetség [National Coalition], an organization devoted to preventing unilateral withdrawal from the war. His behavior caused consternation and disbelief even in the circles that previously identified themselves with him or supported him. Actually there were numerous examples in those days where an improperly defined morality and the weight of already completed actions held the individuals captive and prevented any reassessment of their life's work.[157]

Contrary to the indictment and to the findings of the first trial, on appeal he was found innocent on that point of the indictment that accused him of assisting the Arrow Crossists to power. It was felt that Bárdossy's activities focused on preventing the armistice negotiations. He was insistent on a position of complete cooperation with the Germans to the very end but he did not assist the fascist Arrow Cross Party to power.[158]

- - -

When the front moved closer, he left with his family for Szombathely in 1944. At the beginning of 1945, with the assistance of Minister Edmund Veesenmayer, Hitler's plenipotentiary in Hungary, he settled in Bavaria. On April 25, 1945, during the final hours of Nazi Germany, he saw the Swiss minister and asked him for an entry visa to Switzerland. Hans Frölicher, the minister, considered Bárdossy to be a diplomat who only did what his job required and recommended that the visa be granted. A few days later the former prime minister crossed the border and was swallowed up in one of the reception camps.

His pride was deeply offended by this situation. He believed that holding a diplomatic passport he and his family should be allowed complete freedom of movement. Knowingly or unknowingly he thereby sealed his own fate. His case was reviewed by the Swiss federal minister of justice and the police minister in Berne who were not nearly as forgiving as his foreign minister colleague. Prior to a decision an opinion was requested from Maximillien Jaeger, the former Swiss minister in Budapest and from János Wettstein, the former Hungarian minister in Berne. Even though neither of the diplomats made a derogatory statement, the Swiss Council of Ministers decided to expel Bárdossy. On May 4, he and his family were moved across the border and he found himself in Germany in an area already occupied by American troops. He was arrested and several months later, in the company of a number of other alleged war criminals he was returned to Hungary in handcuffs.[159]

In the Great Hall of the Music Academy

After weeks of preliminary hearings the trial began in the Great Hall of the Music Academy on October 29, 1945.

His hair gleamed in the hall like a rococo wig and he was very pale most of the time. His previously fragile physique had become almost ethereal under the deprivations, tensions and trials of the last few months. He sat behind a small table that was piled high with papers and also held a glass of water and some medications to strengthen his ailing body if need be.

His eyes, the intellectual mirrors of his being, were shining brightly. He paid great attention to everything that was said and immediately assessed the dangers lurking in the questions addressed to him. The gamble was enormous. Much more than his life was at stake since he had already acquiesced that his life would come to a sudden and forceful death. The gamble involved the entire meaning of his life. He fought to prove that while he was responsible for the dreadful tragedy of the country he committed no crime, let alone a series of crimes, and that his responsibility disappeared in the inevitable, historic predestination which led to Hungary's tragedy in World War II.

He could often feel superior to his adversaries, Ákos Major, the presiding judge and until recently a military judge advocate captain, to the public prosecutor and to the political prosecutor. He knew more than they, his knowledge had a much broader base and he could speak much more concisely and attractively. He used his superior linguistic knowledge to baffle the court with foreign expressions and turns of phrase. This was not always successful, the judge immediately responded to his Latin tags and, much to his surprise, Sándor Szalai, the political prosecutor responded in English to his English terminology.

From time to time he felt that he had the support of the audience. He could not know that the presiding judge received threatening anonymous telephone calls almost every evening but he was confident that the people who filled all the seats in the Great Hall would be favorably impressed by his successes in remedying the territorial demands of Trianon Hungary and that, with sympathetic eyes, they would see in him the champion of the revisionist ideal, dressed in the black national costume.[160]

Extraordinary events took place during the trial. It was unusual that justice was not administered by the usual court but by a People's Court established by four prime ministerial directives and elevated to legal status by Act VII, 1945. The trial was extraordinary also because this was the first time that a nationally well known person stood before the People's Court. The case was unusual also because the accused was a former prime minister of Hungary, and as such, under the still prevailing code, principally Act III, 1848, he should have been tried by a specially convoked parliamentary court.

For this reason and to the very end, László Bárdossy questioned the jurisdiction of the People's Court. Actually, in the Armistice Agreement, signed in Moscow on January 20, 1945, and raised to the force of law by Act V, 1945, Hungary agreed to participate in the arrest of persons accused of war crimes, in extraditing them to the appropriate governments and in trying them.[161] From this it would logically ensue that these crimes would be tried by a newly established court. It was also evident that the people responsible for the war crimes had to be sought principally among the people who held the highest positions during the war.

Yet, for the generation that grew up under the old Hungarian legal system, this procedure was unacceptable. It is enough to mention that Vince Nagy, the minister of the interior during the 1918 liberal democratic revolution, refused, for the above reasons to act as political prosecutor against Bárdossy, even though it was clear to him the Bárdossy had to be brought to account before a court. Later, however, Nagy did accept the role of political prosecutor in the later trial of Ferenc Szálasi, the leader of the Nazi puppet government.[162]

The circumstances of the trial were also extraordinary. There was no heat in the hall and those present shivered in winter coats. The judges kept their hats on and showed their bare heads to posterity only when photographs were being taken. The guns had been silent for months, but the deprivations and sufferings undergone during these months were evident everywhere.

The country and the capital were in ruins and the remnants of bridges over the Danube were slowing down the flow of the river. Daily life was very slow to recapture its normal activities and food, clothing, lodging and work all presented almost insuperable difficulties. Even worse than the economic injuries were the injuries suffered in human life. There was hardly any family that was not mourning someone or that was not searching for a lost father, mother, husband, wife or child. Suffering triggers passions and the burning pain urged the intellect to seek out those responsible.

László Bárdossy sat in the hall and these passions were swirling around him. Even the poorly informed were aware of the fact that it was under his prime ministership that Hungary entered the Second World War.

It is always the court's duty to place arguments and counter-arguments objectively and impartially into the balance. Yet under such extremely heavy external pressures the court could not remain free of emotions. The People's Court considered László Bárdossy to be an "evil" person who had committed unheard of crimes that did not have a parallel "anywhere in world history."[163]

On the other hand, Bárdossy's defense was made impressive not only by his superior intellect, his brilliant, quasi literary style of speaking, his widely based preparedness and debating skill, frequently bordering on sophistry, but also by his use of territorial revisions as one of his major arguments. These arguments were so very inflammatory because in the international situation in which the country found itself at the time, the People's Court could not afford to give any consideration to national sensitivities. At the end of the Second World War a peace had to be accepted that was even more disadvantageous from a territorial point of view than the still almost incomprehensible and unacceptable Trianon treaty. At the same time Bárdossy used the First and Second Vienna Awards and the Subcarpathian and Délvidék actions with their undeniable advantageous territorial arrangements as the bastions of his defense.[164]

For these reasons the trial frequently assumed the characteristics of a Sophoclean tragedy. Such an episode occurred when Bárdossy made some slighting and derogatory comments about Bajcsy-Zsilinszky's January 1942 letter and presiding judge shut him up and had him escorted out of the hall in shackles.

In the Still of the Cell

After the excitement of the courtroom, every evening in the still of his cell Bárdossy reviewed the events of the day and, indeed, of his entire life. The key turned in the lock, the guard brought him his usual supper, a tasty bean soup and a large slice of bread. He comfortably finished his dinner and then again started walking up and down within the narrow confines of his cell.

He smiled bitterly. Horthy. The idolized head of the country, the complete gentleman who, allegedly, in 1944 became incensed that Bárdossy had not submitted to him the code cable from the Hungarian minister in Moscow, József Kristóffy, about his conversation with Soviet Commissar of Foreign Affairs Molotov on June 23, 1941.

As though this cable would have made any difference in the way Horthy viewed the campaign against the Soviet Union. He corrected himself: it was not a matter of viewing, it was a matter of an iron determination. Werth and Bartha would have never dared to behave the way they did if they had not been sure that they had the full backing of the regent. He would never utter the term "military revolt" during the trial[165] but he had to admit that the presiding judge was correct in using that terminology. Horthy himself would have let the soldiers loose against him if he had not announced the state of war with the Soviet Union. The regent would have considered it impossible not to enter the war against Moscow on the side of the Germans.

It was true that his phenomenal career was largely due to Horthy. It was the regent who after Csáky's death accepted his nomination as minister of foreign affairs without any demur and later, after Teleki's death, made him the prime minister of the country bypassing even the usual interviews. Yet, what did Horthy do to help him in the terribly awkward situation? Nothing! When Bárdossy wanted to recall Sztójay from Berlin because Sztójay had become the mouthpiece of the Germans instead of the protector of the Hungarian interests in Germany, and when Sztójay himself would have been willing to come home and recoup his health which had been severely impaired by the strains and stresses of his position in Berlin, it was Horthy who decided that there would be no change in the person of the minister.[166] Furthermore, and he must have felt icy shivers run down his back at the thought, instead of gratitude he was entitled to feel bitterness since it was the decision of the regent that placed him into that crucial position. It was easy to see that at the trial they were looking for a scapegoat who could be made responsible not only for his concrete decisions but for all the sins and transgressions of the era hallmarked with the name of Miklós Horthy.

He must have thought with impotent rage, that he could be somewhere far away or, at the worst, could have been called as a witness in such a charade. It would not have been his neck that was being measured for a hempen collar, as it surely was the case. He may have even realized the wisdom of his captors, that they started these people's trials with him instead of Horthy. They knew very well that they would cut off the branch under their slowly evolving power base if they were to insist that the former regent be brought home and placed in such a pillory. Over time the former admiral had truly become for most the haloed head of state who stood beyond the reach of the muddy waves of day-to-day politics and who had become a noble symbol of the Hungarian nation even for those who did not care much for his person or his policies.

Surely the turning point came at the Council of Ministers meeting on June 26, 1941. He knew that it was his will that decided the outcome of the meeting but he also knew that he did not have the freedom of will. He was implementing the decision of the head of state, Regent Miklós Horthy.

Responsibility or Guilt

During the entire trial Bárdossy emphasized the difference between responsibility and guilt. In principle he was correct in making this distinction.

In the concrete situation, however, he would have been correct only if his statement that the rigid international position of the country meant an absolute predestination corresponded to historical facts. This is not so. Simply because the very real international position of the country allowed only a very narrow path, this did not exclude the possibility of some freedom of action. Freedom of action that during the quarter century of the so-called counterrevolutionary system, was sometimes limited and at times considerable.

It is true that the options for making choices became fewer and fewer. Prime Minister István Bethlen still had considerable latitude during the 1920s, but Gömbös in the 30s had much less, partly because of the Bethlen heritage. At the beginning of 1941 Bárdossy had even less and the most difficult situation was inherited by Miklós Kállay. This occurred because Bárdossy lacked the statesmanship to steer the ship of state, drifting toward a whirlpool, toward calmer waters with vigorous strokes of the oar. Instead, he brought the country, during one year of his rule, into war with the three great world powers.

He knew that he lacked the strength and talent to lead his nation and country out of the morass. This is why he said during the trial that all his life he remained an insignificant, low-level official.[167] The fact that he used this to escape from his responsibilities became ever clearer in the light of the passing years. In words he still accepted responsibility but by harping on the distinction between responsibility and guilt he, in fact, denied all responsibility. In order to dispel the conceptual fog created artificially by Bárdossy it is sufficient to point out that guilt, in a historical-political context, is not a moral category. It is a matter of degree.

The confrontation with the Soviet Union could have been avoided at that time. Under Miklós Kállay the country was already in a hopeless situation and for this Bárdossy, in second place behind the head of state, must carry a criminal responsibility. During the trial Bárdossy distorted the truth when he applied a sterile truth to a situation where it did not belong.

During the People's Court proceedings Bárdossy was made to sit on the bench of the accused as the representative of the entire counterrevolutionary system and this was an ignoble endeavor. Bárdossy was correct when he rejected this process. He indicated that looking at the time of his birth and at his career, his role did not seem to fit him into this era as though he could have taken a position among the creators or principal leaders of the period.[168]

Under the excuse of deflecting certain accusations he completely neglected his hardly insignificant role and instead of facing up to his substantial and even criminal responsibility, he depicted the period in a way that suggests that everything that happened had been rigidly pre-ordained. The absolute determinism of the counterrevolutionary period was consistently claimed by Bárdossy in a variety of contexts. He consistently held on to his determination not to say a word in mitigation of his actions and in lessening his responsibility. Actually, a number of the questions that he addressed to witnesses were directed precisely to this purpose. From beginning to end, however, he spoke of the predetermined course of history paralyzing action and offering no alternatives.

- - -

The trial, including the fact that the likelihood of the severest possible sentence was a given right from the beginning, was not a show trial and the accusations were not manufactured. Bárdossy's activities furnished more than enough reason for his condemnation.

It is a different issue that the severity of the sentence was much debated at the time and this debate may be even timelier now. This is suggested by the examination of post-war legal retributions in different countries. It appears that in Austria, for instance, where a large number of people participated in Hitler's suppressive and sadistic agencies, only thirty-two people were executed, while in Hungary 189 persons were executed for such crimes.[169] In all fairness it must be pointed out that a number of additional Austrian war criminals were brought to justice in the countries where they had committed their crimes.

The Bárdossy trial was not conducted irreproachably. The process was made unpleasant and was disfigured by errors, distorted presentations, incredible laxity in the citation of documents, occasional intentional misrepresentations, by the citation of laws no longer in effect and by judicial intemperance.[170]

Yet, in spite of this the People's Court did not violate the basic standards of jurisprudence. This is shown by the fact that neither Bárdossy nor his legal advisers ever used the defense of *nullum crimen sine lege* (no crime in the absence of law) meaning that a legal sentence can be handed down only for an action that, at the time it was performed, was a legally forbidden criminal act.

Bárdossy never recognized the jurisdiction of the People's Court and on appeal his lawyer filed a claim for dismissal of the lower court's verdict on the grounds that the presiding judge, Ákos Major, was not qualified as a judge or attorney. Yet, he never used the *nullum crimen sine lege* argument, presumably because of the logic that Bárdossy persistently held on to vis-à-vis his actions.

It was the *rebus sic stantibus* (this being the case) principle that applied, meaning that all events had to be analyzed and assessed on the basis of their own circumstances. It was this argument that Bárdossy used to explain that the validity of the 1940 Eternal Friendship Pact with Yugoslavia was null and void at the time of the occupation of the Délvidék. Bárdossy was aware of the fact that when the circumstances changed the law tended to follow the new situations and that the obligations assumed under international agreements had a ripple effect on domestic laws.

Standing in the shadow of death he abandoned much of the cynicism that characterized his previous life and, deeply sensitive to the immeasurable suffering caused by World War II, he said, "I admit that the legitimately gathered bitterness and passion must be allowed to dissipate. A way must be found to ease the soul in order that the reawakening spirit may lead to the unification of the nation. No sacrifice is too great that leads to this result."[171] To be sure, he did add, "Even though the sacrifice is in no way related to the dispensing of justice, as in this case."[172] His basic tenet here was evidently the recognition that there was ample justification for passions and bitterness.

The Sentence

The trial came to an end on November 2, 1945. The People's Court found the accused guilty for Hungary's involvement in World War II, for having participated in the enactment of the legislation against the Jewish population and for ordering the deportations to Galicia. He was found guilty also for agitating for the increased participation in the war and for trying to thwart the armistice agreement. The sentence was death by hanging, within walls but without excluding spectators.[173]

The appeal was heard in one of the intact rooms of the Parliament building behind closed doors, but with the press being present. The sentence was announced on December 28. With minor modifications it confirmed the previous sentence.

The execution was scheduled for January 10, 1946. The prisoner, taken to the condemned cell the night before had one last wish. He wished to take his last breakfast in the company of his wife. The guards were watching him very closely. They were evidently concerned about something happening that might prevent the execution of the sentence. This concern proved unnecessary. The physically very frail man did not collapse. With very much bitterness in his heart he defiantly watched the time go by. He asked for paper and pen and sent a message in writing to four people whom he considered important.[174]

- - -

During the night the Nemzeti Főtanács [Supreme National Council] executing the rights of the head of state, commuted the sentence of death by hanging to death by firing squad. Bárdossy learned about this only at the site of execution.

The cruelly handed down gesture of mercy again raised his passions. When the command to fire was given he exclaimed, "May God preserve the country from these..."[175] That was all he could say. He fell, but the bullets aimed at his chest and face did not kill him. He had to be shot from close range with a handgun by the prison commander.[176] The deed was done.

THE DOCUMENTS

THE DOCUMENTS IN THE CASE

The History of Their Publication

The material of the Bárdossy trial was published in a small booklet shortly after the completion of the trial as an official publication of the Magyar Országos Tudósító [Hungarian National Informer] and of the Magyar Távirati Iroda [The Hungarian News Bureau]. Similar volumes were published by these agencies after every major war crime trial.[177] The value of the booklet as source material is limited because it does not render an impartial account of the trial, emphasizing the aspects that show Bárdossy in a very unfavorable light, while the other side of the picture is either not included at all or is presented very sparingly. Yet the booklet became important in historiography because the trial documents survived only in parts in the archives of the Ministry of the Interior and were almost entirely unavailable in all other collections until the change in the political system. They were unavailable even to the professional historians during the era of the so-called People's Democracy.

In 1976, in Switzerland, a small volume was published under the title of *A nemzet védelmében* but it contained essentially only Bárdossy's two carefully constructed speeches[178] which he delivered or planned to deliver at the end of the first trial and at the end of the appeal process. Thus, after almost three decades, the other extreme position that saw the light of day came from abroad.

Biased data are unsuitable to learn the truth about the past. It was the plan in 1945 that the documents relative to the trials of the major war criminals before the People's Court be published in their full extent, as teaching material, so that the new generation could form an accurate historical perspective. The documents of the Bárdossy trial, particularly the justification of the sentence at the end of the initial trial, show clearly that the goal was not only to sentence László Bárdossy, but to pillory the entire Hungarian political system of the interwar period. It seemed therefore particularly appropriate in 1989, the critical year standing like a watershed between the past and the present, to provide the readers with a publication that contained all the available material and that also included notes and comments by a historian to assist the reader over the hurdles in the text. The work was completed in 1989 but funding for publication was made available only after a lengthy struggle and the book was finally published in 1991.[179]

The author of the above book found that the transcripts of the trials were not included in the copious material. He did find, however, numerous transcripts of earlier depositions of witnesses and could also include in the publication the transcripts of the interrogations conducted while Bárdossy was in American captivity. These documents were contained in the first section of the book. The second section dealt with the trial before the lower court. Of this material only the indictment, the sentence and Bárdossy's final speech can be considered completely authentic. The verbal exchanges of the trial, lasting a full week, were reconstructed by the author from the booklet published in 1945 and also from the 118 minute-long tape in the archives of Radio Hungary. The latter is fragmentary and contains material combining unrelated material. It took a considerable amount of very careful analysis to separate the material and reorganize it in a proper sequence. The author also took great pains to indicate very clearly from which of the three sources each part of the material in the publication was taken.

The third section deals with the trial before the Court of Appeals and contains two major texts. The first one is Bárdossy's closing speech. It was not in the 1945 booklet and was taken from the Swiss publication. Bárdossy's closing speech at the end of the first trial was available from the original transcript and comparing it with the material in the Swiss publication showed that except for some very minor differences the two texts were identical. Consequently, and after careful analysis of content and style, it was concluded that the text of the second speech, found only in the Swiss publication was authentic.

The text of the sentence of the Court of Appeals was taken from the archives of the Ministry of the Interior.

The transcript of the trial became available only in 1996 when it was published by László Jaszovszky.[180] Jaszovszky had the material in his possession for several decades and after the change of the system he submitted it to Prime Minister József Antal. From the Prime Minister's Office the transcript was sent to the Library of Parliament and it was only in 2001 that it finally arrived at its proper destination, the National Archives.

The 1996 volume makes it clear why we have been talking about the speech that Bárdossy planned to make under his right to the last word. The actual speech was repeatedly interrupted by the presiding judge who did not permit a proper and full delivery of the last message. Hence the original text has both additions and deletions as shown by the actual transcript.

It ensues from all this that historians in the future will have to assemble all these various fragments and coalesce them into a single volume.[181] The 1991 volume contains about a thousand footnotes to assist the reader. The final future publication will have to be even more extensive.

For the present volume the author felt that it would be appropriate to submit to the reader two larger units in their complete extent. One is the indictment and the other is the speech, planned and also largely delivered, under the right to the last word. The indictment in its stark bareness clearly shows the frequently valid passions that were marshaled against Bárdossy and, on the other side, the lines written in the solitude of the cell equally clearly reflect Bárdossy's point of view in its unvarnished purity. It is not the speech that was so frequently interrupted by the judge.

The Indictment Submitted by the Budapest Public Prosecutor to the Budapest People's Court on October 15, 1945

I charge the accused:
Dr. László Bárdossy
In preliminary detention since the 10th day of October, 1945,

(Born in Budapest* on December 10, 1890, Mother's name Gizella Zalka,** married, former royal Hungarian prime minister and minister of foreign affairs, residing at Virágárok utca 8, Budapest, II) with the following:

1. War crimes under Point 2, Paragraph 11 of Act VII, 1945 (Nbr.) [Népbíróság/Peoples's Court][182] which he committed by

a) as royal Hungarian prime minister and minister of foreign affairs, in Budapest on April 1, 1941, six weeks after the ratification of Eternal Friendship Pact with Yugoslavia, at the meeting of the Supreme Defense Council, he reported and endorsed the request of the German government[183] for Hungary to participate actively in the armed German action against Yugoslavia, then, on April 11[184] at the Council of Ministers meeting he announced that Yugoslavia had disintegrated into its component parts and that this fulfilled the conditions set by the Supreme Defense Council for beginning the military action, and finally he drafted and countersigned the proclamation of the former regent[185] announcing the armed occupation of the Yugoslav districts of Bácska [Bačka], Muraköz [Medjumurje] and Baranya [Baranja], which meant a declaration of war with Yugoslavia without having requested the approval of Parliament, as required by Paragraph 13 of Act I, 1920[186];

b) At the Council of Ministers session, held in Budapest on June 26, 1941 he recommended that a state of war be declared to be in existence between the Soviet Union and Hungary and further recommended the utilization of the Hungarian army beyond the borders of the country.[187] His recommendations were carried by a majority vote in the Council of Ministers. He announced the decision of the Council of Ministers to the Parliament on the following day, prior to the regular agenda of the lower house, that is he announced that he had declared war, without prior approval of the house on a Great Power even though said Great Power had assured our country of its goodwill towards us. The accused withheld the relevant telegram from the regent and from the members of the cabinet and further he announced the deployment of the army beyond the borders of the country only on July 25 at which

*Crossed out. Corrected in pencil to Szombathely.
** Correctly: Zarka.

time, without waiting for action by the house he recessed the house for the summer vacation;

c) On December 12, 1941, in spite of the fact that on the preceding day the Council of Ministers authorized only a statement about the solidarity with the Axis Powers and the severing of diplomatic relations with the United States of America,[188] he, in spite of the Council of Ministers' decision and according to the facts described above, declared that a state of war existed between Hungary and the United States of America. This declaration being made unconstitutionally and on his own decision, finally he falsified the minutes of the two Council of Ministers meetings in question prepared by István Bárczy de Bárcziháza, undersecretary of state in the Prime Minister's Office by omitting from them all comments in opposition to his proposals, thereby, even though he could foresee the consequences, he was the initiator of decisions which carried the Hungarian people into the World War that began in 1939.

2. War crimes under Points 3 and 4 of Paragraph II of the Nbr.[189] which he committed by participating as a member of the executive committee in the formation, in August 1944, of the so-called Nemzeti Szövetség[190] [National Alliance] initiated by Ferenc Szálasi and consisting of extreme right-wing parliamentary deputies devoted to fight alongside Germany to the very end, drafting the charter of said alliance and further, as a member of the executive committee participated in the resolution according to which the regent and the government could not engage in armistice negotiations without the approval of the National alliance, meaning that the regent could initiate armistice negotiations only with the approval of Parliament and agreed that this resolution be communicated to the regent and to the members of the government by a deputation, finally

On October 12, 1944, the United Christian National League, of which he was the president addressed the following question to the that time Minister of Justice Dr. Gábor Vladár, "If the news were true that Gendarmes Superintendent Faraghó was negotiating in Moscow, would he start a treason trial against him even though he was negotiating on instructions of the regent?"[191]

Thereby trying to thwart the establishment of an armistice agreement willfully and by using all his influence, and thereby also using his leadership prerogatives assisted the Arrow Cross movement to come into power and retain that power.

3. War crimes under Point 5. of Paragraph 11 of Nbr.[192] which he committed by, learning, as the royal Hungarian prime minister, of the atrocities committed in January 1942 in Zsablya [Žabalj] and Újvidék [Novi Sad] on the population of the reclaimed territories by the gendarmes and by the military forces he abused his official position by not preventing them and instead of calling the responsible persons to account he even tolerated that the Court of the General Staff, created for the suppression of all opinions contrary to the war, pass death sentences on approximately 150 Serb national residents of those areas.[193]

4. War crimes under Point 1 of Paragraph 13 of Nbr.[194] which he committed by, stating at a reception for the Italian Minister of Foreign Affairs Count Ciano, "Hungary, which again has gone to arms and has joined the ranks of the combatants, fights on the side of its great allies Italy and Germany, like so many times during history, and confronts the demons of destruction and atheism threatening from the East in order to protect European civilization."[195]

In Kolozsvár, on January 18, 1942, he said among other things, as follows, "We are in a serious struggle and we must throw all our strength into it. Our fate and all of Europe's fate is being decided now. We must confront the fact that we must reach the obvious conclusions, we must reach them and we will reach them."[196]

In a speech in Szombathely on June 25, 1944, he said among other things,

> This fight is a fight of freedom and liberation against the harmful foreign influence, chaos, anarchy and Bolshevism, the threatening whirlpools of which we have already beheld with a spinning head. A nation that does not dare to risk its strength when it is a question of its existence abdicates any rights to be considered. Only the cowards and traitors could have believed that Hungary could stay out of this war.[197]

Thereby with his speeches he agitated for continuation and an increased participation in the war.

5. Crimes against the people under Point 1, Paragraph 15 of Nbr.[198] which he committed by initiating legislation severely harmful to the best interests of the nation as royal Hungarian prime minister and min-

ister of foreign affairs, and knowingly participated in their enactment:

2870/1941 ME[199] according to which those who were ordered to forced labor service were forced to serve without rank even though they had previously achieved the rank of officer or noncommissioned officer.

6090/1941. ME[200] which ordinance states that Jews expelled from their business may be paid commission on transactions completed prior to the expropriation only within a limited period of time.

6162/1941 KKM ordinance[201] which removes Jewish merchants from trading in the most essential public consumption items.

6. Crimes against the people under Point 1, Paragraph 17 of Nbr.[202] according to which he as royal Hungarian prime minister and minister of foreign affairs had the legal right to prevent the internment and deportation to Galicia of Jews, allegedly not Hungarian nationals, during July 1941, but made no efforts to do so.[203]

For this indictment the Budapest People's Court has the jurisdiction under Bp. Section 1, Paragraph 16[204] as well as Nbr. Paragraph 20[205] and Nbr. Paragraph 23.[206]

I recommend that the accused be retained in detention until the appropriate decision is rendered by the court.

The list of those to be called as witnesses and the list of the factual proofs is appended at the end of the indictment.

Justification

1/

The accused, László Bárdossy, admits the facts of the events listed in the expository section of the indictment. In the discussion below we will make reference to his defense.

a)

The accused, László Bárdossy, has committed the crimes defined in the expository section of the indictment on multiple occasions and for the first time during the military action against Yugoslavia beginning on April 11, 1941.

In order to furnish evidence for the crimes the following undeniable facts are submitted:

1. On January 22, 1941,[207] following the death of the Minister of Foreign Affairs Count István Csáky, László Bárdossy accepted the portfolio of minister of foreign affairs. On April 3, 1941, following the death of Count Pál Teleki, he also assumed the position of prime minister. When the decision was made to initiate military action against Yugoslavia he was therefore a member of the cabinet.

2. He was the initiator of the decision to begin the military action in as much as at the session of the Crown Council,[208] preceding the death of prime minister Count Pál Teleki, he (Bárdossy) as the minister of foreign affairs submitted and endorsed the request of the German government for Hungary to actively participate in the German military action against Yugoslavia. This is attested to before the people's prosecutor by the witness Lajos Reményi-Schneller. Another initiating step taken by László Bárdossy was to draft, word by word, the entire proclamation signed by Regent Miklós Horthy, on April 11, 1941, in which the orders were issued for the beginning of the military action against Yugoslavia.[209] This action was admitted by the accused, László Bárdossy, in his testimony before the political prosecutor. Another initiating action of the accused was to announce at the session of the Council of Ministers, on April 11, 1941, that Yugoslavia had disintegrated into its component parts and thus the conditions set by the Crown Council for beginning the military action have been fulfilled.[210]

3. As an active participant in the meeting of the Crown Council preceding prime minister Pál Teleki's death and of the meeting of the Council of Ministers on April 11, 1941, he was obviously a participant in the decision-making process even though he could not only have foreseen the results but actually did foresee them. One such consequence was, first of all, that Great Britain, as an ally of Yugoslavia, would sever diplomatic relations with Hungary and would, beyond this action, draw even more serious conclusions vis-à-vis Hungary. This event could have been foreseen by László Bárdossy and, in fact, he did foresee it because the Hungarian minister in London, György Barcza sent him a report along these lines on April 2, 1941,[211] and repeated this message even more emphatically referring to a statement of the British deputy foreign secretary on April 5. (London code cable no. 5.61, April 5, 1941.)[212] Bárdossy realized the probable consequences and informed Minister Barcza on April 6 that, "in case of the severance of diplomat-

ic relations he wished to transfer Barcza to Ireland." (Ministry of Foreign Affairs, code cable, April 6, 1941.)[213] In fact, Great Britain promptly announced the severance of diplomatic relations.

It was also predictable how every free country and the public opinion of the entire free world would view the Hungarian military action evidently following the German aggression and how Hungary would be viewed with particular reference to the Hungarian-Yugoslav Eternal Friendship Pact, ratified only six weeks earlier, on February 27, 1941, and signed by the accused László Bárdossy and Cincar-Marković, the Yugoslav minister of foreign affairs. The fact that László Bárdossy could foresee the danger of the loss of Hungary's prestige and its degradation to being a vassal of Germany is proven by the circular cable of April 10, 1941, addressed to the Hungarian legations in Moscow, Ankara, Berne, Stockholm, Washington, Madrid, Lisbon and Vichy, in which he instructs the Hungarian ministers to "try to understand" his point of view as far as the military action was concerned.[214] Particularly grave was the reaction of American public opinion that was foreseen by Bárdossy (see his response to cables nos. 28 and 29 from the Hungarian minister in Washington)[215] and which led to a declaration that Hungary's aggression was unjustified (see cable no. 39 from the Hungarian minister in Washington).[216] The reaction of the Soviet Union could also be foreseen, that country having signed a mutual assistance agreement with Yugoslavia during these critical days.[217]

4. That the military action against Yugoslavia was one of those events that involved Hungary in the World War that began in 1939, was a matter of public opinion and was also a universally accepted fact that Bárdossy had clearly foreseen. While the reattachment of the Felvidék [Highlands or Southern Slovakia] and of Northern Transylvania was not the result of a coordinated Hungarian-German military action, beginning with the Yugoslav action Hungary was viewed as a comrade-in-arms and satellite of Germany. This is supported by the prompt severance of British-Hungarian diplomatic relations. Independently, Great Britain and her allies promised assistance to Yugoslavia, as an obligation, in case of an attack against that country and such assistance was provided during the later phases of the war.[218]

On the basis of the facts presented above, there could not have been any doubt, even at that time, that the Hungarian military action was viewed as an attack against Yugoslavia.

Bárdossy's personal responsibility is made even more serious by the facts given below.

a) The Crown Council[219] made it a condition of the initiation of the military action against Yugoslavia that Yugoslavia first disintegrates into its components, i.e. cease to be an integral unit. This fact was admitted by László Bárdossy in his deposition to the police[220] and was confirmed by the deposition of witness Lajos Reményi-Schneller before the people's prosecutor. The determination of this condition, namely of the disintegration of Yugoslavia, was deduced by László Bárdossy from the night-time telephone call from the Hungarian Consul László Bartók on April 10, 1941, according to which a person by the name of Kvaternik proclaimed the independence of Croatia in Zagreb.[221] László Bárdossy admitted to the political prosecutor that he was not familiar with the name of Kvaternik and "assumed" that the old Croatian independence movement had taken over. He made no attempt to determine whether Yugoslavia, as such, had really ceased to exist or whether this was simply the establishment of a puppet regime that the Germans frequently used as an alibi to legalize their aggression. He did not even investigate whether the Yugoslav troops had withdrawn from the Délvidék [Vojvodina] and thus the possibility of an armed clash with Hungarian troops had been eliminated, that was also established as an absolute criterion by the Crown Council.[222] These circumstances are admitted by László Bárdossy in his confession to the Political Security Division and this confession is confirmed by the testimony of Lajos Reményi-Schneller before the people's prosecutor. László Bárdossy ignored all of these circumstances and simply concluded that all conditions for a military action against Yugoslavia had been met. The fact is that Yugoslavia did not cease to exist, even during the period of German occupation and that the Hungarian troops had to fight battles in the Délvidék.[223]

In his avid endeavors to justify the military action László Bárdossy did not refrain from falsifying the facts. He concluded in the proclamation, drafted and signed by him that, "On March 26 the legal head of Yugoslavia was forcefully removed."[224] Contrary to this assertion by Bárdossy, the truth was that until March 26, 1941, a three-member council with Prince Paul at its head exercised the royal prerogatives in the name of King Peter who was a minor. On March 26, 1941, King Peter was declared by constitutional means to be an adult and this automatically brought an end to the Regency Council and to the role of Prince Paul. Not only was the legal head of Yugoslavia not removed but, on the contrary, the legal head of the country assumed the rights of the head of state. Dr. József Bölöny, university professor and a witness before the people's prosecutor, in a personal letter advised László Bárdossy at the time of these facts and also of the fact that the secession of Croatia by itself did not mean the disintegration of Yugoslavia. In his response, László Bárdossy admitted the general correctness of Bölöny's assertions and used as an excuse only that in motivating the military action his proclamation "had to make concessions at the expense of precision" because this made the text easier to understand.[225]

It is noteworthy that a superficial assessment of the facts, the willful distortion and dissembling of the true situation, the concealment and suppression of the crucial facts that could be used against the war, and the avoidance of civil and constitutional law can be determined in every instance when Bárdossy again and again started initiatives to embroil Hungary ever deeper in the war that served the goals of Hitler's Germany.

b) When Count Pál Teleki saw clearly that Hungary, having recently signed an Eternal Friendship Pact with Yugoslavia, was drifting into a war with Yugoslavia, he committed suicide. According to the testimony of István Bárczy de Bárcziháza before the people's prosecutor, Count Pál Teleki in his last letter to the regent wrote as follows,

> I accuse myself that I was unable to prevent our participation in the German action against Yugoslavia. I have let the honor of the nation down. The Yugoslav nation is our friend as Your Highness had also stated at Mohács. But we are now allied to scoundrels. The rumor about the atrocities committed against the Hungarian and German minorities in the Délvidék are not true and are but German inventions. Perhaps with my death I can render a service to my country.[226]

The entire Hungarian nation interpreted Pál Teleki's death as the bankruptcy of the nationalist policies that carried Hungary inevitably into the war in the footsteps of the Nazi aggressions and were responsible for Hungary's loss of honor. The shock with which the news of Pál Teleki's death was received by the Hungarian people can never be forgotten. Perhaps the full publication of Teleki's farewell letter and its motivation could have held the country back from the path on which it was engaged, but at the Council of Ministers meeting subsequent to Pál Teleki's death, Bárdossy energetically opposed the suggestion that the full truth be told because, "This would make a painful impression on the Germans and the German public opinion would turn against us." This event is confirmed by the evidence submitted by István Bárczy de Bárcziháza to the people's prosecutor.

Bárdossy, in order to excuse his actions and divert the responsibility from himself, testified before the Political Security Division and the political prosecutor concerning the precursors to Teleki's suicide that Pál Teleki did not commit suicide because of a moral conflict but that it was his neurasthenia and the British threats reported in the cable from the Hungarian Minister Barcza, that drove him into suicide.[227]

This is clearly refuted by Pál Teleki's farewell letter and by the depositions of people close to Pál Teleki such as István Bárczy de Bárcziháza and Lajos Reményi-Schneller.[228] It is noteworthy in this connection that it was evident even to Ribbentrop, the minister of foreign affairs of the German Reich who explained to Döme Sztójay, the Hungarian minister in Berlin, that he regretted Teleki's death saying, "Under the effect of the facts and of the bombardments Teleki's doubts would have disappeared. The moral basis of the action against Yugoslavia is proven beyond any doubt and every concern about it is without foundation." (Sztójay's code cable no. 6239/68).[229]

c) László Bárdossy also endeavors to defend his comportment in the Yugoslav affair by saying that the Eternal Friendship Pact was made with a Yugoslavia that wished to join the Tripartite Pact and thus belonged to the same political grouping as Hungary. Yugoslavia did not, however, ratify its adherence to the Tripartite Pact and this caused such a change in the nature of the contracting party that it nullified the validity of the Eternal Friendship Pact. (Bárdossy's deposition before the police.) This defense of László Bárdossy's and these arguments cannot be accepted and are without legal basis because the nature of a contracting party is not changed by ratifying or not ratifying another and unrelated agreement. This is particularly true in this case because there was no such clause or condition whatever in the Eternal Friendship Pact. This event, however, is a suitable testimony how superficially and irresponsibly László Bárdossy viewed the international agreements and, in general, everything pertaining to international law, civil law and constitutional law.

b)

The crimes committed by László Bárdossy in the armed attack against Yugoslavia pale into insignificance when compared to the whole series of willful misdeeds with which he drove the Hungarian people into the war with the Soviet Union and when he did everything in his power to increase Hungary's involvement in this war. With this activity he met all the criteria of being guilty of war crimes as defined in Point 2, Paragraph 11 of Nbr.[230]

That in the meaning of the above act he, as prime minister and minister of foreign affairs was the initiator and participant of the Council of Minister's decision to begin a military action against the Soviet Union and that he reported this to the Parliament and that Hungary in consequence of these steps became involved in World War II and that these steps led to total defeat and destruction are documented so completely by depositions obtained during the investigation that the above facts require no additional proof beyond this documentation.

In order to establish László Bárdossy's guilt of war crimes under the acts listed in the first section of the indictment only three indisputable historical facts are required.

a) On the recommendation of László Bárdossy, prime minister and minister of foreign affairs, the Council of Ministers at its meeting, held on June 23, 1941, decided to sever diplomatic relations with the Soviet Union.[231]

b) On the recommendation of László Bárdossy, prime minister and minister of foreign affairs, the Council of Ministers at its meeting, held on June 26, 1941, decided that Hungary was in a state of war with the Soviet Union and that Hungary would participate with limited forces in the military action against the Soviet Union.

c) At the meeting of the lower house of Parliament on June 27, 1941, László Bárdossy, prime minister and minister of foreign affairs announced to the house that a state of war existed between Hungary and the Soviet Union.

For the preliminaries of the initiation of war against the Soviet Union and for the appropriate demonstration of László Bárdossy's responsibility and guilt the following facts have been established on the basis of available documents and depositions:

1. There was no international agreement that obliged Hungary to participate in the war against the Soviet Union.

2. Even Germany did not demand that Hungary enter the war against the Soviet Union at that time.

3. The Soviet Union furnished no reasons whatsoever for Hungary to initiate any military action against her.

4. The preparation of the state of war between Hungary and the Soviet Union and its announcement to the House by the prime minister and minister of foreign affairs, László Bárdossy, were unconstitutional acts. Employment of the Hungarian army beyond the borders of the country was equally unconstitutional. For these acts prime minister and minister of foreign affairs, László Bárdossy, is not only politically but also legally responsible.

5. László Bárdossy, prime minister and minister of foreign affairs drove the country into war with the Soviet Union knowingly and maliciously.

ad 1. When Bárdossy, at the June 23, 1941, Council of Ministers meeting, referring to the outbreak of the German-Russian war recommended that the diplomatic relations with the Soviet Union be severed, he used as the justification that under the Tripartite Pact this was Hungary's obligation. (See Council of Ministers minutes.) The Tripartite Pact, in fact, contains no such requirement either literally or morally. This is proven by the fact that even one of the three contracting nations, Japan, did not sever its diplomatic relations with the Soviet Union and neither did Bulgaria that had joined the Tripartite Pact at a later date.

The earlier Anti-Comintern Pact[232] mentions no military obligation of any kind and is distinctly against the so-called Comintern activities and not against the Soviet Union.[233] Hungary was not a signatory to any other international agreement that could have affected the Hungarian-Russian relations.

ad 2. According to the minutes, Bárdossy said at the June 26, 1941, Council of Ministers meeting,

There have been no requests or demands from Germany or from the German policy makers (for participation in a military action). When the German undersecretary of state of the Ministry of Foreign Affairs, Baron Weizsäcker was in Budapest a few weeks ago I attempted to get him to say something. He coolly declined....On Sunday, June 22, the German minister in Budapest transmitted a letter from Hitler to the regent. Hitler, in this letter, informed the regent that a state of war existed between Germany and Russia and added that Germany hoped that Hungary would appreciate Germany's decision. Nothing else was said.[234]

The same day Bárdossy saw the deputy of the German Minister, Werkmeister, and informed him about the decision of the Council of Ministers according to which the Council of Ministers had determined that a state of war existed between the Soviet Union and Hungary. He also mentioned, however, that the German government had offered the Slovak and Romanian governments an opportunity for acting together but had not done so for us. (Ministry of Foreign Affairs note, June 26, 1941, page 2.)[236] Döme Sztójay, the Hungarian minister in Berlin, stated in his code cable (489/conf.–no. 1941) as follows, "In all my reports I wished to point out unmistakably that the German intention was for us not to manifest any activity in this war...." In contrast, he asked in a letter dated June 17, 1941, (84/pol. főn.–1941) that we should definitely enter the German-Russian war because otherwise we would be left behind by the Romanians and Slovaks.[236]

Bárdossy followed Sztójay's advice and, albeit uninvited, made Hungary enter the war against Russia although, as he stated in his deposition before the political prosecutor, he did this because if we entered the war voluntarily we could determine the size of the force committed while if we had to enter later and under pressure we might have had to give more.[237] How honest and successful this policy was became evident later. In any case László Bárdossy's admission is certain. It was he who, without coercion and on his own initiative, declared a state of war between the Soviet Union and Hungary. The fact that

Bárdossy took Hungary into the war against the Soviet Union for fear of later German pressure or fear of Romanian and Slovak competition makes it clear that the Soviet Union had given no cause for Hungary's entry into the war.

László Bárdossy did not look for a cause but for an excuse. He did find an excuse. Allegedly in one or two instances Russian planes machine gunned the railway lines near the border, that is in the area of German deployment, and on June 26, 1941 an air raid was made against Kassa [Košice] in consequence of which five persons lost their life.

Bárdossy made no attempt to verify whether the attack was really made by Russian planes and did not address a question to the Soviet Union via a neutral power (Sweden) to explain this unfriendly act nor did he protest in the name of the Hungarian government against this obvious border violation. There would have been ample time to do so, because in the final analysis the Kassa air raid was quite modest (proven by the number of dead in spite of the fact that the attack was made in bright daylight, no alarm was sounded and people were in the street) and did not justify the immediate declaration of a state of war and the utilization of the Hungarian armed forces in a retaliatory move against the Soviet Union.

László Bárdossy states in his deposition that he had no doubts that the attacking planes were Russian and that the attack was an intentional provocation because the Soviet Union wished to involve Hungary in the war due to its laying claims on Subcarpathia.

This defense of László Bárdossy's is destroyed not only by the legal explanation presented below, but also by simple logic, because the Soviet Union had to consider that it either won or lost the war. If it won the war, a great power like the Soviet Union clearly did not have to inveigle a small country, like Hungary, into the war in order to make a border adjustment particularly since the Soviet Union had given multiple evidence of her wishing to maintain good relations with Hungary and had no territorial demands against her.

This defense of László Bárdossy was also unacceptable because it was before the Kassa bombing that he received the cable from Kristóffy, the Hungarian minister in Moscow, who advised him that he had been officially notified by the Soviet government that the government had no demands from or intentions to attack Hungary and had no comments concerning the realization of the Hungarian demands vis-à-vis Romania and that the Soviet Union would have no comments on this matter in the future. In this cable the minister also advised Bárdossy of his opinion that according to the news from the Hungarian press and radio he considered it unlikely that Hungary had any intention of going to war with the Soviet Union.[238]

Even under the difficulties of war-like conditions, the Soviet government made a Moscow-Ankara cable access available to the Hungarian minister in order to enable him to transmit the above information urgently to prime minister László Bárdossy. (Moscow code cable no. 7026/1941.)[239]

This cable did not make László Bárdossy thoughtful and did not turn him from his decision to attack the Soviet Union. In his deposition before the people's prosecutor, however, Bárdossy defended himself by saying that, "In the nervous atmosphere the significance of the telegram was lost."[240] The facts are that Bárdossy disregarded this telegram intentionally because it would have made it impossible for him to take the country to war against the Soviet Union.[241]

In his deposition before the people's prosecutor, István Bárczy de Bárcziháza, secretary of state in the Prime Minister's Office, stated that Bárdossy did not report this telegram to the Council of Ministers and or to the regent. In August 1944, Horthy found out about this official Russian announcement by accident. Bárdossy even prevented Kristóffy, the Hungarian minister in Moscow, from reporting to the regent after his return to Budapest. When Kristóffy asked Bárdossy about the fate of his telegram, Bárdossy did not answer.[242]

László Bárdossy denied that he had prevented Kristóffy from having an audience with the regent and also denies that he did not report to the regent about the telegram and also insisted that he conveyed the text of the entire telegram to the Council of Ministers. This latter statement was evidently untrue because there is no trace of such a report in the minutes of the Council of Ministers' meeting and if, in fact, the report had been made, those who opposed the immediate entry into the war would have referred to this telegram repeatedly.[243] This claim by László Bárdossy was also nullified by the depositions of István Bárczy de Bárcziháza and Lajos Reményi-Schneller, questioned during the investigation, who were present at the meeting of the Council of Ministers and who in their deposition asserted that the prime minister and minister of foreign affairs Bárdossy did not mention this telegram from Kristóffy, minister in Moscow, at the meeting of the Council of Ministers or anywhere else.

Bárdossy did advise one party, however, of the Moscow telegram… the Germans. According to the written deposition of witness Alajos Béldy (page 4),

> Bárdossy notified the German military leadership of the telegram which redoubled its propaganda toward Hungary and one of its outcomes was the bombing of Kassa, attributed to Russian planes. The German military leadership which, contrary to the German political leadership, as mentioned by Bárdossy at the June 26 Council of Ministers meeting, did indeed wish for Hungary's immediate entry into the war and used a fake-Russian air attack to prevent the peaceful Russian intents from materializing.

Witness Béldy also deposed (page 4) that the regent found out about the Kristóffy telegram only later, in 1944.[241]

The complete publication of the Kristóffy telegram would certainly have delayed the entry into war with the Soviet Union and would surely have presented a solid argument for those members of the Council of Ministers who, according to the minutes of the meeting, even without it argued in favor of delay.

The official Russian announcement appearing in the telegram of the Hungarian minister in Moscow, Kristóffy, was not at all surprising. It could have been expected. The Soviet Union, after some initial anger, even condoned Hungary's adherence to the Anti-Comintern Pact because they knew of the terribly heavy pressure brought on Hungary.[245] Afterwards the Soviet Union made numerous friendly gestures toward the Hungarian people, as for instance the return of the Hungarian military flags of the 1848 freedom fight shortly before the declaration of the state of war.

Who specifically performed the Kassa air raid is still in doubt. It is certain that it was not done by the Russians who had no interest in doing so. It is well known that the Germans frequently used such means of provocation during the conduct of the war. It may be assumed on the basis of the deposition before the people's prosecutor, of witness István

Tarnay that an air force captain Csekmek performed the bombardment under instructions of somebody in the pay of the Germans or by a Hungarian clique friendly to the Germans.[246] From the perspective of Bárdossy's guilt this is immaterial. It is proven that the Soviet Union had done nothing that could have given cause for a declaration of war. But even if the bombing of Kassa was an individual Russian attack, it would have been the duty of László Bárdossy as prime minister and minister of foreign affairs to become assured after an exchange of diplomatic notes that it was really an attack by Russian planes and then express the protest of the Hungarian government to the Soviet government and not immediately declare a state of war out of self-motivated haste.

László Bárdossy's deposition before the people's prosecutor left no doubt that he would have declared war on the Soviet Union even without the Kassa bombing because even prior to it he was coercing the Germans to insist on the desirability of Hungary's entering the war against the Soviet Union.[247] He went even further in his deposition when he stated that it was better for Hungary to enter the war voluntarily on her own than under German pressure later.

ad 4. The will of the nation can be implemented legally only by the governmental structures so empowered by the constitution. According to the Hungarian constitution a declaration of war was the exclusive prerogative of the king. The act temporarily regulating the supreme powers in the state, (Section 5, Paragraph 13 of Act I, 1920), conferred this supreme power on the regent with the sole condition that in order to declare war the preliminary approval of Parliament had to be obtained. Thus a declaration of war was the joint responsibility of the legislature and of the regent and could not be exercised by anyone else. It could not be exercised by the royal Hungarian government or by any other governmental agency.

Contrary to the above, László Bárdossy made the following announcement to the House of Representatives of Parliament at the June 27, 1941, sitting, "The royal Hungarian government concludes that in consequence of the attacks a state of war exists between Hungary and the Soviet Union." In doing so the government clearly acted beyond its authority because a statement of the existence of a state of war was tantamount to a declaration of war and this was the exclusive prerogative of the regent and only with the prior approval of Parliament. The government could not legally exert the powers of the regent and the legislature's legally mandated prior approval could not be replaced by the hurrahs and applause that followed the prime minister's unconstitutional announcement. The law demanded prior approval by the legislature in order that the members of the legislature not be confronted with a fait accompli that they were unable to change and even less to prevent and be forced to acknowledge in the interest of the country that the country had been taken to war. It must be noted that the house took no action relative to the government's announcement and in the upper house, at the July 4 sitting, it was not the prime minister, but only the president of the upper house who announced that the country was at war with the Soviet Union and that military action had already begun.[248] The determination of the existence of a state of war, being equivalent to a declaration of war, was done by a structure unauthorized by the constitution and also with the unconstitutional disregard of the prescribed conditions. It must therefore be considered legally null and void. László Bárdossy's responsibility was not limited to his violation of the constitution but extended also to the fact that this illegal and thus legally null and void action in fact took the country into the war.

László Bárdossy also carried not only political but legal responsibility for the deployment of the Hungarian army beyond the borders of the country. According to Paragraph 2 of Act XVII, 1920, the regent could order this only in the presence of imminent danger and that it was the responsibility of the entire government to seek the Parliament's ex post facto approval without any delay. If in his capacity as commander in chief, the regent ordered the deployment of Hungarian soldiers beyond the borders of the country without ministerial approval, every member of the government was responsible under the law to determine whether there really was an imminent danger and whether the approval of Parliament had been obtained without delay. For this the principal responsibility rested on the prime minister, László Bárdossy, whose duty it was to seek parliamentary approval. After having announced the existence of the state of war at the June 27 sitting of the house, it was only at the July 25 sitting that the president submitted to the house the prime minister's pertinent message.[249] Since the house adjourned at that sitting, it was not until October 23 that it gave its approval.[250] It wasn't only the lack of following the legal requirements in submitting to the house the request for approval without any delay, but it would have been the government's duty to prevent the adjournment of the house prior to rendering its approval and to permit that a decision on the request be made only three months later.

Bárdossy's defense that he was unfamiliar with the constitutional law and that it was for this reason that he did not follow his constitutionally prescribed duties, namely to obtain prior parliamentary approval for the existence of a state of war and permission of Parliament for deployment of the army beyond the borders immediately and with no delay, was unacceptable.

ad 5. The deposition of István Bárczy de Bárcziháza before the people's prosecutor demonstrates that László Bárdossy knew that his forcing an announcement of the state of war with the Soviet Union was completely unconstitutional. According to the witness, Bárdossy willfully and knowingly falsified the minutes of the June 26, 1941, Council of Ministers meeting by omitting from the minutes taken by István Bárczy de Bárcziháza, the secretary of the Council of Ministers, important comments concerning the existence of a state of war. He expunged several comments by Ferenc Keresztes-Fischer, minister of the interior, the comment by Minister of Defense Károly Bartha and the comments of two other ministers who shared Keresztes-Fischer's point of view. Minister Dezső Laky was not present at the meeting, being away from the capital and Ministers Dániel Bánffy and József Varga joined Ferenc Keresztes-Fischer's views opposing the immediate announcement of a state of war with the Soviet Union. Bárdossy at this meeting of the Council of Ministers forcefully insisted on the immediate declaration of a state of war and was determined to coerce the Council of Ministers to make a decision in this matter. These intentions of László Bárdossy appear much more clearly in the original minutes prepared by István Bárczy de Bárcziháza and which faithfully recorded all comments than the minutes that Bárdossy revised and edited nine months later and which he then dictated at the Ministry of Foreign Affairs.[251] He falsified other sets of minutes of Council of Ministers meetings as well, according to Bárczy's deposition. The minutes were first to be signed by the secretary who then submitted them to the prime minister for signature and only then to the ministers who were present at the meeting for their signature. For his later defense Bárdossy reversed this order. He took the minutes submitted to him by Secretary István Bárczy de Bárcziháza, redictated them in the Ministry of Foreign Affairs, signed them and then sent them on via the cabinet chief of the Ministry of Foreign Affairs to members of the government with a request for their signature. This made it possible that the ministers who were asked to sign not only the minutes of the last two session of the Council of Ministers, edited by László Bárdossy, but a number of other sets of minutes from other Council of Ministers meetings, also edited by László Bárdossy, not to take the time for careful perusal of the minutes. And it was this that made it possible for the signature of Minister Dezső Laky to appear on the cover of the Council of Minister minutes as participant when he could have signed that only by mistake, because he did not have to sign it at all, having not been present at the June 26 meeting of the Council of Ministers.

c)

In a radio address on December 11, 1941, Adolf Hitler announced that Germany considered itself to be in a state of war with the United States. On the same day Italy also announced that it was in a state of war with the United States of America.

László Bárdossy on receiving this news that same day, i.e. December 11, 1941, summoned an extraordinary meeting of the Council of Ministers at which, after announcing the news, declared that the newly established situation created obligations for Hungary under the terms of the Tripartite Pact.[252] This is what Baron Weizsäcker, the German undersecretary of state for foreign affairs, had referred to when he told the Hungarian minister in Berlin, Sztójay that he (Weizsäcker) hoped that Hungary would draw the appropriate conclusions from the action of the German Reich government, under the terms of the Tripartite Pact.[253] Bárdossy continued his comments by saying that Hungary had two alternatives. One was to sever diplomatic relations with the United States and the other was to go all the way and declare that a state of war existed between Hungary and the United States. Bárdossy expressed his desire that the government make a decision promptly that very day. He considered it desirable that Hungary not wait until the German government expressed its request, beyond what Baron Weizsäcker had already told Sztójay and that he (Bárdossy) recommended that Hungary declare its solidarity with the Axis Powers. This would satisfy the obligations under the Tripartite Pact.[254]

Bárdossy tried to get around Minister of the Interior Keresztes-Fischer's objections by saying that the declaration of solidarity imposed no obligations on Hungary except for the severance of diplomatic relations.

It was at this meeting of the Council of Ministers that the minister of defense declared his views according to which the severance of diplomatic relations or the declaration of a state of war by the Hungarian government should be decided on the basis of what was better for the Germans. If the declaration of a state of war was better, let Hungary make that declaration. After several comments and objections the Council of Ministers accepted the prime minister's proposal according to which the severance of the diplomatic relations with the United States of America was announced. Bárdossy added the comment that this decision was flexible and could be expanded. It was this decision that László Bárdossy conveyed that day, December 11, to Mr. Pell, the minister of the United States of America in Budapest.

That same night László Bárdossy learned from a report by Döme Sztójay, the Hungarian Minister in Berlin, that Romania and Bulgaria went further and not only severed diplomatic relations with the United States of America but declared a state of war with that country.[255] This cable led László Bárdossy, trying to compete for the favor of the Germans, to take steps that were unconstitutional and meant the total violation of constitutional law. The following day, December 12, he again asked Mr. Pell, the American minister, to come and see him and told him that the Hungarian government was acting in the spirit of the Tripartite Pact when it not only severed diplomatic relations, as announced yesterday, but if it declared that a state of war existed between Hungary and the United States of America, as he was doing today. When the American minister expressed his astonishment that László Bárdossy had announced only the severance of diplomatic relations the previous day, while today he arbitrarily advised him that a state of war had been declared, Pell said, "prime minister Bárdossy, you have announced the existence of a state of war under severe German pressure." Bárdossy responded to this statement by Pell indignantly and told the American Minister that Hungary was a sovereign and independent country and it was as such that the Hungarian government declared that the country was in a state of war with the United States of America, as of that very day.[256]

Thus László Bárdossy, on his own, announced the existence of a state of war between Hungary and the United States on December 12, without the approval of the regent, the Hungarian government or the legislature and even without prior notification.[257]

On December 12, the regular meeting of the Council of Ministers, which started at 5:00 P.M., dealt with routine matters with minor interruptions until midnight. At the end of the meeting Bárdossy simply announced to the Council of Ministers that he would announce to the House on December 16 that Hungary considered itself to be in a state of war with the United States.

Even before the meeting of the Council of Ministers, the Hungarian News Bureau was authorized to release the following news item,

The Royal Hungarian Ministry of Foreign Affairs has addressed the following note to the minister of the United States of America in Budapest…: The royal Hungarian government, in accordance with its principles of solidarity in existence on December 12 of the present year, considers that the state of war existing between the United States of America on one side and the German Reich, Italy and Japan on the other side, was equally existing vis-à-vis Hungary.[258]

The cable sent on December 13 to the Hungarian minister in Stockholm proves that the Council of Ministers meeting on December 11 only expressed Hungary's solidarity with the Axis Powers and declared the severance of diplomatic relations with the United States. Bárdossy stated in this cable that this decision, for the time being, did not mean that a state of war existed or was declared. Bárdossy continued the cable by referring to the Reuter Agency's release which stated that when Bárdossy announced the severance of diplomatic relations to the American minister, he said that "we had to." Bárdossy tried to deny this in his telegram by saying that he had never used that expression and only stated that he made common cause with the Axis Powers.[259]

In his telegrams of December 13, 1941, to the Hungarian ministers in Berlin and Rome, Bárdossy advised the Hungarian ministers in

Berlin and Rome that the announcement of the severance of diplomatic relations between Hungary and the United States could be interpreted by them, if they so wished, to include a declaration of a state of war. The Hungarian government originally did not believe that it would be necessary but, in the spirit of the Tripartite Pact, it was obviously ready to do this and was also ready to draw all the consequences inherent in our declaration of solidarity. This actually is a logical consequence of our having identified ourselves with the Axis Powers immediately after the German announcement. The Hungarian press will make this clear. I have brought this interpretation of solidarity to the attention of the American minister in Budapest....The Hungarian government is not planning to issue any further communiqué.[260]

Bárdossy's deliberate crime in knowingly and criminally converting the decision of the Council of Ministers of December 11 into a declaration of a state of war becomes evident from the code cable he sent to all Hungarian legations on December 14, 1941, "...I advise you that on the basis of the Tripartite Pact and of the declaration of solidarity on the 11th inst., the royal Hungarian government considers that the state of war existing between the United States on one side and Germany, Italy and Japan on the other, was equally applicable to itself."[261]

This criminal and unconstitutional act of Bárdossy is made evident by his code cable, no. 7952/62, addressed to all legations, in which he knowingly falsifies the December 11 decision by the Council of Ministers when he writes, "The decision of the government was precisely in agreement with the official statement issued via the Hungarian News Bureau." In this telegram Bárdossy told the ministers that Hungary, in the spirit of solidarity, had only severed diplomatic relations with the United States.[262]

On the basis of all this Bárdossy's guilt is clearly established. He committed such grievous crimes and unconstitutional acts that are unparalleled not only in Hungarian history but in the history of the whole world. He unconstitutionally and illegally took the December 11 decision of the Council of Ministers in which the government announced only the severance of diplomatic relations with the United States of America and converted it, without authority or prior approval, into the existence of a state of war.

Bárdossy's defense is that at the December 19, 1941, sitting of the house he announced that the government had determined that the state of war existing between the United States of America on one side and Germany, Italy and Japan on the other side, was applicable to Hungary as well. This act does not relieve him of the grave responsibility that he violated the existing and clear mandate of the constitution when in violation of Section 5, Paragraph 13 of Act I, 1920, he arbitrarily assumed the powers of the government and of the regent and also omitted to obtain the prior approval of Parliament.

The fact that in contrast to the announcement of the state of war with the Soviet Union the house, in this instance, acknowledged the announcement of the prime minister, this does not make it legal and the acknowledgment was legally just as unconstitutional and null and void as the announcement by the prime minister.

Concerning these matters, the witness, Dr. Bölöny submitted a legal opinion in December 1941 to Mr. Pell, the American minister, in which he explained in detail to the American minister that the unconstitutional act of the prime minister cannot lead to a de jure state of war between Hungary and the United States. With the armed attack against Yugoslavia and with the declaration of a state of war with the Soviet Union and the United States of America, the accused Bárdossy, as prime minister and minister of foreign affairs of the Hungarian government, initiated and participated in the making of decisions that swept the Hungarian nation into the World War that broke out in 1939, even though he could foresee the consequences of said actions.

2–3/

After being head of government and minister of foreign affairs for eleven months during which time he involved Hungary in war with a neighbor and with three major powers, he developed a difference of opinion with the regent about the proposed deputy regent legislation. Consequently he resigned on March 7 and turned over his chair to Miklós Kállay.

Prime minister Miklós Kállay enthusiastically pursued the war with the Soviet Union, the Nazification of public opinion, the legal deprivation of the Jews and their elimination from commerce and trade which was the inheritance of Bárdossy.[263] As long as he followed this line Bárdossy was not active. He saw that the government was in good hands.

When in the spring of 1942, immediately after his resignation, Ferenc Szálasi sent a messenger to him wishing to establish contact with Bárdossy, the latter gave him a dilatory answer, saying that he would be pleased to establish a political relationship with Szálasi, but that at the present moment he was still too close to his abdication, was in the limelight of domestic policies and was therefore regretfully unable to do so. If the interest swirling around him would dissipate, he would have the opportunity to establish political relations with Ferenc Szálasi. (See Ferenc Szálasi's deposition before the people's prosecutor.)[264]

A major turn, however, was imminent. The New Year of 1943, the German defeat at Stalingrad, the Don breakthrough in the middle of January and the destruction of the Second Hungarian Army made Prime Minister Kállay lose his belief in the certain victory of Germany and made him undertake the well-known, so-called "shuttlecock policy" in which he maintained the formula of loyalty to his allies but also began an orientation toward the Anglo-Saxons. Kállay announced in Parliament that he did not start the war with the Soviet Union and laid the responsibility for the declaration of war at Bárdossy's feet.[265] In order to prevent the awkward and painful parliamentary questions about the Don catastrophe and about Hungarian foreign policy in general, Kállay recessed the house for an indefinite period.

Seeing this, Bárdossy believed that it was time for him to take action. He wished to make certain that the active, pro-Nazi, belligerent line would be followed without a break. Having no party he wished to start some societal organization to bolster this policy in the wavering national public opinion. Filled with offended vanity and pride, he admitted in his deposition that Kállay had put the responsibility for the war and for the Újvidék massacre squarely on his shoulders.[266] Bárdossy was anxious to demonstrate that he very much wanted to be associated with the political avalanche that he had initiated.

It was for this reason that in March 1943 he accepted the presidency of the United Christian National League when it was offered to him. This league was well known as a right-wing organization masquerading as a Christian association which served as a meeting place for mostly higher ranking public officials to exchange ideas. Bárdossy attempted to make a political organization of this social body and when in June 1943 Prime Minister Kállay called for a retreat and announced that hence forward "Hungarian policies will be guided exclusively by Hungarian perspectives," László Bárdossy made a major speech at a meeting of the league stating that "Hungary had to stand unconditionally with the Axis Powers" and that only the Axis could be the basis for any Hungarian perspective. This speech by Bárdossy caused major attention and Ferenc Szálasi made a special note of it in his diary. ("Diary of the Hungarist Movement," July 4, 1943, p. 4.)[267] From this moment on, László Bárdossy was regarded as the statesman representing absolute friendship toward Germany and loyalty toward the Axis in opposition to the vacillating policies of the government.

His activities in the United Christian National League added to his performance as prime minister raised the curiosity of the Germans. When in May 1943 Ferenc Szálasi sent an official delegation to Berlin, the Germans asked about the relationship between the Arrow Cross Party and László Bárdossy. ("Diary of the Hungarist Movement," May 1943, p. 55.)[268]

Recognition was forthcoming from the other political extreme as well. In September 1943 the circle around the regent was considering the possibility of doing away with the shuttlecock policy and were considering Lipót Baranyai or Count István Bethlen as potential heads of government in case of an allied victory and Béla Imrédy or László Bárdossy for the same post in case of an Axis victory. ("Diary of the Hungarist Movement," September 1943, p. 8.)[269] A similar combination with Géza Bornemissza and László Bárdossy had already been considered several months earlier. (Addendum to the April 1943 "Diary of the Hungarist Movement.")[270]

In the fall of 1943 the Germans were beginning to get ready for the possible disloyalty of the Kállay government. They sent the Reich representative designate Edmund Veesenmayer for an exploratory visit and he was introduced by András Mecsér to "possible" politicians and other men. It is obvious after the above that Mecsér would take this outstanding and notorious enslaver and despoiler of occupied countries to meet Bárdossy with whom he had a thorough discussion. We are not familiar with the subject of the discussion but very much so with its results. (See László Bárdossy's deposition before the people's prosecutor.)

On March 19, 1944, Hungary was occupied by Germany. Bárdossy immediately began a feverish activity to buttress the puppet government led by Döme Sztójay and also the general situation.

Immediately after March 19, 1944, Bárdossy received an invitation from the German minister and plenipotentiary Veesenmayer for a political discussion to which a number of other prominent Germanophile politicians were also invited. According to his defense, Bárdossy did not attend this meeting.

During this period, however, Bárdossy consulted with the Gestapo General Otto Winkelmann and with Veesenmayer's deputy, Kurt Haller, to whom he suggested that a military government be set up for Hungary.

As soon as Döme Sztójay was appointed prime minister Bárdossy hastened to the assistance of his old friend and comrade in the fight for the German interests. The proclamation issued on April 2, 1944, by the Sztójay government in which the government committed itself to a joint German-Hungarian fate, was drafted by László Bárdossy. Bárdossy denied this but the written deposition of Mrs. Péter Zánkay, prime minister Sztójay's secretary nullifies Bárdossy's defense.[271]

The witnesses László Baky and Béla Imrédy in their deposition before the people's prosecutor stated that Bárdossy was prime minister Sztójay's confidential advisor and frequently hastened to Sztójay's assistance with his advice. According to the witness László Baky, Bárdossy enjoyed the confidence of both the right-wing parties and of the Germans and was an extreme right-wing Germanophile politician.[272]

In possession of this confidence, Bárdossy set out to organize a wide right-wing coalition, extending from MÉP [Magyar Élet Pártja (Party of Hungarian Life)] to the Arrow Cross Party, to buttress the Sztójay government and insure the political reign of the Germans over Hungary. According to Baky's deposition this endeavor of Bárdossy's was undertaken on Sztójay's request. In his deposition before the people's prosecutor Bárdossy denied that he acted on Sztójay's instructions. According to him it was done on the written request of the right-wing parties. The intent was quite evident regardless.

This endeavor of Bárdossy's failed because of the disputes between the leaders of the extreme right-wing parties and their incompatible demands for cabinet positions. Bárdossy, according to his deposition before the people's prosecutor, unselfishly did not seek a portfolio for himself. Evidently because in this way he could serve the cause better and with less publicity.

The best evidence for the extent of his activities and negotiations on behalf of the consolidation of the Nazi stooge government was the list given below which shows by how many politicians and how often his name was entered as a candidate for a portfolio to serve the interests of the Germans and of the Germanophile politicians:

a) On April 28, 1944, on Ferenc Szálasi's behest, his assistant, Jenő Szőlősi, went to see Veesenmayer and told him that Bárdossy would be willing to head up a new united party and in this case the new party would have to be created by Szálasi and Bárdossy. The difficulty might be that Bárdossy had not considered the role of the Hungarist leader in the planned coalition. ("Diary of the Hungarist Movement," May 1, 1944.)[273]

b) On May 1, 1944, Ferenc Szálasi held a highest-ranking, secret party council meeting in Csobánka and announced that the next day, Sunday, he would be received by the regent. Szálasi also stated that on that occasion he would submit to the regent the plans for a coalition government in which Bárdossy would be the minister of foreign affairs and his deputy would be Baron Gábor Kemény. (Addendum to the May 1944 "Diary of the Hungarist Movement.")[274]

c) On May 4, 1944, Prime Minister Sztójay told Ferenc Szálasi that László Bárdossy was the link between MÉP, the Hungarian Party of Renewal, the Hungarian National Socialist Party and the Transylvanian Party. Bárdossy wished to establish a new political structure, the Nemzeti Összfogás Partja [The Party of National Union]. ("Diary of the Hungarist Movement," May 5, 1944.)[275] At the same time Szálasi told Sztójay that it would be better if two right-wing party blocs were set up, one would be led by Szálasi with his own party and the other by Bárdossy with Prime Minister Sztójay standing above them and forming the link between the two groups. Thus the important matters affecting the country could then be discussed by the three of them, Sztójay, Bárdossy and Szálasi. These facts are attested by the deposition of Ferenc Szálasi before the people's prosecutor.[276]

d) On May 13, 1944, Prime Minister Sztójay again received Ferenc Szálasi and regretfully informed him that the Bárdossy National Union

Party negotiations had broken down because the Szálasi group was unwilling to join the Bárdossy configuration and was willing only to cooperate with it. This was not satisfactory to Bárdossy. ("Diary of the Hungarist Movement," May 13, 1944.)[277]

e) As a recognition of his efforts László Bárdossy was given a parliamentary mandate through the good will of Prime Minister Sztójay and Ferenc Szálasi. Because of his high regards for Bárdossy, Szálasi did not nominate an opponent and thus the election was unanimous. (Deposition of Ferenc Szálasi before the people's prosecutor.)

f) Toward the middle of July Sztójay wished to abdicate. András Mecsér negotiated with the German minister, Veesenmayer, and recommended Jurcsek as prime minister, Beregfy as minister of defense and László Bárdossy as minister of foreign affairs. ("Diary of the Hungarist Movement," July 1944, pp. 154–155.)[278]

g) On July 25, 1944, Szálasi negotiated with Veesenmayer and this time recommended András Mecsér as prime minister and László Bárdossy as minister of foreign affairs. ("Diary of the Hungarist Movement," July 1944, pp. 288–299.)[279]

h) On August 2, the German minister, Veesenmayer, sent Secretary of State Dániel Mocsáry as an intermediary to Ferenc Szálasi with the recommendation for a new coalition in which, characteristically, the future Szálasi cabinet members were mentioned (e.g. Pálffy, Hellebronth, Szemák as president of the Supreme Court and, again, Bárdossy as minister of foreign affairs.) ("Diary of the Hungarist Movement," August 10, 1944, p. 17.)[280]

i) On August 3, László Baky endeavored to set up a coalition government and the minister of foreign affairs designate was again László Bárdossy. ("Diary of the Hungarist Movement," August 1944, pp. 60–61.)[281]

j) In his deposition before the people's prosecutor László Bárdossy admitted that he had repeatedly conferred with prominent German persons such as Gestapo General Winkelmann and others. (This fact is attested to by the "Diary of the Hungarist Movement," August, 1944, pp. 48–49.)[282] Bárdossy claimed in his defense, that during these discussions he had stated emphatically that he did not wish to accept any position. This claim is incomprehensible because his name was mentioned again and again in connection with the prime minister or minister of foreign affairs portfolio.

László Baky in his deposition before the people's prosecutor states that he participated in a conference in August 1944, where the participants included Lajos Szász, Fidél Pálffy, Jurcsek, Count Mihály Teleki and Bárdossy. At this conference, in the discussion of a coalition government, Bárdossy was designated as prime minister and he did accept this nomination but made conditions which made it impossible to reach an agreement. What Bárdossy's conditions were, witness Baky did not recall.[283]

k) On August 9, 1944, Ferenc Szálasi negotiated yet another possible cabinet with the German minister, Veesenmayer. Here the entire future Szálasi government took shape (deputy prime minister: Szőlősi, minister of justice: Budinszky, minister of public supplies: Jurcsek and minister of foreign affairs, naturally: László Bárdossy.) "Diary of the Hungarist Movement," August 1944, pp. 85–86.)[284]

According to the above list, during the Döme Sztójay regime, László Bárdossy was in the center of all the endeavors that were directed toward strengthening and securing the Nazi rule over Hungary.

On August 20, 1944, an attempt was made on Hitler's life. On August 23, 1944, Romania asked for an armistice with the Soviet Union, the Sztójay government fell and the Lakatos government took over. It was a last naive attempt in the shadow of collapse to resuscitate the shuttlecock policy with more modest means and to extend feelers toward an armistice. The rumors that the regent had sent negotiators across the front lines to the Russians were increasing in political and private circles and the rule of the Germans and their stooges in the country was weakening. Bárdossy again initiated a major endeavor. Even though the frequently attempted coalition party did not come about, he, together with two prominent Nazi stooges, András Tasnádi Nagy and Lajos Szász proceeded to pull together the extreme right-wing and right-wing parliamentary fractions so that they might prevent Hungary's getting out of the war and prevent the regent from making an armistice agreement without their approval. Under Bárdossy's spiritual leadership the National Alliance was established.[285] It was Bárdossy who, via the National Alliance, insisted that for any armistice negotiation the regent had to seek the approval and consent of Parliament, or more precisely, of the National Alliance. The Bárdossy who made this demand was the same

Bárdossy who, ignoring both civil and constitutional law, on three occasions took Hungary into a state of war.

The facts are that the demands were not motivated by constitutional legal concerns but solely by the intent to prevent any armistice negotiations because it was obvious that in an occupied country no parliamentary armistice negotiations can be conducted with the enemy of the occupying power. Furthermore, such a constitutional legal stance by a large public body like the National Alliance, incorporating all the extreme right-wing parties, served no other purpose than to give the secret armistice feelers wide publicity. All of the démarches of the National Alliance with Regent Horthy and Prime Minister Lakatos had the sole purpose of uncovering and exposing the secret of the armistice negotiations. László Bárdossy admits in his deposition before the people's prosecutor, that the reason why he approved the action of the representatives of the National Alliance before the "higher authorities" was because he wished to ascertain the facts.

In his deposition before the people's prosecutor, Ferenc Szálasi declared that the basic idea behind the National Alliance was his, but that the negotiations with Bárdossy and others were conducted by his deputy Jenő Szőlősi. According to Jenő Szőlősi's deposition before the people's prosecutor, Bárdossy, as a distinct Germanophile and right-wing politician, was active on the committee drafting the charter for the National Alliance. According to witness Szőlősi, the goal of the National Alliance was to make sure that the rights of Parliament, or rather of the National Alliance, be secured as far as any armistice negotiations were concerned. According to witness Szőlősi it was a subject for discussion that Bárdossy would become the president of the National Alliance.[286]

Béla Imrédy spoke even more openly in his deposition before the people's prosecutor and called the National Alliance an association of Germanophile politician committed to the continuation of the war.[287]

It is shown in the diary of the National Alliance (pp. 123–124),[288] and it was also admitted by László Bárdossy in his deposition before the people's prosecutor, that the charter of the National Alliance was prepared within a larger committee by Jenő Szőlősi, Ferenc Rajniss, and himself and that, in effect, the committee essentially accepted the draft prepared by him.

László Bárdossy admitted in his deposition before the people's prosecutor that he was present as a member of the executive committee at the meeting of that committee when it sent a deputation to Prime Minister Lakatos in order to convey the protests of the National Alliance against the armistice negotiations and further to learn the facts about these negotiations. At an earlier executive committee meeting that sent András Tasnádi Nagy to the regent for the same purpose, it was Bárdossy who with Szálasi's representative, Jenő Szőlősi, moved that the National Alliance make a strong demarche to the regent demanding that the regent make no decision about an armistice or about the conduct of the war without the concurrence of Parliament. ("Diary of the Hungarist Movement," September 1944, 2nd Suppl.)[289] Witness Lajos Reményi-Schneller was also aware that Bárdossy had been very active in the National Alliance.[290] In order to supplement and support the above and particularly to show the goals of the National Alliance in whose creation László Bárdossy had such a critical role, I must cite the shorthand diary of Lajos Szász that includes the entire history of this lamentable organization as seen by its leadership:

> In his introductory speech, prime minister Lakatos wisely and openly took a position in favor of a forceful continuation of the war....Yet his role was viewed with suspicion since his actions were not consistent with his statements and he never emphasized his loyalty to our allies. The discussion of the fusion of the right-wing forces continued....The National Alliance was established....It did not include parties but politicians who thought along the same lines and who wished to enable the government to realize its proclaimed program and force it to bring its actions in conformance with its statements...it endeavored with full force it to make it possible...that we keep up the war in complete loyalty with our allies...much to the astonishment and dismay of the National Alliance the Hungarian radio aired the regent's proclamation on October 15....dismay did not, however, control our souls. In these most difficult hours the members of the National Alliance risked their life to remain faithful to their point of view and made sure that the revolution imposed from above did not take control of the country....It was thus that the National Alliance maintained

order in the country and preserved the possibility of making the guilty accountable. (pp. 72–74.)[291]

The order to be maintained, that Lajos Szász was talking about, was the Nazi Arrow Crossist order and making the guilty accountable meant to place them before the Szálasi retribution courts. This is what the National Alliance was to maintain. Jenő Szőlősi, Szálasi's deputy was correct when he stated that, "The National Alliance must be taken for a serious right-wing organization because it had a major role in the evolution of the events of October 16."[292]

The National Alliance, created with Bárdossy's assistance also fulfilled its tasks when it transferred its headquarters from Budapest to Sopron. Ferenc Rajniss concluded that when there was no more cohesive force, soul and confidence in the army and in a huge segment of the soldiers…"the National Alliance had the important task of helping to the best of its ability, insight, will and belief" (p. 42).[293]

What did this "help" consist of? On December 27, 1944, the Germans asked the National Alliance to start an intensive propaganda campaign against listening to the broadcasts from the enemy countries. (p. 74.) Its parliamentary deputy members were to hold propaganda meetings at county seats, establish propaganda centers in certain regions and drive the desperate people into the final battles on the side of the Germans (p. 26).[294]

Ferenc Szálasi and his associates started organizing the preparations for the October 15 coup in September, with German money, German weapons and under German protection.

According to the deposition of witness László Baky before the people's prosecutor, Baky was on bad terms with Szálasi at the time and it was for this reason that he informed László Bárdossy about Szálasi's preparations for the coup. According to the witness, Bárdossy did nothing to try to prevent the coup by bringing the facts out into the open.[295] Bárdossy undoubtedly expected to be given a role in the political leadership after the coup.

His expectations were not without foundation. Gábor Kemény, the chief of the Foreign Service Section of the Hungarist Movement reported to Ferenc Szálasi on September 22, 1944, that he had conferred with József Friedel, the leader of the German security services in southern Hungary, who had indicated that in the near future major changes would take place in that area. According to Kemény, this would have no impediments because Szálasi had created a right-wing front which included Ferenc Rajniss's Hungarian Renewal Party, Károly Ney's Eastern Front Fraternal Organization and could also count on László Bárdossy's adherence. "No one could say that the Germans are forcing a Hungarist solution on the country. It is now to be a Szálasi government supported by a large segment of the country." ("Diary of the Hungarist Movement," report of the leader of the Foreign Affairs Section about a discussion with Dr. Friedel).[296]

According to this, the Hungarist Movement counted on László Bárdossy's former prime minister position to make the Szálasi regime "constitutional."

On October 1, 1944, Emil Kovarcz, the organizer of the armed activities went to see Ferenc Szálasi and informed him that the decision to take over the government had been made and was to be implemented within a few days. He asked Szálasi to let him have the "General Order for the Armed Nation" so that he might take it to Vienna and have several hundred thousand copies printed. After taking over the government these would be widely distributed. Szálasi handed over the manuscript copy of the "General Orders" to Emil Kovarcz and then hastened to the apartment of Ferenc Rajniss to discuss with him, as an intermediary to the National Alliance created by Bárdossy, the role of the National Alliance in having the Parliament give legality to the takeover.

On October 2, Szálasi visited the president of the House of Representatives. On this occasion Jenő Szőlősi and Ferenc Rajniss summoned the reliable deputies such as Andor Jaross, Mecsér, Jurcsek, Bárdossy, etc. From there András Tasnádi Nagy, Bárdossy, Szőlősi and Jaross went, as a deputation, to prime minister Lakatos and took a position, as a parliamentary majority in opposition to the prime minister. Thus, in reference to the change in regime, other than a potential armed coup, "The Hungarian National Socialist change of regime has secured its parliamentary basis of power and none of the old-timers[297] will be able to say that there has been any injury done to the constitutional continuity." ("Diary of the Hungarist Movement," October, 1944, p 18.)[298]

It is evident from this that in Ferenc Szálasi's plans the National Alliance and Bárdossy no longer figured merely as political factors trying to prevent the armistice, but as legalizing factors behind the Arrow Cross coup.

When on October 4, 1944, Ferenc Szálasi negotiated about the cabinet to be set up with the German minister, Veesenmayer, the list included Bárdossy as a person acceptable to Veesenmayer. ("Diary of the Hungarist Movement," October 1944, pp. 24–30.)[299]

At the October 12 meeting of the United Christian National League, Bárdossy vehemently attacked the secretary of state in the Prime Ministers Office, Fáy, and the Minister of Justice Gábor Vladár. Bárdossy addressed the following question to Gábor Vladár, "If the rumor is true that Gendarmes Superintendent Faraghó was negotiating in Moscow, will you start a trial for treason against him?" Then Bárdossy asked Vladár, "Will you start a trial for treason even if Faraghó is in Moscow on the regent's instructions?" ("Diary of the Hungarist Movement," October 1944, pp. 64–69.)[300] (This is what László Bárdossy, former royal Hungarian prime minister and minister of foreign affairs did on October 12, 1944.) He asked whether a regental directive could be the subject of a treason trial. He could not tolerate that the regent at least made an attempt to conclude an illegal war that led the whole nation to destruction and which he, Bárdossy, started unconstitutionally as the head of state's prime minister.

This was approximately the highpoint of Bárdossy's career as a major war criminal. After this he was largely pushed aside.

Three days later, on October 15, 1944, Szálasi assumed the power and Bárdossy, whose name was on every proposed cabinet list since the German occupation, was left out of the Szálasi cabinet. There is an explanation for this. He was maneuvering too long between the various extreme right-wing factions and it was for too long that he played the gray eminence, puppet master who would never come out into the open. On October 26, 1944, Ferenc Szálasi characterized Bárdossy to Veesenmayer as a man who says, "Please restrain me or I will become a hero." ("Diary of the Hungarist Movement," September 26, 1944. [301]

It is characteristic of Bárdossy's personality and political orientation that shortly after Szálasi came to power, Bárdossy signed up for a courtesy visit to the "Nemzetvezető"[Nation's Leader] (Szálasi's deposition before the people's prosecutor).

Szálasi was too busy and did not receive him. According to Szálasi's deposition Bárdossy again came to see him in Brennberg-bánya and at this time was received. At this discussion, lasting more than an hour, Szálasi discussed the war situation and the German military action directed toward liberating the Transdanube.

This was the first personal encounter between the two principal Hungarian war criminals. Szálasi, in order to preserve his mystical halo, preferred to deal with mere mortals, vain, fallen and ambitious diplomats through intermediaries even though their role might have fit into his political goals. Bárdossy also preferred to remain in the wings rather than on center stage.

This brings to an end the story of the accused László Bárdossy who was the initiator of three declarations of war and who was a planner of the October 15, 1944, Szálasi coup. He was more than "just" a war criminal. He was the principal Hungarian criminal of the entire war. No other person carried the same responsibility for the destruction of the Hungarian nation.

With his activities detailed above, it was he who endeavored to prevent the signing of the armistice with all his influence and all his efforts. (Nbr. Par. 11, Point 3.)[302]

He was the one who with his leadership activities assisted the Arrow Cross movement in their revolt to grasp power and then in their retaining the power. (Nbr. Par. 11, point 4.)[303]

Feketehalmy-Czeydner, Grassy and others, who, because of their actions, were demoted and sentenced to the penitentiary under the old regime and who are now considered to be war criminals, were high-ranking military officers. In consequence of their abuse of power and their totally inhuman vileness there were serious massacres and looting in the Délvidék occupied by Hungarian military forces. The most notorious of these were the Zsablya massacre and the Újvidék mass murders which perhaps, during the entire war, sullied the Hungarian honor more than anything else and which caused a severe consternation of the entire civilized world's opinion.

Bárdossy was reluctant to talk about these events because, as he explained in his deposition before the people's prosecutor, the public discussion of this affair would have done more harm then good for Hungary.[304] The truth is that it is only the presentation of the unvarnished truth, the assignment of guilt and the merciless prosecution and punishment of the criminals which can prevent the whole nation, from being held responsible for the crimes of a small group of infamous criminals.

As far as the Zsablya massacre was concerned, Bárdossy in his deposition claimed that he knew only what Károly Bartha, the minister of defense at the time reported, namely that it was a "defensive act" at the time of a partisan attack. According to his deposition he knew nothing about the story that was echoed on all foreign radio broadcasts and that was common knowledge in Budapest that in retaliation for a minor incident, gendarmes and Hungarian soldiers, contrary to the rules of war and law, murdered men, women and children, essentially exterminating the entire population of a Serb village.

The accused László Bárdossy stated in the proclamation drafted by himself that the Hungarian military action was not directed against the Serb people "with whom we have no quarrel and with whom we wish to live in peace in the future."[305] As the responsible prime minister and minister of foreign affairs, he did not ask Károly Bartha, the minister of defense, what the nature of the "defensive actions" had been and whether retributions had been performed after the partisan incursion. László Bárdossy had to know, and in fact knew, that even the smallest excesses against the Serb nationals would irretrievably demolish the very fragile moral construction with which the Hungarian government endeavored to justify before the world the military action designed to reattach the Délvidék.

The Council of Ministers authorized a raid by the military in Újvidék against a partisan action because the police were not strong enough to do so. A few days later, on a day that cannot be identified accurately, eminent Hungarian politicians (Károly Rassay and Endre Bajcsy-Zsilinszky) asked László Bárdossy over the telephone to look into what had happened in Újvidék because dreadful news was circulating and a flood of refugees had arrived in Budapest.[306] The radios of the free world again went on the air and the world press reported with great indignation that in Újvidék Serbs, Jews and even Hungarians were murdered by the thousands. Bárdossy did not take the situation seriously and issued only bureaucratic orders. He instructed the Chief of the General Staff Szombathelyi, once directly and once over the telephone, to investigate and act according to the law.[307] According to the deposition of the Chief of the General Staff Ferenc Szombathelyi, Bárdossy was satisfied with this. Since the Újvidék massacres continued and public opinion loudly and insistently demanded an investigation Bárdossy ordered the commanding officer in Újvidék, Feketehalmy-Czeydner to Budapest to report. He was again satisfied.

As the responsible Hungarian prime minister and minister of foreign affairs he was satisfied with the endless vacillation of the military investigation that was apparent to him. He did not go to visit the area, he did not dispatch an investigating committee, he did not arrest a single one of the guilty people and only asked for reports even though the entire world was aware of the facts and talked about them. The investigations and reports were delayed. Bárdossy stated in his deposition before the people's prosecutor, that during that time he was very busy with other activities and that it was only much later that he received the requested reports that contained inappropriate, inadequate facts which shed no light on the issue at hand. After a delay of several months he transmitted the reports to the minister of defense at a Council of Ministers meeting and asked for a report via the minister of defense. He never saw the report because he had resigned in the meantime.

As the responsible prime minister, László Bárdossy tolerated the serious violations of international legal requirements pertaining to war that were committed by the military and gendarmes authorities in the cruel and inhuman treatment of the inhabitants of the occupied areas. Bárdossy also tolerated that the military courts, established by the leadership of the General Staff to suppress any anti-war sentiment, executed a very large number of people in these areas.

4/

The accused László Bárdossy was in general agreement with the crimes listed in the expository part of my indictment. He admitted that he did deliver the speeches listed above. In doing so the accused László Bárdossy committed a crime against the people when before the house he agitated for entry into the war and for increased participation in the war.

5/

The accused admitted that he had committed the crimes listed in the expository part of my indictment but states in his defense that he was unfamiliar with some of the ordinances promulgated against certain segments of the population at the time that he was the prime minister or rather that he knew only what was presented at the Council of Ministers meeting. Other than having general information he never even read these ordinances. In response to a question by the prosecutor he stated that even at the present time he did not know which of the ordinances promulgated while he was prime minister affected the interests of the people adversely.

This defense of the accused cannot be accepted because László Bárdossy, as the responsible prime minister and minister of foreign affairs, was instrumental in initiating the said ordinances, harmful to the interests of the people, and knowingly participated in their enactment.

6/

The accused as royal Hungarian prime minister and minister of foreign affairs had to know that beginning in July 1941 thousands of allegedly non-Hungarian Jewish residents, Jews of doubtful citizenship and Jews who were unable to produce the hard-to-obtain citizenship papers were interned and deported to Galicia under the most inhuman conditions and that there most of them were executed or died of starvation. Further, during the tenure of the accused as prime minister there was a major increase in the cruel ordinances against the forced labor battalion troops, of which as prime minister he had to know.

By not endeavoring to prevent or stop these acts even though in his legal position he had the authority to do so, the accused committed crimes against the people.

The accused László Bárdossy in his defense alleges that he had no knowledge about these ordinances or about their inhuman implementation.

The defense of the accused is unacceptable. It would have been his legal obligation as the responsible prime minister to prevent the implementation of these ordinances.

Because these acts of László Bárdossy fully meets the statutory elements of war crimes and crimes against the people, as outlined in the expository part of my indictment and the accusations are fully justified.

I request that the preliminary detention of the accused be continued because all the reasons for ordering said detention are still extant.

(The surviving copy of the indictment was signed by the chief people's prosecutor and by Ferenc Fenesi, people's prosecutor. The indictment requests that fifteen persons be subpoenaed: László Bárdossy, István Bárczy de Bárcziháza, József Bölöny, Mrs. Péter Zankay, Zoltán Bencs, Ferenc Szálasi, László Baky, Béla Imrédy, Lajos Reményi-Schneller, Jenő Szőlősi, Lajos Szász, István Antal, Ferenc Szombathelyi, Alajos Béldy-Bruckner and István Tarnay.)

THE SPEECH OF LÁSZLÓ BÁRDOSSY BEFORE THE PEOPLE'S COURT BY HIS RIGHT, AS DEFENDANT, TO THE LAST WORD

November 2, 1945

If I avail myself of the privilege granted, I believe, everywhere in the world to the defendant to speak, without the barrier of questions and the yoke of answers, to his case I do not avail myself of this right in order to defend myself. Neither in the preliminary phases of the process against me nor at the trial did I defend myself, looked for excuses or mitigating circumstances and I never tried to disclaim my responsibilities. I know that I am responsible and I will understand if the People's Court will draw the final conclusions of my responsibility. I protest, however, against being considered a criminal. Guilt and responsibility are two fundamentally different concepts. One has nothing to do with the other. In a guilty person the knowingly and willfully committed crimes wait for retribution; conclusions about responsibilities undertaken in matters of state must be judged with full consideration being given to the political necessities and to the pertinent circumstances and conditions. Be that as it may, I am not defending myself because it is my conviction that after the dreadful storm that crushed so many young lives, scattered so many families and destroyed so much of value, the fate and future of those who are now to be held accountable have no significance. The only thing of importance today is peace, the peace of the soul and if this requires a sacrifice, a sacrifice must be made. It all depends on whether the inner peace and the peace of the country in the international arena will be honest, solid and lasting. Everything hinges today on not repeating what happened in 1919 when the country was torn to pieces, when hundreds of thousands of Hungarians were torn from the land of their fathers as though they were no more than cattle or pawns on a chess board in a game played by powerful hands.

I have another reason for not defending myself. I have claimed at the beginning of the trial that according to the ordinance which serves as the legal basis for the People's Court's activities, the court has no right to pass judgment on me. The indictment has accused me of a number of violations of the constitution. Hungarian constitutional law, as reflected in the legal code, states clearly that if a government or an individual is accused of the violation of the constitution, the right to file suit and the preparation of the indictment are the prerogative of a duly elected legislature and rendering judgment is the task of a court established and empowered for that purpose under the law. The People's Court ordinance did not rescind the validity of the applicable laws, nor could it legally do so. The pertinent laws are therefore still in effect and will remain so until a legally elected legislature does not order otherwise. I am not asking for any special court, or as the president of the People's Court had said, a "feudal court." Could there possibly be a more democratic way of adjudicating a violation of the constitution than when a duly elected legislature exercises its right to file suit and to draw up the indictment as it had been mandated by Act III, 1848. This act has been sustained in subsequent legislation and a court, legally established by the legislature, must rule on the violation of the constitution serving as the basis for the indictment. If the adjudication of the violation of the constitution is not performed according to the legally prescribed procedures then, as in the present case we find an irreconcilable contradiction inasmuch as a violation of the constitution is adjudicated by a process that in itself is a violation of the constitution. This is what I have come face to face with and this is what forces me to reject the authority of the People's Court and prevents me from defending myself before the People's Court even if it had been my intent to do so, which it wasn't.

Why am I then speaking? Because it is my feeling that under the circumstances and conditions of the situation it is my duty to cooperate in uncovering the truth as I have lived through and suffered through the truth of the events. It is my duty to give information so that the nation may see and understand what happened and why it happened and that with rendering such information I may serve the cause of domestic peace.

The indictment sought a connection between my activities and the spirit of the entire period. Without claiming the wish to identify myself with the principles of the period let me speak about this period that we could call Hungary's Trianon period. It is indeed true that that this period established a path along which Hungarian policies progressed as though in the bed of a river. Let there be no misunderstanding. What I am going to say is not said to exonerate myself or to lessen my responsibility. My activities took place in the last, or perhaps more accurately the penultimate phase of the period. Can it be argued that during this period it was not a dictator who forced his arbitrary will onto the nation and it was not some party politician implementing his program in order to secure power for himself and for his party? Everything that took place during this brief period took place in complete concordance with constitutional factors. During the trial the issue of public opinion was raised repeatedly. I am fully aware of the fact that there is both an overt and a silent public opinion. If there is a conflict between the two it is impossible to determine what force and weight the silent public opinion might represent, precisely because it is silent. It is also impossible to make a determination because the silent public opinion is usually amorphous, changeable and vacillating and thus no decisions can be based on it. It is certainly not in the interest of the nation to try to determine now whether in 1941 the overt or the silent public opinion represented a majority of the national forces. The only thing that could give directives to the government was public opinion that was manifest and that sought, and even demanded, implementation of its ideas and wishes. According to the basic principles of parliamentary procedure and keeping in mind the options of practical politics, the government had to heed the overt public opinion and also heed official Hungary that held the power in its hands. These latter included the Parliament, the county legislatures, the village councils and the national organizations and it also included the national will. The national will was assessed by monitoring the sale of the daily papers and the percentage of sales contributed by each paper. This gave an indication of the popular support for the political orientation of the paper. Such an outstanding expert of Hungarian parliamentary life as Károly Rassay stated, under oath, in his testimony before this court that 95% of the Members of Parliament wished for and approved what the government had accomplished. It was he who also said that those who were of an opposite opinion were so few in number that because of this they felt that it would be better if they did not voice their concerns and opposition openly in order not to show and document the weakness of the opposition. It is true beyond any doubt that, regardless what any individual may think about the Hungarian parliamentary system, nobody could have governed in opposition to the desires of a significant majority in Parliament. In addition to the Parliament other national forces also had to be taken into consideration. I admit that the Trianon period was rife with faults and omissions. Principally that it neglected and delayed the solution of social problems and that it maintained a threadbare and obsolete administrative system and its rusty and fitfully active machinery. Yet who would question that the entire generation of this period lived with the will and the inextinguishable desire for the reestablishment of national unity. A disabled soldier could have the same wish that pervaded and kept active the entire Hungarian nation: to be once again whole, healthy and united. Once again to recapture and reclaim all that the war and brute force tore away from the lacerated trunk. The Trianon Hungarians were similar in this desire to the disabled veteran who with the shining medals of past glory on his chest, but without arms and legs, poor and orphaned, always in deadly peril, is at the crossroads of the world where the ambitions of the great powers of the world intersect and clash. This is what the entire Hungarian nation felt and this was similarly felt by the Hungarians who led a miserable existence in the areas wrested away from the country. The Hungarians of the crippled but surviving country had the duty to try to change this situation with all their might. Can there be a better and more convincing proof for showing how universal and overwhelming the desire for this change really was in all of Hungary than the fact that it was the government of the Hungarian Soviet Communist Republic, together with the Hungarian proletariat, that first accepted the responsibility and duty to make this change and the first one to be willing to use arms in its accomplishment. It was

Béla Kun who started two wars, against Czechoslovakia and Romania to recover the lost eastern and northern territories.[308]

To be technical we could say that Béla Kun should be sitting next to me in the dock for these two bellicose undertakings because, Paragraph 9 of the ordinance governing the People's Courts recognizes no statute of limitation for this "crime."[309] What do these two bellicose undertakings of the communist Hungarian Soviet Republic prove? They prove that the Hungarian workers and the Hungarian proletariat also did not accept the forceful rending apart of the Hungarian nation and would not resign itself to the situation. When the weight and responsibility of governing came to rest on the proletariat, the government of the Hungarian Soviet Republic, contrary to communist ideology, and not waiting for other possible solutions, took up the weapons and made the young Hungarian soldiers of the Hungarian Soviet Republic face rifles and canons to retake with arms what was wrested away illegally and with violence. After Béla Kun's bellicose endeavors there was not and could not have been a Hungarian government, social class or party that would have declined the service of trying to reestablish the unity of the Hungarian nation.[310] With the passing of time after the so-called Trianon peace the accomplishment of this task became ever more urgent and pressing. The Hungarians in the separated area were rapidly becoming weaker, fewer and more oppressed. They had to be saved or, at the very least, confidence and trust had to be maintained in them in order to prevent them from undertaking a suicidal attempt for liberation, relying only on their own very limited strength. Anyone who visited the separated areas before 1938 knows that all the burning Hungarian eyes focused on them had only one question, "When will you come? When? How soon?" Anyone who saw the awe with which, on the other side of the "borders," young Hungarian men and women, and the elder generation as well, kissed the national flag in spite of the fact that this was likely to followed by the hands of the gendarmes falling on their shoulder, realized that this situation could not prevail, that it had to be changed and that the task rested on the shoulders of the Hungarians in the mutilated country.

The successive Hungarian governments during the Trianon period tried to accomplish this task with every means and method at their disposal. They first tried peaceful negotiations with their neighbors.

The Bruck, Marienbad and Karlsbad negotiations were way stations of the discussions with the Czechoslovaks.[311] The regent's speech in Mohács was an attempt toward the Serbs.[312] But in the mean time the concerned nations around us formed a defensive and defiant union with the slogan that whoever raises the matter of revision, even if only before the League of Nations, starts a war. There was not a single one of the interested parties with whom we could talk because it was they and not Hungary who made the revision a matter of war. Successive governments thereafter tried to find understanding and some support in the West. Indeed, there was an echo in the press and in the political literature of the Western countries. The increasing signs of sympathy and of understanding further strengthened the feeling in the Hungarians that their cause was just. It is a painful fact, however, that the official agencies of the Western countries rigidly refused even to investigate the matter and this made the bitterness of the Hungarians increasingly insupportable. At one time, a Hungarian minister of foreign affairs, Lajos Walkó, was told in Geneva in a very friendly fashion what Hungary could expect from the Western nations,[313]

> When a road is being repaved and it happens during the work that one of the paving stones has less space assigned to it than its dimensions required, the result will be that this stone will jut out beyond the surface of the road. Yet, who could expect that for the sake of this single stone the entire road would be dismantled again and the work restarted from the beginning? No, no one could expect that since nature will eventually remedy the situation anyway. The stone rising above the level of the others will be gradually worn down, chipped off and hammered by everything passing along the road until the difference in height between the stone and the road is eventually eliminated and the problem is resolved. Everything can be left to the passing of time. Just as every wheel of every cart, every shoe of every horse and every sole of every passer-by will hammer on the extruding stone, every difficulty of every situation "necessarily" affects the nation dissatisfied with its position until, finally, the nation acquiesces and settles into the place that greater powers have assigned to it.

This is the fate that they planned for Hungary. And, in fact, this was the lot of Hungary. If the king of one of the countries was killed, far away in France,[314] the innocent Hungarians of that country were shoved across the border by the thousands after the women and the children had been shamefully abused.[315] The minister of the interior of another neighboring country was boasting in an open session of its parliament that unscrupulous emigration agents managed to persuade several thousand poor Hungarian farmers to go to South America where the killing climate and the unfamiliar conditions would inevitably destroy them. The minister admitted openly that with this emigration policy he wished to make the ethnic balance of the country more favorable for his own people.[316]

When in the 30s the economic crisis reached Europe from overseas and the commercial and industrial enterprises in the neighboring states were in increasing difficulties the Hungarian workers were dismissed. It was then that the "*numerus vallachius*" was created with the intent that it rapidly progress to a "*numerus nullus.*"[317] But, in addition to the Hungarian agricultural and industrial workers, the Hungarians of all classes were heavily burdened by the miseries that the administration of their new countries endeavored to make even more bitter and more insupportable. Officials, independent professionals and landowners all suffered for being Hungarians. If we consider how rapidly the Hungarians in the annexed territories lost their strength and their livelihood and that these Hungarians represented approximately one third of all the Hungarians in the world, it becomes readily comprehensible that the urgency with which this situation had to be changed weighed heavily on the Hungarians on both sides of the borders. Until 1938 Italy was the only European country that recognized the legitimacy of the Hungarian demands. In 1938, unexpectedly, a new political situation arose in Europe that opened the doors for Hungarian revisionism.[318] For the Hungarian people this was a vital and critical turning point. The turning point was the Munich agreement. If, after resolving the Sudeten question, the Western Powers had addressed an equitable solution for the Hungarian revision demands, the subsequent behavior of Hungary would have been quite different. But in Munich, and even more strongly afterward, the Western Powers declared their intention that they did not wish to tackle the issues pending in the southeastern part of Central

Europe.[319] They even gave up protecting their own interests in these areas. In spite of her alliance with Czechoslovakia, France showed no further interest in the fate of the country. The Soviet Union also showed no interest and watched the events in complete inertia even though she did have a pact of mutual assistance with Czechoslovakia.[320] Thus, both from the West and from the East the resolution of the problems in southeast Europe was left to or, perhaps, handed over to the German Reich and to her ally Italy. No reliance could be put on the Western countries who had abandoned southeast Europe either as the guardians of the old order as established after World War I, or as a power bloc willing to participate in the creation of a new, more equitable and more healthy arrangement. With the silent acquiescence of the Western Powers and of the Soviet Union, southeast Europe and the entire Danube Basin came under the leadership of a militarily very powerful Germany. Hungary did not create this situation but drew the obvious conclusions. This is what all the other countries in the Danube Basin did as well. Forgetting the ties that linked them for twenty years to the Western Powers, forgetting that they owed their existence or great enlargement to those countries, every one of them turned toward the rising sun of Berlin and it was there that they looked for protection. The Czech Republic, under the leadership of her democratically elected president and without the least sign of resistance became a German protectorate. Romania realigned her national life according to the German model as early as 1937. At the beginning of 1939 Romania committed almost her entire agricultural production to Germany under the so-called Wohltat agreement.[321] This was followed in rapid succession by an expansion of the agreement, the ostentatious rejection of the territorial guarantees offered earlier by Great Britain, the renunciation of her obligations under the Balkan Pact and, to top it all off, the unsolicited invitation to German military forces to be stationed in Romania. Yugoslavia also developed intimate economic and political ties with the German Reich. Everything had changed around Hungary. Those who until recently were walking on the leash of the Western Powers and were seeking only the favors of the Western Powers now did the same thing, with all their might, but toward Berlin. They hoped for Berlin's favor and voluntarily subjected themselves to Germany. Prior to this they were leaning on the Western Powers and it was with their help that they were successful in making good their interests at the cost of Hungary and of the Hungarian nation. Now, in the changed situation, they wished to thwart the Hungarian demands with Berlin's assistance, even though they had to honestly admit the legitimacy of these demands while they denied them loudly.

Is it imaginable that in this changed situation, surrounded by neighbors clamoring for Germany's good will, Hungary should be the one which, contrary to all the logic of the new political constellation, would tie her fate to the Western Powers which had shown no indication whatever in the past that they appreciated the Hungarian interests and demands or that they were willing to do anything to further their accomplishment? Is it imaginable that Hungary should do this when this country by virtue of its geographic position, historic, emotional and economic ties had a stronger attraction toward the German sphere than any other country in the Danube Basin? It is sufficient to cast a single glance at the map to see the centuries-old requirements of our geographic location. Toward the west Hungary is open, toward the east it is enclosed by a mighty mountain chain which can be traversed only by very narrow passes. As a consequence of these geographic realities Hungary had sent the majority of her surpluses to the west, primarily to German markets where they were sold. Conversely, it was from there that she imported what she could not produce or for the production of which she was not yet ready. The raw materials required by the Hungarian industries, giving work to hundreds of thousands of Hungarian workers, were also imported from Germany. It was from there that almost one hundred percent of the coke, essential in the production of iron and other metals, was imported as well as a significant amount of anthracite coal. It was from there that we received all the artificial fibers, essential for the functioning of our extensive textile industry. I could continue, but there is no point. The decisive issue is that the intelligent Hungarian agriculturalist knew that he was just as dependent on the easily reached German markets to sell his products as the well-informed Hungarian industrial work force that knew from where the raw materials and some of the more intricate machines came that were essential to keep industry going. It was not political calculation that established and maintained these contacts but the interdependence of neighboring territories. There is no question that this interdependence also influenced the political behavior of the working and thinking Hungarian nation. This influence was augmented by the fact that after World War I the situation of the two countries evolved similarly or, more accurately, in parallel, and that in the face of the indifference and disinterest demonstrated by the governments and official agencies of the Western Powers, Hungary could hope only that a change in the power position of the German Reich would allow it [Hungary] to unite her people and recover her strength. All this was affected by the strong spiritual influence of Germany to which we had been exposed for centuries and also by the memory of alliance in World War I that remained particularly strong among the military organizations of the two countries and that fostered intimate relationships between them. It was important in this regard that the German military leadership was Hungarophile and thus could be counted upon to counterbalance the not always friendly attitude of other German factors.

In addition to that, there was another most important factor affecting the evolution of the Hungarian-German relationship. In the southeast European area the Hungarian nation lived not only abandoned to itself, but surrounded by hostile peoples. In the south, beyond the historic borders as well as in the northwest beyond the Carpathians there were Slavic peoples who in their struggle for national advancement regretfully frequently came into conflict with the Hungarian nation. In the political striving of these people they could always count on the support of the ethnically related Russia which ever since the seventeenth century kept growing in strength and power and which usually provided the requested support. In this respect Germany and Hungary were natural allies. In the isolated and exposed situation of the Hungarian nation it needed some balance vis-à-vis the pressure exerted by the Slavic nations while the Germans in protecting their interests in the Danube Basin could rely only on Hungary among the several nations of Slavic origin. The strongest evidence for the proposition that Germany could never turn against Hungary and that she always had to respect Hungary's interests, was in the fact that Germany needed Hungary and that it would severely affect her own interests if she would weaken Hungary or permit that Hungary be weakened by others. This political interdependence was advantageous for Hungary because our national dynamics and birth rate were greater than Germany's but unfortunately much smaller than of the people living to the north and south of us. Another problem was that among the people living in the area of southeast Europe the Germans were assimilated and large numbers became Hungarians while in the process of assimilation of Hungarians in other countries the Hungarians were usually the losers.

These were essentially the geographic, economic and political factors which determined Hungary's behavior and position in the sequence of events starting in 1938 and which then took such a fateful turn. Is it imaginable that this generation, fully aware of the above, could have declined the return of the areas inhabited totally or partially by Hungarians just because said return was accomplished with the assistance of Germany and Italy? This question cannot be raised seriously.[322] The generation of the Trianon era had to follow the path that was determined for it by the possibility of leading to the achievement of its rightful national goals and any deviation from this path would have meant the denial and falsity of our aspirations. Yet, with all this we are in the world of assumptions. In the fall of 1938 the German and Italian governments assumed control of the implementation of our claims concerning those areas of the Felvidék inhabited by Hungarians. In March 1939 Hungary reattached Subcarpathia to which action the German government had given preliminary approval in the fall of 1938. The award by the German and Italian governments returned Northern Transylvania and the Székelyföld [Székely Counties] to Hungary in August of 1940. This brought to fruition one part of the Hungarian revisionist aspirations. The awards were followed by Hungary's joining the Tripartite Pact on November 20, 1940, which step changed the relationship between Hungary and the so-called Axis Powers from a previously voluntary cooperation into a contractual relationship bringing with it mutual obligations.

The realization of some of our revisionist demands meant a significant increase in strength but, at the same time also imposed a certain burden. The reattachment of a strip of territory north of the Danube created a feeling of hostility in the leadership of the newly created Slovakia and a part of its population that made the Hungarian-Slovak relations very tense and even inimical. The recovery of Subcarpathia had even graver consequences. It is well known that Russia had declared a claim to Subcarpathia even before World War I. It is also known that while Subcarpathia was a part of Czechoslovakia, Edvard Beneš, both as minister of foreign affairs and as prime minister repeatedly emphasized that the Czechoslovak Republic held Subcarpathia "in trust" for the Soviet Union. The Soviet Union herself never made a secret of the fact that she claimed Subcarpathia for herself. The reattachment of Subcarpathia thus created a debated issue and a temporarily latent animosity between Hungary and the Soviet Union. The recovery of Northern Transylvania completely poisoned Hungarian-Romanian relations that was bad to begin with. There were numerous armed clashes along the entire new border and it could be expected that one day the entire armed forces of the two countries would be launched against each other.

It was also part of the picture that one part of Hungarian public opinion was dissatisfied with the First and Second Vienna Awards because it was felt that the returned territories were too small. This part of public opinion expressed its dissatisfaction by the loudly stated demand of "mindent vissza!" [All of it back]. The ones who took this position were mostly from among those who viewed the increasingly firm Hungarian-German relations with disfavor. This part of the Hungarian public opinion was anti-German, or at least had grave concerns about Hungarian-German relations. It was not yet of the opinion that nothing should have been accepted from the hands of the German government but felt rather that the German government should have given all of the former Hungarian territory back to Hungary or, at the very least, considerably more than what they had given. While one part of Hungarian public opinion was dissatisfied and wished to push for the very maximum in the realization of the Hungarian revisionist demands, another part of the public opinion felt that in view of the Realpolitik of the situation no further returns of territories could be expected and that the return of the territories already accomplished created a position of dependency for Hungary versus Germany. This was the first time that a rift appeared in Hungarian revisionist policies in the sense that one group wanted everything or at least considerably more, while another group was willing to settle for what we had received. There was no voice, not even in the most careful and covert way that would have taken a position completely opposed to the realization of any revisionist goals. It is undoubtedly true that the part of Hungarian public relations unfriendly to Germany was strengthened by the two Vienna awards and that the disappointment and bitterness over the Vienna awards moved many into the anti-German camp.[323]

The importance of all this for future developments was that the return of the Southern Slovakia and Northern Transylvania territories did indeed create a dependency relationship between Hungary and the German Reich. In order to assure the trouble-free possession of the recovered territories vis-à-vis the neighboring countries and the Western Powers Hungary became increasingly dependent on the strength of Germany. This was made manifest by Hungary's joining the Tripartite Pact.

In the meantime the German-Polish war was started and was brought to a surprisingly rapid end. In 1940 the great military successes in Norway, Belgium, Holland and France, Denmark's occupation and the fact that the Danish nation made no resistance whatever against the occupation and that the Danish constitutional bodies were willing to cooperate with the occupying forces, at least until the middle of 1944, strengthened the feeling in increasingly wide circles that Germany's military strength could not be overcome, at least not on the Continent. While during the Polish campaign many still doubted that Germany could attain the same results against other opponents, such as the Western Powers, after the results of 1940 these voices were completely silenced.

From the perspective of Germany the most unfavorable consideration was that if the Western Powers truly threw all their resources into the fight, the struggle would be greatly prolonged and the final outcome might depend on how many forces could be marshaled until the final phase. Even the political and military leaders of the Western Powers were not optimistic in their utterances[324]

Following the course of events we now arrive at the middle of 1940 when, after the end of the military action against France, the war shifted to the Balkans. The Italians attacked Greece but since the military action dragged out and its outcome became increasingly doubtful, Berlin came to the conclusion that the Italian military action had to be brought to an urgent and successful end with German assistance so that the Western Powers could not establish a foothold on the Greek peninsula like they did in World War I. Because of the conflict initiated by the Italians it became Germany's prime interest to secure a military position in the Balkans even though the interests of two world powers, Great Britain and the Soviet Union were already engaged in that area.

The German army could approach the Greek theater of war only through Yugoslavia and for this it was necessary to obtain either Yugoslav participation or at least Yugoslav government permission for German troop transit. This is what German diplomacy had to achieve in Yugoslavia. One part of Yugoslav public opinion that was otherwise friendly toward Germany was reluctant to join the Axis forces for fear that the Axis Powers would support Hungary's revisionist goals vis-à-vis Yugoslavia to a degree that might jeopardize the cohesion of Yugoslavia's component parts. It was therefore the task of German diplomacy to allay this apprehension of the Yugoslav government. This was the reason for the German government's request to the Hungarian government to establish a more peaceful relationship with Yugoslavia. This did not require that the Hungarian government give up all attempts to achieve territorial revision but would serve as surety that all future steps in this direction would be toward a peaceful solution by mutual agreement between the Hungarian and Yugoslav governments.[325]

It was according to this German request and in this spirit that in December 1940 the Hungarian-Yugoslav friendship pact was signed in Belgrade. Prior to signing the pact, the Hungarian minister of foreign affairs made it unmistakably clear that Hungary maintained its claims for the Hungarian areas of the Délvidék but was willing to submit the resolution of this problem to mutual agreement.[326]

The pact was understood in the same way by the Yugoslav government and the representatives of both governments stated and confirmed this when the documents were signed. After Germany allayed the Yugoslav concerns and promised that other Yugoslav wishes would be honored the Cvetković government was ready to join the Tripartite Pact on Yugoslavia's part and permit the transit of German troops through Yugoslav territory. The adherence to the pact was solemnly announced in March 1941 but very shortly after the prime minister and the minister of foreign affairs returned from this ceremony to Belgrade a military coup forcefully removed the government and also forcefully disbanded the highest constitutional body, the Regency Council. Its members and the members of the government were arrested and the young king was declared to be an adult. In his name the powers were bestowed on a group that declared the adherence to the Tripartite Pact null and void which also meant that the Yugoslavs would resist all German attempts to cross Yugoslavia.

The war had now reached Hungary's doorstep. It was now that the Hungarian government was confronted with the tragic question, what should Hungary do in this situation? In deciding the question the following points had to be considered. If Hungary were to remain strictly neutral in the war against Yugoslavia and deny the German troops permission to cross Hungarian territory, this would inevitably cause the German government to take armed action against Hungary as well. Ignoring the fact that an overwhelming majority of Parliament and of Hungarian public opinion would have opposed such a provocation and that there was practically no way in which such a decision could have been carried out, the answer to the question evidently had to be that a German military action against Hungary would have had the most fatal consequences for the Hungarian nation.[327] There is no doubt that the German army would have overrun and destroyed the country in a very short period of time and there was no defense against an attack from the west. The entire country would have been under German control within a few days and the occupying force would have detached the recently regained Hungarian territories. As far as those areas of Hungary were concerned where the inhabitants were mostly Germans it is likely that they would have also been separated from the country. Additionally all resources and products of the country would have been used for German purposes until the end of the war.

Those who believe that the suffering and destruction undertaken in that way would have been a good investment for the period after the Germans had lost the war are greatly mistaken. We are again, inevitably, in the realm of assumptions but, examining the issue theoretically, we must conclude that the stronger the Hungarian resistance, the greater the loss of life and assets which in view of our low birth rate could never have been recovered after four years of German occupation.[329] If the resistance would have been brief and pro forma, the German occupying forces would have entrusted the management of the country to a new Hungarian government and thus in addition to losses suffered, the Hungarian nation could not have counted on a postwar recognition of its resistance to Germany. The winners would have viewed the government installed by the Germans as representatives of the entire nation and the only difference would be that others would be the "war criminals" and that the effects of the German occupation could never be made up. It is an equally grave mistake to assume that for these sacrifices and sufferings the victors would have compensated the Hungarian nation with additional territories. There is no territory in the Danube Basin that is not claimed by one of the neighboring countries and because the economic strength of the surrounding countries and their military and territorial strength is much more important for the victors than Hungary's strength and situation, there is no doubt that the disputed territories would not have been used for the benefit of the Hungarian nation. In politics there is no gratitude and there are no gifts. It is all about the protection of interests and it would have been in nobody's interest to return territories to a Hungary bled out by serious resistance and unable to even manage such territories.

The second theoretically possible option would have been to yield to the request of the German government and permit the transit of German troops across Hungarian territory but in no way and no form take part in any military action against Yugoslavia. This solution would have essentially meant the same thing as if the government had resisted but yielded to brute force. The consequences would also have been the same. In control of the transportation system and of the industrial centers of the country the German army could have done with the country whatever it wanted and whatever would have been beneficial for it. Taking control of the political power and bestowing it on a group that was willing to assume that responsibility under the circumstances would have presented no difficulties and everything that was said above in connection with slight or apparent resistance, would apply to this situation as well.

All this is empty speculation because in 1941 there could have been no government that remained in position for more than twenty-four hours, had they seriously considered any one of the above options. Nobody would have backed a government that had such intentions regardless how honorable the concerns were that lived in the heart of some Hungarian patriots. They also viewed the situation and concluded that it would have been unwise to voice their doubts and concerns because there was nothing they could do to change the events and because the nation had to make its decisions on the basis of more elevated considerations.

South of the Trianon border, in the territory awarded to the Serb-Croat-Slovene state in 1919,[329] almost half a million Hungarians were waiting for liberation, waiting to be united again with Hungary and to live in its national life in freedom from which they had been deprived for twenty years.

The Trianon generation proclaimed for twenty years that mutilation of the Hungarian nation was unjust and that it would use every means available to remedy this injustice. This generation was committed to this task on behalf of the Hungarians in the mutilated country and the Hungarians in the territories annexed by its neighbors. The German-Yugoslav war, beginning shortly, was a way to achieve the liberation of the Délvidék Hungarians. It would have been the denial and abandonment of the entire past twenty years and of the legitimacy of the claims voiced many thousands of times if the nation did not take advantage of this opportunity. It would have been the final abdication of the correctness of the principle that those belonging to one nation should live in one country. A lasting peace in the Danube Basin could be assured only by eliminating the causes of the injustice and of antagonism. Looked at from a more distant perspective, this was the ultimate goal of Hungarian revisionism.

What was it that could have prevented the liberation of the Délvidék Hungarians under these circumstances? The Hungarian-Yugoslav pact, signed in Belgrade is mentioned in this context. But this pact came into being with the expressed preservation of the Hungarian revisionist goals, with the plan of Yugoslavia joining the political configuration of which Hungary was a member and with the intent that the Yugoslav government, jointly with the Hungarian government, would find a solution of the revision issue in the form of a mutual and friendly understanding. Every international agreement is reached with a *rebus sic stantibus* [under the prevailing conditions] clause. If the conditions considered at the time of signing and serving as the basis for the agreement change or cease to exist, the validity of the agreement is also gone. Nobody makes an agreement to achieve unachievable goals and if the possibility of achieving reasonable goals disappears any agreement made for that purpose looses its legitimacy. If an agreement no longer regulates the activities of the parties it can no longer be a hindrance to other decisions. The Yugoslav state never ratified the Hungarian- Yugoslav pact, signed in Belgrade, and thus never gave it the power of a mandate. It was the Yugoslav state that revoked its adherence to the Tripartite Pact and since the Hungarian-Yugoslav pact was part of the political system represented by the Tripartite Pact and was an essential component of that pact, according to Yugoslavia, the new Yugoslav government revoked not only their adherence to the Tripartite Pact but simultaneously rescinded the validity of Hungarian-Yugoslav pact, they had never ratified.

The pact had become meaningless by the decisions of the Simović government and by the fundamentally altered conditions and thus could in no way impede the decisions of the Hungarian government. The possibility of peacefully settling the problem of where and to whom the Hungarian areas of northern Yugoslavia should belong had disappeared and this gave the Hungarian government the freedom to act on behalf of the Hungarians in the Délvidék as it saw fit. If the prison in which my sister and my brother are unlawfully detained catches fire I would not wait to get them out until the jailers set them free.

If Hungarian public opinion would not have undertaken the liberation of the Hungarians in the Délvidék, then under the conditions sketched above, this reluctance would have resulted in these Délvidék Hungarians going from Yugoslav rule to German rule. It also had to be taken into account that Germany might combine the mixed German-Hungarian population of the so-called Schwäbische Türkei, including parts of Baranya County and Tolna County with the Délvidék and set up another Schutzstaat [Protectorate]. None of this was decisive! The decisive issue was that the Hungarians in the Délvidék had to be liberated and that this liberation could be achieved only by the Hungarians.

It is an insult to Count Pál Teleki's memory to assume that he did not feel and think in this way. Pál Teleki devoted almost every effort of his most productive twenty years to the issue of Hungarian revisionism. This is what he lived for. During the critical negotiations concerning the liberation of the Hungarians in the Délvidék, he repeatedly stated that the recovery of the territory inhabited by Hungarians could not be expected from peaceful reassignment. He said frequently, "We deserve the freedom of our brothers and the recovery of our territories only if we are willing to make sacrifices for them." Pál Teleki would have been in opposition with himself and would have denied his loyalty to his personal goals and to the national goals of the Hungarian nation if he would have doubted, even for a second, what he had to do for the Délvidék Hungarians. His death is his personal tragedy. His doubts and struggles are not a part of this trial but cannot be used as argument against the decisions in the making of which he had a dominant role. It was his principal concern that if we use the German-Yugoslav war to free the Hungarians in the Délvidék then our actions must serve that goal only. It should not begin before this was absolutely necessary, offend no other interests and that our military action be terminated as soon as the territory inhabited by Hungarians had been reattached.

The chancellor of the German Reich turned to the Hungarian head of state on March 26, 1941, and asked for the approval of the Hungarian government for the transit of the German army across Hungarian territory against Yugoslavia.[330] The message, which stated emphatically that Germany would use forces that would guarantee decisive results in a very short period of time, also included that if Hungary participated in the action, a move welcomed by Germany, it could gain back everything that was torn away from the country in 1919 and was attached to Yugoslavia. The Hungarian government granted permission for the German army to cross Hungary. Concerning other matters, the government decided that it would not participate in the war against Yugoslavia and only reserved the right to perform a strictly limited military action between the Danube and the Tisza to reclaim those Hungarian areas that were outside Croatia, Slavonia and Dalmatia. The Hungarian government tied even this very limited action to three alternative conditions, meaning that it would not enter the fray until at least one of the conditions was met. According to this stipulation military action would be initiated only if the Yugoslav kingdom, known originally as the Serb-Croat-Slovene state would cease to exist as a political unit and fell apart into its constituents, a fact that could reasonably be expected, or if to the south of the Trianon border a vacuum would develop, i.e. the Yugoslav army abandoned this area or reliable news was received that the Hungarians in the Délvidék were mistreated in which case immediate assistance would be rendered to the persecuted people. This, in principle, was the government's decision. In fact the liberation of the Délvidék was performed in accordance with these principles and entirely in agreement with them.

The German campaign began on April 5, 1941,[331] and immediately moved forward at a rapid rate. On April 9, the Hungarian General Staff, evidently on urging by the German military leadership, protested to the regent about tying the campaign to conditions of which it was virtually impossible to determine whether or when they were met. It requested the immediate initiation of the military action. The stated request was ignored and the original decision was confirmed.[332] Late at night, on April 10, a telephone call was received from the Hungarian consul general in Zagreb.[333] The consul general reported that the independent Croat state was proclaimed that day in the Croatian capital and that, according to reliable information, every responsible Croat organization was participating in the creation of the new state. The unexpectedly poor showing of the Yugoslav army was claimed to be due to the fact that units under the command of Croat officers or consisting mostly of Croat soldiers would not fight and that from units with a mixed crew the Croat and Slovene officers and men were deserting and returning home. The same was being done by Croat and Slovene officials who were assigned to Serb areas outside their homeland. The rapid advance of the German forces could be attributed to this general disintegration.

The proclamation of an independent Croatia fulfilled the first condition that the Hungarian government demanded prior to liberating the Délvidék. According to the official report received by the government there could be no doubt that the Yugoslav state had fallen apart into its various constituents and ceased to exist as a political unit. The one place where there could be no doubt that the creation of national independence was based on autochthonous national forces was Croatia. This drive for independence had been alive for twenty years beginning shortly after the formation of the Serb-Croat-Slovene kingdom and the ensuing disappointments. They had martyrs. They made significant international connections. The leaders of the movement appeared before international meetings, the diplomats of the Western Powers took notice of the strength of the movement and its significance was not questioned by the Serbs either.[334] Could the argument that the proclamation of independent Croatia was just an excuse used by the

Hungarian government be maintained and that as long the government of the Yugoslav kingdom was functioning in the nation's capital or elsewhere, Yugoslavia could not be regarded as extinct and that the German "occupation" of Croatia was just a loss of territory?

The surprisingly weak and in some areas non-existent resistance of the Yugoslav army was the most eloquent proof that the retreating army not only yielded the evacuated territory to the enemy but that the state based on administration and defense had almost chemically disintegrated into its constituent elements. Nobody argued that the Serb nation no longer existed but this was a very different proposition from the Serb-Croat-Slovene nation which its creators in 1918 wished to make into a federation.

If on September 18, 1939, the government of the Soviet Union claimed[335] that its army entered Poland because "Poland had ceased to exist" then it should be impossible to deny the Hungarian government the right to occupy the Hungarian areas of the Délvidék using an analogous argument. Other than the disintegration of the Yugoslav state there were other conditions that gave the Hungarian government the right to initiate military action according to its original conditions. By April 10 the bulk of the German army was beyond Újvidék and the Serb military leadership had evacuated the southern area between the Danube and the Tisza. Only small partisan groups remained which did not alter the fact that politically and militarily this area was a vacuum in which there was no longer any personal or material security.

The Hungarian military action began in the early afternoon of April 11[336] fully six days after the beginning of the German campaign from which it was thus clearly distinct. The Hungarian action came to an end with the occupation of the Bácska, well before the end of the German campaign. The soldiers mobilized for the Hungarian action were demobilized and sent home after the occupation of the Bácska, with the exception of a small number of security troops left in the area. The entire action was thus strictly within the originally determined framework and boundaries. By performing this action Hungary did not become one of the belligerents and in no way became a "comrade in arms" of the German Reich, nor was its action in any way coordinated with the German Yugoslavia campaign. This was exactly like the armed action of the Soviet Union in Poland in 1939 which was not coordinated with the German military action in that country.[337] The position of the Hungarian government that Hungary had not waged war against Yugoslavia and thus was not a belligerent party was conveyed to the German Reich government on several occasions, for the last time when the Yugoslav national assets were liquidated and distributed. Even though the belligerent parties received a larger share, the Hungarian government insisted that it should not be considered as one of the belligerent parties.

In one of the speeches for the prosecution there was a long discussion as to how we could have taken part in the German war against Yugoslavia. I must admit that I was shocked in listening to this because I thought that it was inconceivable that in the capital of Hungary, in Hungarian, this question could be discussed as though in 1941 we had engaged in a robber campaign for the occupation of foreign lands. In the speech there was no mention at all of the half million Hungarians in the Délvidék who were waiting for liberation and that the occupied territories had been ethnically and economically an integral part of Hungary for a thousand years. The speech to its end never said that the area and its people were not strangers to Hungary and that they were like the branch of a tree that reaches over into the neighbor's yard but remains a part of the tree even though they may erect a fence between the trunk of the tree and the branch. It was not I but the honestly pacifist, but truly Hungarian Mihály Babits who wrote angrily that he did not understand why it was called an "enlargement of the country" when it was a process that brought our blood relations back to us, driven by a natural affinity.[338]

Returning to the chain of events, it could be seen as early as the beginning of April when, following the Italians, the Germans engaged in warfare in the Balkans that something had affected the relationship between Germany and the Soviet Union. Germany was first secretive about this but this secretiveness itself suggested that she was preparing for some action. The antagonism between Germany and the Soviet Union was not new. Being unable to arrange for an eastern Locarno,[339] the German government openly asked for a free hand toward the east. The difference in philosophy and the parallel German-Slav antagonism made it clear that the so-called Third Reich saw Russia as its principle enemy.

In Hungary it was the military leadership that received the first intimation that the Reich chancellor had decided to resolve this antagonism with the force of arms. In a lengthy memorandum, submitted to the Hungarian government on May 6, presumably on suggestions from the German military leadership, the Hungarian General Staff stated its opinion that a German-Soviet war was likely and then complemented this information with the recommendation that the Hungarian government should spontaneously offer armed cooperation in the war against the Soviet Union, which might result in substantial benefits for Hungary, including additional territorial adjustments.[340] The government did not accept the recommendation of the General Staff and only started a careful exploration, by diplomatic routes, to ascertain the plans of the German government in order to be informed about the probable future course of events. The German Ministry of Foreign Affairs not only refused to give any information but denied the existence of any German-Soviet opposition by stating that for it there was no "Russian question," even though there was a succession of signals indicating the increasingly venomous differences.

While the German Ministry of Foreign Affairs thus refused to give out any information, the Hungarian General Staff, alleging reliable information, never stopped to urge and pursue that the Hungarian government should prepare itself for a war against the Soviets and agree that the Hungarian military leadership issue the appropriate orders within the military establishment. It was evident that the German government did not wish to engage in negotiations with the Hungarian government on the *do ut des* [I give so that you give] principle, but still considered our cooperation very important and wished to ensure it by utilizing the military routes to exploit Hungarian-German relations. It was very important for the German Reich, initially more along political rather than military lines that all European countries, but particularly the countries neighboring on the Soviet Union participate in the war against that country. Germany knew the philosophical basis of the present Hungarian regime and its continued strong anti-Bolshevist stance and realized that forcing the Soviets back toward the east was an eminent Hungarian desideratum in order to maintain undisturbed control over Subcarpathia that the Russian had laid a claim to. In Berlin they were evidently assuming that Hungary would participate in the war and that therefore it would be a mistake to give the Hungarian government the opportunity to demand additional territorial compensation as the price of cooperation. Any such additional territorial demand would only increase the trouble and the restlessness which because of the complex and probably irresolvable territorial problems poisoned relations between the nations in southeast Europe and created a difficult and awkward problem for Germany. The German policy hence endeavored to make it mandatory for the Hungarian government, perhaps by military pressure or by stirring up the anti-Bolshevist public opinion, to participate in the war without demanding any compensation for this action. It is only this rationale that would explain why the Germans protested by diplomatic routes against having this matter be raised while along military routes they increasingly urged Hungary to get ready and participate. The German government even held out the possibility of some territorial gifts but this was done only along the military lines, i.e. without the government accepting any responsibility for it.

There is no question that in Hungary the factors that determined the participation of the country in the war were given just as the German government had figured. After a brief communist experiment, the system of government evolved from the so-called conterrevolutionary movement. It was first of all the head of state who was committed, after twenty years of service and innumerable statements, on the side of the anti-Bolshevik endeavors, and who, since the beginning of the Polish campaign, in his messages to Berlin reiterated his convictions. These are facts which do not, however, decrease the Hungarian government's responsibility.

The same view of the world and the same political orientation determined the position of the Hungarian military leadership and of the officer corps. Prior to the beginning of the war the large majority of the military leadership and of the officer corps showed a boundless optimism concerning the outcome of a Russian campaign and this affected their position as much as their desire that the Hungarian army demonstrate its strength and that the standing of the army not be overshadowed by the armies of the neighboring countries.

In a large portion of public opinion the following facts played a role and while it is impossible to state today how large this portion was, it was the portion that stated its position loudly and clearly. The factors were fear from the so-called Slav peril that had been a bugaboo of Hungarian public opinion for more than a hundred years, ever since the publication of Wessélenyi's famous pamphlet.[341] During this trial Lajos Kossuth was cited repeatedly. A large part of Hungarian public opinion was aware that Lajos Kossuth's utterances in Great Britain and America were directed primarily to the issues of Hungary but, immediately second to that, he wished to draw attention to the Pan-Slav peril and to the need of strengthening Hungary because of this peril.

Awareness of the peril made it a moral obligation that Hungary had to participate in efforts to avert the peril. Similarly, the memories of the communist experiment right after World War I contributed to the position taken by Hungarian public opinion as did the news about the events that had recently taken place in the Baltic States.[342] There were not a few who felt that if Hungary did not participate in the war it jeopardized the recently regained territories while participation might result in obtaining additional territories. In a number of critical discussions the argument was used repeatedly that the voluntary participation of Hungary would strengthen its claims for the return of Hungarian territories still under foreign rule and also that the return of the Felvidék and of Northern Transylvania placed an obligation on Hungary vis-à-vis Germany to now stand at the side of Germany armed with weapons. Even before the return of Subcarpathia voices were raised in the anti-German Hungarian press according to which Hungary would know her obligations and live up to them in the fight against the Soviet Union if Hungary would once again be given control of Subcarpathia (Tibor Eckhardt's editorial in the October 15, 1938, issue of *Magyar Nemzet*).[343]

These were the elements that determined the behavior of the power-based Hungarian officialdom, of the army and of the vociferous public opinion in the matter of a war against the Soviet Union. Even more so, consideration had to be given to the interests and power relationships under which the war against the Soviets was to be fought.

With the attack against the Soviet Union the war moved into a new and decisive phase. Natural enemies confronted each other. On the one side an experienced and huge military force, on the other an unknown military preparedness, but an almost incomprehensibly enormous territory and an unparalleled wealth in raw materials and sources of power that gave essentially unlimited opportunities for defense.

The fact that the Soviet Union was brought into the war broadened the scope of the war and prolonged its probable duration. It became predictable that the Great Powers that hitherto stayed out of the conflict, Japan and the United States, sooner or later would also become involved. The opportunity arose for Great Britain and for the United States to build up a military machinery with which they could strike the enemy at the most appropriate location and the most suitable time. The weight of the fight for the time being moved to the east and it was clearly in the best interests of the Western Powers to have the German army tied down in that area until a favorable opportunity arose in the west. It was clear that in order to accomplish this goal, the Western Powers were prepared to make great sacrifices in favor of the Soviet Union.

Germany once again assumed the grave risks of a war on two fronts and even though she was confident in her own strength she had to be aware of the great dangers she exposed herself to. It was important for this reason that Germany line up the other European countries on her side right from the beginning. This was easier to accomplish during the early successful phases of the attack than it would have been later when the élan slackened or the situation became unfavorable. Every small and mid-size European country had to be fully aware that it was to the interest of Germany, politically and militarily, to line up the largest number of countries behind herself, primarily those which were readily accessible to her and which could easily be bent to her will. The small and mid-sized European countries had to be very clear on the fact that there was no way in which they could emerge from this war with any profit. In this unpredictable battle of the giants the small countries could not gain any benefits and were likely to see their strength ground away. This being the case it became less important who came out of the war victorious but it became supremely important how long the war would go on and even more so, whether it would be possible to preserve their strength and assets until the end of the war. Their greatest dangers could be averted only if, indeed, they could preserve their strength and their assets to the end.

In view of the complexity of the relative strengths and weaknesses of the major belligerents it would have been very difficult to predict the probable victor in such a fashion that this prophecy, and it was no more than just that, would be generally believed by public opinion. In politics it matters less whether such prophecies ultimately turn out to be correct than how much of the prophecy could be made believable to public opinion and thus how could the behavior of public opinion be then adjusted accordingly. There was no man in Hungary, regardless how well founded and powerfully explained his concerns about the ultimate outcome of the war might have been, who could have lined up public opinion behind him.[344] Until 1943 nobody tried the ungrateful task of prophecy in any public forum.[345] For us and for other states in a similar position the prediction issued at the beginning of the war were decisive and at that time all the experts agreed that Germany would conclude this war successfully. The various components of Hungarian public opinion accepted this view. If somebody doubted this prediction, he still had to consider the fact that Germany acquired enormous bargaining chips in 1939–1940 which it could have cashed in when things turned against it. It could have chosen which opponent to lose the war to. During the course of history very few wars resulted in either total victory or total defeat.[346] In the past every warring nation that could determine its own behavior, whenever it came into a critical situation attempted to save its remaining forces and to escape total collapse in a timely fashion. Of the opportunities available to the Germans this option had to be preserved. If Germany came to its senses in the face of a threatening catastrophe and stopped on the down-hill course then her loss of control over the countries in her sphere of influence would not have been either total or permanent. It was important for Hungary to realize that Germany would remain even then a player of potential power. If we now consider all that was available to Hungarian public opinion concerning the possible outcome of the war and all that an objective examination of this issue would have revealed, we reach the following conclusions.

It was in Germany's interest and therefore she demanded that Hungary, true to its anti-Bolshevik traditions and statements, participate in the war against the Soviet Union as soon as possible. The various components of official Hungary viewed this either as a necessity, a moral obligation or a beneficial thing to do. There were proponents of each of these choices particularly among the military and among the vociferous part of public opinion. These mutually supportive approaches and the goal that they shared inevitably and necessarily had to lead to Hungary's joining the action. Even the indictment admits that this was just a question of time.

Besides the reasons mentioned, Germany had a special reason for wanting Hungary to enter the war as soon as possible. This special reason is related to the very sharply hostile Hungarian-Romanian relationship. The continued reluctance of Hungary would have rapidly put the brakes on Romania's participation in the war. In Bucharest it was considered that if Hungary could preserve her forces while Romania had to suffer the inescapable losses of war, Hungary's relative strength would increase steadily. Sooner or later, conditions permitting, this would make Hungary attack Romania from the back, while she was fighting in the east. Thus, if Germany wished to keep Romania among the belligerents, she had to enlist Hungary among them as well.[348] If, in May 1939,[348] Hungary had not retaken Subcarpathia with full German agreement, it could have been claimed that she had no direct interest in the outcome of the German-Russian war. In possession of Subcarpathia even this fairly ineffective argument was lost.[349]

There were only two possibilities. If, right from the beginning of the campaign the German army achieved decisive results or results that appeared to be decisive, the Hungarian factions and public opinion demanding participation in the war would have done everything to avoid the disadvantages that the delay in participation might have caused for Hungary. If, however, the German army was bogged down and it became necessary to use auxiliary forces then the German government could have and would have used a whole series of direct and indirect coercive measures to get military assistance from Hungary. These measures were given from the peculiar position of Hungary. As far as the defensive position of the country was concerned it was in a less favorable situation in June 1941 than at the time of the Yugoslav action. At this time Hungary was surrounded on all sides by countries that had significant concentrations of German troops. The hostile feeling of the neighboring countries had also increased in the interval. In 1918 Franchet d'Espérey, the French general told Mihály Károlyi, visiting him in Belgrade, "I hold the Serbs, the Romanians and the Slovaks in the palm of my hand. If Hungary does not follow orders I will let them loose against you." In 1918 there was a sharp point to this threat even though at the time the neighboring countries were exhausted and poorly armed. Having been given large territories already, they had no major incentive to attack the despoiled Hungary.[350] In 1941 the leaders of every neighboring country fostered the feeling that their country had been seriously injured to Hungary's benefit and that these illegal injuries had to be avenged. In 1941 the neighboring states were fully armed and could have engaged Hungary at any time. Thus Hungary was surrounded not only by the iron hoops of the German army but by the ring of her own enemies. If exposed to their attack, the country would have been irreparably destroyed.[351] If we assume for the sake of argument that in 1941 at least a part of Hungarian public opinion could have been enlisted in favor of refusing to participate in the war,[352] this step, impossible to implement in 1941 or later, would have resulted in Hungary being torn in two and among the horrors of a civil war the unity of the nation, its greatest treasure, would have been irretrievably lost. It was this unity that had to be preserved at all costs.[353]

Regardless how much somebody believes in resurrection it is still improper to recommend that he commit suicide. It is even less permissible to start or to force a nation down the road toward suicide in the hope that it would be followed by resurrection. The generation that came into conflict with itself and committed suicide can never be resurrected again and it is an open question whether there would be another generation and also what kind of generation it was likely to be. Yugoslavia is usually mentioned in this context and it is alleged that it will be very well off now. Yet, I tell you, do not envy Yugoslavia. For four years it was the scene of a dreadful and destructive civil war with everybody seemingly against everybody else. The related Slav groups slaughtered each other and it is very difficult to assess all the losses they suffered. It is possible that at the peace conference Yugoslavia will be given a beautiful gown but the question is whether there will be anybody sufficiently alive to wear it?[354]

Only a very selfish person can envy the fate of the Yugoslav people, a person who says that if he survived the civil war what did he care about the ones who didn't and that those who remained would enjoy the spoils. Could a government that was responsible for a whole generation and its unity have used the same philosophy? A government that was responsible for the protection of both the present and the future generation?

If Hungary by hesitation or indecisiveness had invoked, in 1941, the fate that befell it in 1944 as the result of a disastrously faulty policy, how many of you who applauded the indictment speech of the people's prosecutor so loudly in this court room would be alive today?

All in all, in the extremely difficult, sensitive and fragile situation in which Hungary found herself there was only one narrow path that could be followed. Not to antagonize Germany, not to raise suspicion or resentment in Germany as long as Germany was in a position where using the coercive tools at her disposal she could enforce her will or directly take over the entire country. The German demands had to be met minimally in order to avoid Germany demanding more or demanding everything. Above all, national unity had to be preserved. Raising any question that in any way whatever could cause internal opposition or sunder national unity had to be avoided. The government had to carry the Hungarian nation forward in the best possible unity and with the optimal preservation of the national strength and assets until the end of the war so that the nation united could confront the end of the war and whatever came afterward in unaltered unity. This was the only possible way to avoid the greatest danger, namely first the direct intervention of Germany and everything that would mean and later, after Germany had lost the war, falling victim to the unbridled will of the victors. It was from this twofold death, the twofold death of opposite and successive trials that we had to protect the nation.

These were the considerations that led the government in considering the questions relative to the German-Soviet war and that directed its decisions.

After receiving the warnings and recommendations of the General Staff, it came as no surprise when the German minister informed me early on June 22, 1941, that the German armed forces had made their move against the Soviet Union. The minister added the comment that the Hungarian government would surely draw the obvious conclusions. On the same day the minister handed the regent a letter from the Reich chancellor which concluded with the comment that hopefully the Hungarian head of state would respect the decisions made by Germany.

After all the above there can be no doubt about what this really meant. Still, the impossible had to be attempted. If for no other reason than to gain time and also if a decision became inevitable, so that the decision of the Hungarian government not follow the German action instantly. Only one decision had to be made right away in order to prevent a provocation of the German government and the avoidance of a forceful and immediate development. Hungarian-Soviet diplomatic relations had to be severed. It was unimaginable that the German government would tolerate, even for a very short time, that behind the front and among the lines of supply Soviet intelligence gathering services be active at the Soviet Legation in Budapest. It only shows ignorance of the conditions if somebody, in this context, cites Japan and Bulgaria which maintained their diplomatic relations with the Soviet Union. The Soviet Embassy in Tokyo was many thousands of kilometers away from the German-Russian front lines. Also at the time the German-Russian war began it was not in Germany's interest that Japan would become involved in this war and tie up its forces on the Asiatic part of the Soviet Union. According to the ideas of the German politicians it was Japan's primary responsibility at this time to use its entire strength to balance the United States which clearly was making preparations to enter the war. For the conduct of the war and for the provision of supplies, the information gathering services of the Soviet Legation in Sofia represented no danger. Other than this no parallels can be drawn between Bulgaria and Hungary, the situation and assessment of the two countries was quite different. The Slav population of Bulgaria had very strong emotional ties to the Russian people to the point where the Bulgarian nation could not be placed in opposition to Soviet Russia. Knowing this, the German government used Bulgaria to protect its interests during the war. For Bulgaria to be able to do this it had to maintain diplomatic relations with the Soviet Union.

The deputy minister of foreign affairs, Minister János Vörnle, who informed the Soviet minister in Budapest about the severance of diplomatic relations reported that Minister Nikolay I. Sharanov was very surprised that the Hungarian government only severed the diplomatic relations. The Soviet minister admitted that he expected a declaration of war and thus he evidently anticipated that the severance of diplomatic relations would not be the last step of the Hungarian government and that further steps would follow. In his last telegram from Budapest he must have reported accordingly.

When the German minister in Budapest was handed the official notification about the severance of diplomatic relations he said, "Das ist wohl das allerwenigste was Sie haben tun können." [This is the very least that you could have done].[355] At the same time and referring to instructions from the Italian government, he confidentially and amicably warned the Hungarian deputy minister of foreign affairs that withholding the Hungarian declaration of war made a very painful impression in Rome and in Berlin.

The Hungarian government still did not give up hope that it would not have to go beyond the severance of diplomatic relations. It might even have kept this position if first the Budapest-Kőrösmező rail line and then the city of Kassa had not been bombed by planes carrying Soviet markings. The first bombing between Rahó and Tiszaborkút occurred on June 25, the same day when the telegram from the Hungarian minister in Moscow, which was sent three days earlier on June 22, arrived. In the telegram the minister reported that the Soviet commissar for foreign affairs, referring to the rapid progression of events, wished to know immediately whether Hungary was going to remain neutral in the German-Russian war. This was the essence of the telegram and of the query of the Soviet commissar of foreign affairs. Because of the technical difficulties[356] the urgent request could not be answered, nor did it have to be. The answer should have been in the hands of the Soviet government because its minister in Budapest had reported on June 22 that Hungary had severed the diplomatic relations[357] and thus gave up its neutrality. After the severance of the diplomatic relations, Hungary could at best be regarded as a "non-belligerent." It could no longer be regarded as neutral, because the term implied that it regarded both warring nations equally. Furthermore, the Soviet government could have learned of the severance of the Hungarian-Soviet diplomatic relations and of Hungary having ceased being a neutral from the regular broadcasts of Radio Budapest on June 22. Consequently the question of the Soviet commissar of foreign affairs required no answer.[358] The question became immaterial, events had gone beyond it. But, even if the Hungarian government had made no decision concerning the severance of diplomatic relations and wished to maintain its neutrality when the Moscow telegram arrived on June 25, no definite answer could have been given to the commissar of foreign affairs because of the obligations that such an answer would have placed on the country. In view of the situation discussed in detail above and knowing the spheres of interest and the relative strength of the belligerents it would have been impossible to undertake an obligation on behalf of the country as far as neutrality was concerned. Moscow had to be clear about this. When Hungary joined the Anti-Comintern Pact, Moscow justified the severance of diplomatic relations, initiated by her on that occasion, by declaring that Hungary had become a dependent of the so-called Axis Powers and therefore would be unable to conduct an independent policy in the future.[359] With the question the Soviet commissar of foreign affairs addressed to the Hungarian minister, he wished to accomplish nothing else but to force the Hungarian government to show its true colors so that the Soviet government would have a free hand to act against Hungary and against the German troops during their transit through Hungary. As far as the material content of the response of the Hungarian government was concerned there could have been no doubt about it and giving no answer was an answer as well. If the Hungarian government had said in its answer that it wished to maintain its neutrality, but would then shortly be forced to enter the war against the Soviet Union, this would have been considered a breach of faith by the Soviet Union.

The telegram from the Hungarian minister in Moscow had lost its meaning by the time it arrived. This was further indicated by the Russian air raids which occurred the same day and which seemed to fit well into the scheme of things. The air raids meant that in Moscow it was considered as settled that Hungary would enter the war and the Soviet air force acted accordingly. If the Hungarian government still hoped that it could gain some time, the Kassa air raid on June 26 irrevocably frustrated it. The reports from Kassa indicated that the attacking planes carried Soviet markings. One of the witnesses in this trial questioned by the people's prosecutor stated that much later, in 1944 in Moscow, he saw written documentation showing that the attacking planes had been repainted but did carry the Soviet markings.

If the hitherto completely unsupported assertion that the Kassa bombing was arranged by a German hand were to prove true, this would be the strongest evidence for Hungary's oppressed situation. If it can be assumed that the Germans did not refrain from using such a tool they certainly would not have refrained from using even more drastic methods to achieve their goal. Initially there was no doubt that the bombing was done by the Soviet air force and therefore there was no need to verify where the planes came from. In fact this would not have been technically possible. It was only several days later that the rumors started alleging that perhaps the attack was not performed by Soviet planes. On orders from the government, the military authorities started an investigation and concluded from the recovered bomb fragments that the damage had been done by bombs manufactured in Russia.

The repeated attacks were undoubtedly attacks against Hungary. The intentional and offensive nature of the bombings could not be questioned knowing that the Soviet Union had laid a claim to Subcarpathia. The official press release published by the Soviet government at the time of the Bácska liberation, in April 1941, went even further. It threatened Hungary openly and said that Hungary could also be torn into pieces because there were minorities living in Hungary as well.[360] It was therefore evident that Hungary had to defend herself. If Hungary wished to protect its territory, Subcarpathia that she claimed as her own and other territories inhabited by minorities, a duty that every country has toward its own, it could not remain inactive after the Kassa bombings.

There are some who argue that during the war the British and American air force bombed Swiss and Swedish territory. Switzerland and Sweden did not consider this a war-like act and did not consider it necessary to respond in a belligerent fashion. If anybody wished to draw a parallel in this context between Hungary and Switzerland or Hungary and Sweden they would just reveal that they had no understanding of Hungary's problems or of the constituent factors of these problems. Switzerland and Sweden are thousands of kilometers distant from Great Britain and from the United States. Great Britain and the United States had never claimed any Swiss or Swedish territory. It was also never the case that the United States or Great Britain wished to transfer certain territories from Switzerland or Sweden to their neighboring countries. Swiss and Swedish public opinion regarded the safety of their national life only in a victory by the Western Powers. The great majority of Hungarian public opinion was fully aware that Hungary could not stay out of the life and death conflict of the two neighboring Great Powers, for the simple reason of its geographic location. It would have been in vain to try to remain neutral when she could not have defended her neutrality. Thus, in order to protect her interests she had to side with one or the other, preferably with the one less dangerous to her territorial integrity. It was for this reason that the bombing attack had a decisive effect on the steps taken by official Hungary and by public opinion effectively expressing its sentiments. Suddenly all the forces, all the considerations and all the points of view that were discussed above made themselves heard. It was as though the waiting and the delay of reaching a decision had built a dike in front of these forces and it appeared as though the Kassa bombings tore a breach in this dike. The attack touched upon the most sensitive spot in the emotional make-up of the regent, of the Hungarian military leadership and of the officers' corps. For them it became a matter of military honor and bravery that Hungary not remain idle after the unprovoked attack. The military leadership stated bluntly that it would consider it an unbearable shame if Hungary would not participate in the war. The same thing was stated by the regent.

In addition to its own responsibility, the Hungarian government had to take all this into account and weigh it carefully. It was also impossible to ignore the further evolution of events. Italy, having declared war on the Soviet Union as early as June 22, decided to dispatch a separate force to the Russian front without delay. Slovakia decided to make its entire army available. There was a serious endeavor to set up French, Flemish and Spanish armed formations and this was further clear proof for the great weight the German government placed on having participation from all possible European countries. Even more important was the fact that on June 26 the highest German military leadership put a direct request before the Hungarian General Staff, "Die deutsche Heeresleitung wäre dankbar, wenn Ungarn mittun würde" [The German military leadership would be grateful if Hungary would participate].361 Now they no longer suggested that Hungary offer its participation but explicitly asked for Hungary to join in. We now had to acknowledge what had never been in doubt, namely that it was the German leadership which wanted our participation. Within the totally centralized governmental structure in Germany it was not possible that in such an important issue the stance of the political and military sectors not overlap completely and that the German military leadership, on its own responsibility, could have experimented with assuring the participation of the Hungarian army.[362] The only Hungarian minister[363] who initially, during the decisive discussion, recommended that a decision be postponed also stated that if the German political direction became identical with the German military one then the situation would be different and he would also withdraw his opposition. In fact, there never was a difference between the German political and military directions and there could not have been.

With the forces becoming active in this matter it was no longer a question whether Hungary should participate in the war but rather whether the participation could be held to an irreducible minimum. Henceforth the task of the government was to act as a brake and if the decision had been postponed even for a short period of time it might have led to a complete collapse of the dike. If the government wished to maintain its unfettered initiative and maintain a free hand in deciding what forces to make available and how to do it, it had to make its decision promptly. Delaying would have exposed the government to such external and internal pressures that yielding to them once would have made it impossible to ever again resist in the future. This was the reason for rigidly avoiding any query to the German government or to the German military about the strength of Hungarian forces that they expected to receive. It would have been just as impossible to ignore the provoked response as it had become impossible to maintain Hungary's continued inactivity.

Nothing would have been simpler than to step back and resign, but this would have meant a faithless surrender of the responsibilities entrusted to the government at the precise moment when these responsibilities required the most careful protection. Protecting them meant that no suspicion and mistrust be generated in the German government because such would have made the position of this and successive Hungarian governments infinitely more difficult and by virtue of the logic of the situation would have forced said governments to make increased sacrifices.

Resignation of the government would have started an open debate in Hungarian public life concerning German-Hungarian relations and this, again by virtue of the logic of the situation would have strengthened the opponents of passivity. If we loosen a stone on a slope, the stone will roll downward and not upward. Every change at that time would have brought those into the foreground and into power who were committed to participation in the war and who would have to demonstrate that their position was the valid one. The members of the government could have escaped only from their personal responsibilities, the responsibility that I have to account for here. At the same time they would have had to assume the very much heavier responsibility which, in order to save their person would have exposed the entire country to the trials and dangers to which it, regretfully, had fallen a victim. Even in this regard their responsibility would have been increased by the fact that in 1941 Germany was standing at the peak of her powers and in Hungary and the Continent the feeling was almost universal that Germany would be the victor in the conflict. In this status of power and in an atmosphere of certainty of victory during four long years, would it not have been easy to change Hungarian existence radically and totally realign it in the image and likeness of Germany? This question requires no answer.

I admit that after all the suffering and tribulations that have fallen particularly severely on the residents of Budapest during the past years it is difficult for this urban population to recall the 1941 situation and it is even more difficult to relive the events of that day. The suffering, the blows, the pains and the thousand tortures of sleepless nights lie like a veil and an impenetrable cloud on the eyes and on the hearts. It is this veil, woven by suffering that makes it impossible for the inhabitants of Budapest to once again clearly see the picture of the Hungarian situation as it was four years ago and the way we lived then with our ideas, hopes, problems, difficulties and possibilities. Viewed through the bitterness of suffering everything, in retrospect, seems to have been a crime, an omission, a recklessness and a mistake.[364]

This is similar to the situation where we revisit a place where we lived recently but have trouble recognizing it. Because in the meantime a deluge had changed it. It is hard to recognize even though the major features are still there, the hills, the house in which we lived, the lands that gave us bread and the trees that gave us fruit, the paths, the hedges and the road signs that pointed us on our way. But now everything is covered by a black flood. Our churches and houses are destroyed, the barns are empty and we cannot see the path that, we believed, would lead us through difficulties to a better future. We had to stay together and preserve our strength.

Those who did not have to struggle with internal agony, concerns and doubts to reach crucial decisions, seeing the perils from the right and from the left, whose heart is filled with the memories of pain and the desire for vengeance truly cannot understand what happened and why.

If the government had not decided on June 26 to participate with minimal force, assuming that such a decision could have been sustained for which there was little evidence, then the first and least reaction to our passivity would have been that the Germans took control of Subcarpathia in order to direct their fight against the Soviet from there. The Hungarian General Staff had repeatedly warned us about this. Let us remember that it was Subcarpathia from where, in 1944, the German military first directly interfered with Hungarian civil life and from where this interference rapidly spread to the entire country.

The decision made by the government on June 26 created a situation that made it possible for us to take part in the campaign with only moderate forces. The total number of personnel dispatched to Russia was no more than 30–35,000 men.[365] The president of the People's Court cited documents which indicated that the German military leadership later made the request that larger Hungarian units be made available to it. The Hungarian government did not honor this request and the forces committed remained at the earlier level. This was possible only because of the atmosphere created by the June 26 decision. It was also possible to arrange, albeit not easily, that the Hungarian government could call back the Hungarian military units from the front prior to the onset of winter and replace them with rear area occupation forces. Even though the troops fighting at the front had suffered painful losses, these losses, thanks to God, were relatively minor as the population saw with great joy when the returning troops paraded in Nyíregyháza and in Budapest.

All this was possible only if the Hungarian government made it very plain to the German government that under the given circumstances it would do all that was inevitable but would not go beyond this and also expected that its independence would be respected. It was only this Hungarian-German relationship, maintained within the boundaries of Realpolitik that made it possible to husband our national forces, maintain a relative freedom of action and, most importantly, preserve Hungary's national unity.

If there were some who were dissatisfied with the situation, no matter how many or where, they also considered it prudent not to demonstrate their objections and concerns openly. If they had a reason for not jeopardizing their person and the cause they wished to serve by taking an open stance, this must lead to the admission that a change in our policy would have exposed the whole country to great danger. While some were worried about their person, perhaps the government had good reason to be worried about the interests of the entire nation.

The only matter left to discuss are the effects of the state of war between the United States and the so-called Axis Powers on Hungary. When we liberated the Bácska, we simply performed our national duty. It was done at a time and under conditions dictated by international events in which we had no part.

Our participation in the war against the Soviet Union was the result of the situation in which our country found itself and of the spheres of influence and power that produced this situation.

In the war between the United States and the Axis Powers it was our solidarity with the Axis Powers and the interpretation that this solidarity required our being at war as well, simply meant that we were living up to the obligations that Hungary assumed when she joined the Tripartite Pact.

In this war the Axis Powers considered themselves to be the aggrieved party, but on what basis this was done is not a matter for this trial. It again ensued from the situation of the country and from the disparity of the forces that established the rules, that unless it wished to confront the German government, the Hungarian government, could not argue as to who was the attacker and who was the attacked. If then the Hungarian government tacitly agreed with the interpretation of the German government that the war was initiated by the United States, then according to the letter and the spirit of the Tripartite Pact, Hungary was obligated to provide the Axis Powers with military, economic and political assistance, which also meant that she had to declare war on the United States.

The Hungarian government, being aware of this and also keeping in mind that for the well-known reasons it could not clash with the German Reich over this issue, decided to sever diplomatic relations with the United States and, at the same time, declare that the country considered itself to be loyal to the Axis Powers. The declaration of solidarity was made because the government hoped that perhaps this would satisfy the Axis Powers. Even if these powers were not satisfied, perhaps the declaration of solidarity could be interpreted as meeting the requirements of the Tripartite Pact and still be less harmful to the interests of the Hungarians in America than a declaration of war. Simultaneously with the issuance of the declaration of solidarity the Hungarian government approached the German and Italian governments and, openly discussing all aspects of the situation, asked them to be satisfied with our declaration of solidarity. The government used the following arguments: 1) There was no antagonism between Hungary and the United States and the Hungarian government did not wish to create any. 2) The government wished to maintain a situation in which, after the war, the Hungarian-American economic and other contacts could be resumed without any difficulties. 3) A declaration of war would be an empty and shallow formality because Hungary could obviously give no military assistance and no such could be expected of her. 4) The declaration of solidarity satisfied the demands of the Tripartite Pact that obligated Hungary to provide political support. 5) Considering the enormous difference in power and strength between the United States and Hungary a declaration of war would put Hungary into a ludicrous position. 6) There were a large number of Hungarians living in the United States whom a declaration of war would place into a very difficult position. 7) The Axis Powers evidently accepted the risks of the war because they expected benefits from the outcome of an armed conflict. Hungary could expect no such benefits and a declaration of war would bring only calamities that she would prefer to avoid.

The Hungarian ministers in Berlin and Rome were instructed that, using these arguments, they should endeavor to get the German and Italian governments to understand and refrain from insisting that Hungary declare war. On the urgent request of the Hungarian government the German and Italian ministers in Budapest agreed to bring the Hungarian position to the attention of their governments.

In the meantime the German deputy minister of foreign affairs, Baron Weizsäcker, told the Hungarian minister in Berlin that the Reich government wanted Hungary to declare war according to the requirements of the Tripartite Pact.[366] Also, in answer to the Hungarian government's proposition, the German, Italian and Japanese ministers in Budapest jointly and clearly explained that their governments had to insist on a declaration of war and demanded the immediate compliance with their demand. It was pointed out that, in accordance with the requirements of the Tripartite Pact, the Romanian and Bulgarian governments had already declared war on the United States and that therefore the Axis Powers could not consent to Hungary taking a different position. This would inadmissibly disrupt the uniformity of action of the countries united within the framework of the Tripartite Pact.

It is unnecessary to again recapitulate at this point the reasons why the Hungarian government had to avoid a conflict with the German Reich. The request of the Axis Powers could be foreseen and, pro forma, was consistent with the stipulations of the Tripartite Pact. The government therefore tried to reach a compromise, using the second line of defense, according to which the declaration of solidarity would bring into harmony our obligations under the Tripartite Pact and be the best possible protection of the interests of the Hungarian-Americans. On heavy pressure from the Axis Powers, the government was willing to interpret the declaration of solidarity as though a state of war had been established with the United States. This interpretation was accepted by the Axis Powers as meeting the obligation under the Tripartite Pact.

What this accomplished was that while Romania and Bulgaria had declared war, Hungary initially only declared its solidarity with the Axis Powers and interpreted this solidarity to mean that attack against the Axis Powers was an attack against her as well.

Under the given conditions this represented a success that was appreciated by the American minister who was still in Budapest at that time. At the least it succeeded in indicating that the Hungarian government wished to spare the sensitivities of the American government.

The government was fully aware of the fact that all this meant very little since the behavior of the powers, particularly after a victory, was not determined by consideration of the position and intentions of their former foes. In this regard the public statement of the official British sources, as early as January 1941, is typical. According to this statement Great Britain would regulate the arrangement of the Continent after the victory with full consideration being given to the interests of their faithful allies, Czechoslovakia and occupied Romania. (Report from the Hungarian Minister in London, 1/pol–1941.)[367] This declaration was made at a time when Hungary was still neutral[368] three months before the liberation of the Bácska. This showed more clearly than anything else what Hungary could expect in case of a victory by the Western Powers. How often have we seen in the past, and see it again now, that the victors give favorable consideration to those countries which could hardly have merited it by their behavior during the war, and it was done only because it was in the interest of the victors.

A country, that while still in full possession of its independence, under the leadership of its constitutionally elected president and with its administrative staff in full control, served the German military industry better and with less resistance than all the other European countries taken together, is held in high honor today. Similarly, other victors give better treatment to countries where the organization of national socialism was stronger then even in Germany and where a higher percentage of the population belonged to the party.

The fate of the losers is determined by the interests of the victors and only the unity of the nation may provide some protection. This was the reason why the government of which I was the prime minister considered it its first and foremost duty to preserve a solid national unity above everything else.

It was my feeling even later on that it was my duty, in every thing and at all times, to serve this unity. Only by being united can a country be led through the maelstroms of fateful times. The Bible teaches us that, "If a kingdom is divided against itself that kingdom cannot stand" [Mark 3:24]. In a fragmented country the forces consume each other and the opposing forces, unwillingly, become the tools of foreign interests.

If we go in six different directions we get nowhere.

During the past few years the leadership of Hungary, regretfully, frequently ignored this principle. It did not realize that it was impossible to implement decisive political changes affecting the convictions and fate of millions, while leaning only on a small clique. This can be done only in cooperation with the majority. It has to be convinced and nothing must be done until this is accomplished. The outcome of a failed experiment is the greatest disaster.

Bodies can be moved only if their center of gravity moves with them. It is the same thing in the world of politics and if, because of an irresponsibly executed and failed experiment, the slide of the nation can no longer be halted on the slope on which it found itself largely due to the force of circumstances, national unity must be preserved even in the face of a fall. There is no more dreadful and repellent sight than passengers on a sinking ship killing each other.

It is again unity that alone can lead away from the fall toward a new life. This is why unity is so important even today. Allow a man saying goodbye to tell you that even among the ruins you must not look for opposition. Look for what binds together not for what divides. With a hand in a fist you cannot build, with a heart full of hate you cannot heal. I admit that rightful passions and bitterness must find an outlet. A way must be found to ease the soul so that it may emerge from its pain and find its way back to national unity. No sacrifice is too great if it leads to this. Even if bringing the sacrifice has no relationship to rendering justice.

After six months of suffering in body and soul and exposed to continuous attempts to humiliate me, I stand here with a clear and calm conscience.

It is only the immense pain and bitterness that this unfortunate nation has suffered that bows my head and fills my heart. I still believe and avow that God will help this nation.

Now I am asking you to do your duty.

ENDNOTES

1. Piroska Poth, "Rákosi Mátyás előadása Moszkvában 1945 júniusában," *Múltunk* 44, no. 4 (1999): 219–220.

2. Quoted in Elek Karsai, *Itél a nép* (Budapest: Kossuth Könyvkiadó, 1977), p. 15.

3. Gyula Illyés, *Naplójegyzetek*, vol. 1, *1929–1945*, ed. Gyuláné Illyés (Budapest: Szépirodalmi Könyvkiadó, 1986), p. 396.

4. Ibid., p. 403.

5. László Bárdossy, *Bárdossy László a népbíróság előtt*, ed. Pál Pritz (Budapest: Maecenas Kiadó, 1991), p. 24.

6. Tibor Zs. Lukács, "Magyarország és az 1933-as négyhatalmi paktum," PhD diss., Eötvös Loránd University, 2000, pp. 245–249.

7. László Zsigmond ed., *Diplomáciai iratok Magyarország külpolitikájához 1936–1945*, vol. 5, *Magyarország külpolitikája a nyugati hadjárattól a Szovjetunió megtámadásáig 1940–1941*, ed. Gyula Juhász (Budapest: Akadémiai Kiadó, 1982), p. 772.

8. Gyula Juhász, *A Teleki kormány külpolitikája 1939–1941* (Budapest: Kossuth Könyvkiadó, 1964), pp. 281–282.

9. Zsigmond, ed., *Diplomáciai iratok*, vol. 5, pp. 860–862.

10. Ibid., p. 871.

11. Ibid., pp. 864–865.

12. Ibid., p. 865.

13. Ibid.

14. See Andreas Hillgruber, *Hitlers Strategie. Politik und Kriegsführung 1940–1941* (Frankfurt am Main: Bernard & Graefe Verlag führ Wehrwesen, 1965); and Bernd Martin, *Friedensinitiativen und Machtpolitik im Zweiten Weltkrieg 1939–1942* (Düsseldorf: Droste Verlag, 1976).

15. Zsigmond, ed., *Diplomáciai iratok*, vol. 5, p. 930.

16. Ibid., p. 931.

17. Ibid., p. 932.

18. Ibid., p. 933.

19. Juhász, *A Teleki kormány külpolitikája*, p. 286.

20. Zsigmond, ed., *Diplomáciai iratok*, vol. 5, p. 943.

21. Juhász, *A Teleki kormány külpolitikája*, p. 286.

22. György Barcza, *Diplomata emlékeim* (Budapest: Európa Kiadó, 1994), vol. 1, p. 481.

23. Zsigmond, ed., *Diplomáciai iratok*, vol. 5, p. 952; and György Ránki, Ervin Pamlényi, Loránt Tilkovszky, and Gyula Juhász, eds., *Wilhelmstrasse és Magyarország. Német diplomáciai iratok Magyarországról 1933–1944* (Budapest: Kossuth Könyvkiadó, 1968), 556.

24. Juhász, *A Teleki kormány külpolitikája*, p. 288.

25. Ibid., p. 289.

26. Ibid., p. 288.

27. C. A. Macartney, *October Fifteenth. A History of Modern Hungary 1927–1945* (Edinburgh: Edinburgh University Press, 1956–1957), vol. 1, p. 474 and Juhász, *A Teleki kormány külpolitikája*, p. 288.

28. Elisabeth Barker, *British Foreign Policy in South-East Europe in the Second World War* (London: Macmillan, 1976), p. 87 and Géza Perjés, "Bárdossy László és pere," *Hadtörténelmi Közlemények* 113, no. 4 (2000): 774–840.

29. Zsigmond, ed., *Diplomáciai iratok*, vol. 5, p. 966–968 and Ránki, Pamlényi, Tilkovszky, and Juhász, eds., *Wilhelmstrasse és Magyarország*, 560–561.

30. Macartney, *October Fifteenth*, vol. 1, p. 475; Juhász, *A Teleki kormány külpolitikája*, p. 293 and Antal Czettler, *Teleki Pál és a magyar külpolitika 1939–1941* (Budapest: Magvető Kiadó, 1997), p. 273.

31. A letter written by Pál Teleki to Baron Gábor Apor, Hungarian envoy at the Holy See in which he states that Horthy "became fiery and burst into flames." Quoted in Mihály Fülöp and Péter Sípos, *Magyarország külpolitikája a XX. században* (Budapest: Aula Kiadó, 1998), p. 231.

32. Quoted in Macartney, *October Fifteenth*, vol. 1, p. 475.

33. Ibid.

34. Miklós Horthy, *Horthy Miklós titkos iratai*, ed. Miklós Szinai and László Szűcs (Budapest: Kossuth Könyvkiadó, 1962), p. 54.

35. Zsigmond, ed., *Diplomáciai iratok*, vol. 5, p. 971.

36. See L. Nagy, *Bethlen liberális ellenzéke. A liberális polgári pártok 1919–1931* (Budapest: Akadémiai Kiadó, 1980).

37. See Károly Rassay's deposition in the Bárdossy trial. Bárdossy, *Bárdossy László a népbíróság előtt*, p. 174.

38. Zsigmond, ed., *Diplomáciai iratok*, vol. 5, pp. 971–972.

39. Ibid., pp. 980–981.

40. Ibid.

41. Antal Náray, *Náray Antal visszaemlékezése 1945*, ed. Sándor Szakály (Budapest: Zrinyi Kiadó 1988).

42. Juhász, *A Teleki kormány külpolitikája*, pp. 301–302 and Loránd Dombrády, *Katonapolitika és hadsereg 1938–1944* (Budapest: Ister, 2000), p. 73.

43. Náray, *Náray Antal visszaemlékezése*, pp. 44–45.

44. Ibid., p. 45.

45. Ibid., pp. 46–47.

46. Ibid., pp. 47–48.

47. Ibid., p. 52.

48. Ibid., p. 53.

49. Juhász, *A Teleki kormány külpolitikája*, p. 307.

50. Zsigmond, ed., *Diplomáciai iratok*, vol. 5, pp. 991–992.

51. Ibid.

52. Juhász, *A Teleki kormány külpolitikája*, p. 314 and Czettler, *Teleki Pál*, p. 307.

53. Macartney, *October Fifteenth*, vol. 2, p. 8 and Juhász, *A Teleki kormány külpolitikája*, pp. 318–319.

54. Zsigmond, ed., *Diplomáciai iratok*, vol. 5, pp. 1017–1018.

55. Ibid. ed., and Juhász, *A Teleki kormány külpolitikája*, p. 319.

56. Bárdossy, *Bárdossy László a népbíróság előtt*, p. 91.

57. Ibid., p. 124.

58. Zsigmond, ed., *Diplomáciai iratok*, vol. 5, pp. 1035–1038.

59. Ibid., pp. 1097–1100

60. Ibid., p. 1097.

61. Ibid., p. 1099.

62. Ibid., pp. 1114–1116.

63. See, Pál Pritz, "A kieli találkozó (forráskritikai tanulmány)," in Pál Pritz, *Magyar diplomácia a két világháború között. Tanulmányok*

(Budapest: Magyar Történelmi Társulat, 1996), pp. 291–333 and Thomas Sakmyster, *Hungary's Admiral on Horseback Miklós Horthy, 1918–1944*, (Boulder, CO: East European Monographs, 2001), pp. 214–217.

64. Adolf Hitler, *Hitlers Weisungen für die Kriegsführung. Dokumente des Oberkommandos der Wehrmacht* (Frankfurt am Main: Walther Hubatsch, 1962), pp. 84–88.

65. Dombrády, *Katonapolitika és hadsereg*, p. 101 and p. 106.

66. Zsigmond, ed., *Diplomáciai iratok*, vol. 5, pp. 1142–1143, and pp. 1176–1180.

67. Ibid., pp. 1134–1135.

68. Ibid., pp. 1174–1175, and p. 1181.

69. See Ernst von Weizsäcker, *Die Weizsäcker-Papiere, 1933–1950* (Berlin: Propyläen, 1974).

70. Zsigmond, ed., *Diplomáciai iratok*, vol. 5, pp. 1174–1175.

71. Ibid.

72. Ibid., pp. 1180–1182.

73. Ibid., p. 1180.

74. Ibid., pp. 1180–1181.

75. Ibid., p. 1181.

76. Ibid., p. 1182.

77. Dombrády, *Katonapolitika és hadsereg*, p. 113

78. On June 15 Ribbentrop sent the following telegram to his minister in Budapest: "Please advise the Hungarian prime minister as follows: In view of the strong concentration of Russian troops along the eastern borders of Germany, the Führer will be forced, probably not later than the beginning of July, to unmistakably clarify German-Russian relations and, in connection with this, make certain demands. Since the outcome of these negotiations is doubtful, the German minister considers it essential that Hungary take the necessary steps for the protection of her borders.

The above instructions are of a top secret nature. Please be sure to emphasize this to the Hungarian Prime Minister." In Ránki, Pamlényi, Tilkovszky, and Juhász, eds., *Wilhelmstrasse és Magyarország*, p. 591. (This is included in a Hungarian collection of documents with minimal variations due to minor variations in the translations. Cf. Zsigmond, ed., *Diplomáciai iratok*, vol. 5, p. 1184.)

79. Zsigmond, ed., *Diplomáciai iratok*, vol. 5, pp. 1190–1191 and Dombrády, *Katonapolitika és hadsereg*, p. 133.

80. Zsigmond, ed., *Diplomáciai iratok*, vol. 5, pp. 1202–1203.

81. Ránki, Pamlényi, Tilkovszky, and Juhász, eds., *Wilhelmstrasse és Magyarország*, pp. 593–594 and Macartney, *October Fifteenth*, vol. 1, p. 21.

82. Ránki, Pamlényi, Tilkovszky, and Juhász, eds., *Wilhelmstrasse és Magyarország*, p. 594.

83. Antal Ullein-Reviczky, *Német háború-orosz béke* (Budapest: Európa Kiadó, 1993), p. 94.

84. Bárdossy, *Bárdossy László a népbíróság előtt*, pp. 93–95.

85. Dombrády, *Katonapolitika és hadsereg*, p. 135.

86. József Kun, "A m. kir. honvédség fővezérségéhez beosztott német tábornok naplója," *Századok* 99, no. 6 (1965):1240; quoted in Juhász, *A Teleki kormány külpolitikája*, pp. 345–346 and Dombrády, *Katonapolitika és hadsereg*, p. 139.

87. Kun, "A m. kir. Honvédség," p. 1240. Also in Dombrády, *Katonapolitika és hadsereg*, p. 139.

88. Gyula Kádár, *A Ludovikától Sopronkőhidáig* (Budapest: Magvető Kiadó, 1978), p. 144.

89. Dombrády, *Katonapolitika és hadsereg*, p. 144.

90. Ibid.

91. Miklós Horthy, *Emlékirataim* (Budapest: Európa Kiadó,1990), pp. 251–252 and Miklós Horthy, *Horthy Miklós dokumentumok tükrében*, ed. Éva H. Haraszti (Budapest: Balassi Kiadó, 1993), pp. 32 and 68.

92. Bárdossy, *Bárdossy László a népbíróság előtt*, p. 145 and László Jaszovszky, ed., *Bűnös volt-e Bárdossy László* (Budapest: Püski, 1996), p. 86.

93. Paragraph 5 of section13 of Act I of 1920 reads, "For a declaration of war, for deployment of troops beyond the borders of the country and for signing a peace treaty the prior approval of Parliament is required." This was amended by section 2 of Act XVII of 1920 to read, "In case of imminent danger, the regent may order deployment of troops beyond the borders of the country, provided the Joint Ministries accept the responsibility and the Parliament is requested, without any delay, to approve the move retroactively."

94. Bárdossy, *Bárdossy László a népbíróság előtt*, pp. 78–82.

95. Hungary, Parliament, House of Representatives, *Napló*, vol. 10 (Budapest: Athenaeum Kiadó, 1941), p. 305.

96. See endnote 93.

97. Jaszovszky, ed., *Bűnös volt-e Bárdossy László*, p. 88.

98. Ibid. and Bárdossy, *Bárdossy László a népbíróság előtt*, p. 127.

99. Ákos Major, *Népbíráskodás, forradalmi törvényesség. Egy népbíró visszaemlékezései*, ed. Tibor Zinner (Budapest: Minerva Kiadó, 1988), p. 211. Cf. Jaszovszky, ed., *Bűnös volt-e Bárdossy László*, p. 88.

100. Bárdossy, *Bárdossy László a népbíróság előtt*, p. 127 and end note # 157.

101. Jaszovszky, ed., *Bűnos volt-e Bárdossy László*, p. 193.

102. House of Representatives, *Napló*, vol. 10, pp. 3–8.

103. Ibid. vol. 13, (1942), p. 7.

104. Horthy, *Horthy Miklós titkos iratai*, p. 301.

105. Ibid. and cf. Bárdossy, *Bárdossy László a népbíróság előtt*, p. 142.

106. Horthy, *Horthy Miklós titkos iratai*, p. 301.

107. We are not familiar with the memorandum. It must be reconstructed from the letter from Bárdossy to Horthy. See *Horthy Miklós titkos iratai*, p. 59.

108. Ibid.

109. Ibid., p. 302.

110. Ibid., p. 303.

111. Ibid., p. 303.

112. Ibid., p. 306.

113. Ibid., pp. 306–307.

114. Ibid., p. 307.

115. Loránd Dombrády, *Hadsereg és politika Magyarországon 1938–1944* (Budapest: Kossuth Könyvkiadó, 1986), p. 255.

116. Ibid., p. 256 and Antal Czettler, *A mi kis élet-halál kérdéseink. A magyar külpolitika a hadba lépéstől a német megszálásig* (Budapest: Magvető Kiadó, 2000), p. 84.

117. Ránki, Pamlényi, Tilkovszky, and Juhász, eds., *Wilhelmstrasse és Magyarország*, p. 615.

118. Zsigmond, ed., *Diplomáciai iratok*, vol. 5, pp. 12–14. The telegram has an extensive literature. Previously it was customary to present it so as to show very clearly that in view of the existence of this

telegram the entry into war with the Soviet Union was criminal. Today the trend is to make light of Moscow's gesture. We believe that the earlier approach was exaggerated and completely ignored the tactical nature of the Soviet action. Yet, the other extreme is equally faulty and the Hungarian foreign policy of that time must be faulted because good diplomacy does not act exclusively under the influence of the moment but must think of the unpredictable future. Clearly some answer acknowledging the gesture should properly have been given.

119. Czettler, *A mi kis élet-halál kérdéseink*, p. 93.

120. Ibid., p. 92 and Macartney, *October Fifteenth*, vol. 2, p. 60.

121. Ibid.

122. Ránki, Pamlényi, Tilkovszky, and Juhász, eds., *Wilhelmstrasse és Magyarország*, p. 631.

123. Hungary. National Archives. Szent-Iványi Kézirat. "Csonka-Magyarország külpolitikája 1919 júniusától 1944. március 19-ig," p. 674.

124. Bárdossy, *Bárdossy László a népbíróság előtt*, p. 141.

125. House of Representatives, *Napló*, vol. 12 (1942), pp. 470–471 and Antal Ullein-Reviczky, *Német háború-orosz béke*, p. 104.

126. Magda Ádám, Gyula Juhász, and Lajos Kerekes, eds. *Magyarország és a második világháború. Titkos diplomáciai okmányok a háború előzményeihez és történetéhez* (Budapest: Akadémiai Kiadó, 1959), p. 383.

127. Lukács, "Magyarország és az 1933-as négyhatalmi paktum," pp. 165–168.

128. Bárdossy, *Bárdossy László a népbíróság előtt*, p. 83.

129. Ibid., pp. 83–85.

130. Ibid., pp. 83–94.

131. Ibid., p. 84.

132. Ibid.

133. Ibid.

134. Horthy, *Emlékirataim*, p. 255.

135. Czettler, *A mi kis élet-halál kérdéseink*, p. 99.

136. Jaszovszky, ed., *Bűnös volt-e Bárdossy László*, p. 410.

137. Ibid., pp. 410–411.

138. Miklós Kállay, *Magyarország miniszterelnöke voltam 1942–1944* (Budapest:Európa Kiadó, 1991), vol. 1, p. 38.

139. Ibid, pp. 38–39.

140. Dombrády, *Hadsereg és politika Magyarországon*, p. 271.

141. Hungary, National Archives, Szent-Iványi Manuscript, "Cson-ka-Magyarország külpolitikája," p. 702.

142. Ránki, Pamlényi, Tilkovszky, and Juhász, eds., *Wilhelmstrasse és Magyarország*, pp. 646–647.

143. Czettler, *A mi kis élet-halál kérdéseink*, p. 105.

144. Ránki, Pamlényi, Tilkovszky, and Juhász, eds., *Wilhelmstrasse és Magyarország*, pp. 646–647.

145. Endre Bajcsy-Zsilinszky, *Írások tőle és róla*, ed. Loránt Til-kovszky (Budapest: Kossuth Kiadó, 1986), pp. 153–160.

146. Ibid. pp. 87–88.

147. Bárdossy, Bárdossy, *Bárdossy László a népbíróság előtt*, pp. 86 and 240.

148. Ibid, pp. 293–299.

149. Major, *Népbíráskodás, forradalmi törvényesség*, pp. 221–223.

150. Horthy, *Horthy Miklós titkos iratai*, pp. 309–312.

151. Jusztinian Serédi, *Serédi Jusztinian hercegprímás feljegyzései 1941–1944,* ed. Sándor Orbán and István Vida (Budapest: Zrínyi Kiadó, 1990), pp. 260–274 and Czettler, *A mi kis élet-halál kérdéseink*, pp. 55–74.

152. Randolph L. Braham, *The Politics of Genocide: the Holocaust in Hungary* (Boulder, CO: Social Science Monographs, 1994), vol. 1, pp. 99–207 and Mária Ormos, *Egy magyar médiavezér: Kozma Mik-lós* (Budapest: PolgArt Kiadó, 2000), vol. 2, pp. 753–767. According to Ormos the Einsatzgruppe C. murdered 23,600 people, mostly local residents.

153. Miklós Kállay, *Magyarország miniszterelnöke voltam*, p. 52.

154. Ibid.

155. László Bárdossy, *Magyar politika a Mohácsi Vész után* (Buda-pest: Egyetemi Nyomda, 1943), p. 334.

156. Bajcsy-Zsilinszky, *Írások tőle és róla*, p. 203.

157. And all along he already knows-suspects that he would have to pay for this with his life. See, Illyés, *Naplójegyzetek*, vol. 1, p. 396.

158. Bárdossy, *Bárdossy László a népbíróság előtt*, pp. 85 and 354.

159. Péter Gosztonyi, "Bárdossy Svájcban," *Élet és Irodalom*, Ja-nuary 20, 1987, p. 20.

160. Major is critical for the mood at the trial and for the reconstruction of numerous components that were important but were omitted from the documents. See Major, *Népbíráskodás*.

161. Dénes Halmosy, ed., *Nemzetközi szerződések 1918–1945. A két világháború közötti korszak és a második világháború legfontosabb külpolitikai szerződései* (Budapest: Közgazdasági és Jogi Kiadó, 1983), p. 588.

162. Vince Nagy, *Októbertől októberig* (Budapest: Európa Kiadó, 1991), p. 335.

163. See p. 99 of this book. Cf. Bárdossy, *Bárdossy László a népbíróság előtt*, p. 304.

164. Major, *Népbíráskodás*, 199, 203 and 213–215.

165. Jaszovszky, ed., *Bűnös volt-e Bárdossy László*, p. 145.

166. Ibid., p. 205 (Jenő Ghyczy's deposition).

167. Ibid., p. 276.

168. Ibid., p. 276.

169. Péter Gosztonyi, "Interjú Gosztonyi Péterrel," *168 óra*, July 4, 1989.

170. A significant percentage of the approximately 1,000 footnotes of the 1991 edition of the People's Court proceedings deal with these mistakes. See Bárdossy, *Bárdossy László a népbíróság előtt*.

171. Ibid. p. 370.

172. Ibid.

173. Ibid. pp. 238–239.

174. Tibor Zinner and Péter Róna, *Szálasiék bilincsben* (Budapest: Lapkiadó Vállalat, 1986), vol. 2, p. 288.

175. Ibid.

176. Major, *Népbíráskodás*, p. 238.

177. Ábrahám, Ferenc and Endre Kussinszky. *Ítél a történelem. A Bárdossy-per; a vád, a vallomások és az ítélet* (Budapest: Híradó Könyvtár, 1945).

178. László Bárdossy; *Bárdossy László, a nemzet védelmében*, ed. Sándor Esső (Fahrwagen: Duna, 1976). It should be noted that in Hungary *Hunnia* (November-December 1989) also published Bárdossy's speech at his first trial before the sentence was handed down. This was based on the Swiss publication with some abridgements.

179. See Bárdossy, *Bárdossy László a népbíróság előtt.*

180. See Jaszovszky, ed., *Bűnös volt-e Bárdossy László.*

181. In his work, Géza Perjés carefully considers the discrepancies in the text of the two publications. See Géza Perjés, "Bárdossy László és pere," *Hadtörténelmi Közlemények* 113, no. 4 (2000): 771–840.

182. Act VII of 1945, enacted by the Interim Legislature on September 13, 1945, raises the governmental ordinance concerning the People's Court to the level of a statute. There are four such ordinances which became appendices to Act VII of 1945. Ordinance 81/1945 ME became appendix I. It states: "The interim national government, led by the necessity of punishing those who were responsible for or participated in the historic catastrophe that befell the Hungarian nation at the earliest possible moment and until jury trials can be reestablished by legislative process, rules in the matter of the People's Court as follows:…"

Ordinance 81/1945 ME was entitled briefly as Nbr. Its Section 11 describes the concept of a war criminal. According to Point 2, a war criminal is defined as, "a member of the government or of the legislature, or a high-ranking civil servant who, being able to foretell the consequences, initiated or participated in decisions which took the Hungarian nation into the World War that broke out in 1939."

183. See Ordinance 81/ 1945 ME, pp. 22–23.

184. The session was held on the 10th.

185. For the proclamation, see Zsigmond, ed., *Diplomáciai iratok*, vol. 5, pp. 1029–1030.

186. See endnote 93.

187. The Minutes of the meeting survived in two versions.

1. Bárdossy's version:

"Those present: László Bárdossy, Ferenc Keresztes-Fischer, Minister of the Interior, Lajos Reményi-Schneller, Minister of Finance, Dániel Bánffy, Minister of Agriculture, József Varga, Minister Industry and Commerce, Bálint Hóman, Minister of Religion and Education, László Radocsay, Minister of Justice, Károly Bartha, Minister of Defense, Dezső Laky, Minister of Public Supplies without Portfolio, Ferenc Zsindely, undersecretary of state in the Prime Minister's Office and István Bárczy de Bárciháza, undersecretary of state in the Prime Minister's Office, secretary. [In the available copy the notation s.k. (m.p.) appears in lieu of signatures and after Laky and Zsindely the notation in parenthesis "Not present." It is thus evidently not identical with the copy returned by Bárdossy.]

"The prime minister stated that he called the Council of Ministers into the present extraordinary session in order for the council to take a position vis-à-vis the unwarranted and unprovoked attack that Soviet planes had delivered that afternoon against the city of Kassa and in consequence of which there were not only great material losses suffered by the city of Kassa and by the Treasury but there was also a great loss of human life.

"In addition to the attack against Kassa, at 12 noon, Soviet planes machine gunned an express train heading from Kőrösmező toward Budapest between Tiszaborkút and Rahó, causing one death and numerous injuries.

"We have already severed diplomatic relations with the Soviet government. In consequence of this unprovoked attack we must now decide whether we should consider that we are in a state of war with Soviet Russia. In his view these attacks created a novel situation to which we must react immediately. In his view it was essential that we declare that we consider ourselves to be in a state of war with the Soviet Russia.

"The minister of defense informed the Council of Ministers about the circumstances of the aerial attacks against Kassa and against the express train going from Kőrösmező to Budapest as well as about the number of casualties. We had to see it as a hostile act and, according to him, we had to react promptly. We had to strike back in retaliation with our own planes and we also had to declare that because Soviet Russia had launched an unjustified and unprovoked attack against Hungary, it thus created a state of war between us and, therefore, we acknowledge that a state of war was in existence.

"He would consider that a partial mobilization, principally of the Rapid Deployment Division, was essential. Hungary was the only country that was not in a state of war with Soviet Russia. Romania and Slovakia have already entered in the war against Soviet Russia on the side of Germany. The Italians were preparing to participate with several armed brigades and with a mounted division and would soon march through Hungary against the Russians. This unprovoked attack was an appropriate opportunity for Hungary to participate in the war against

Russia, the more so because it was the regent of Hungary who was the first one to call for a war against Bolshevism.

"The minister of the interior considered a declaration of a state of war with Russia premature. He did not consider the aerial attack against Kassa a serious enough action that would justify our regarding ourselves to be at war with Soviet Russia. He agreed that our borders facing Russia should be strengthened. He did not believe that this issue had been discussed appropriately with the Germans. He believed that declaring that a state of war existed today was premature. We had to consider that we were declaring war on a Great Power. It was not in Hungary's interest to wage war with Russia. He considered it reasonable that we react with a few planes in retaliation to the Russian attack of this day. He did not believe that our army was strong enough for an offensive or that we could participate in a war against Russia with significant forces. Yet we would have to bear all the consequences of having initiated (sic) a war against a Great Power. We had to consider the nation's interests. It would not improve the situation in Transylvania if we entered the war against the Russians. He opposed the mobilization and was opposed to a declaration of a state of war without first consulting Germany. The situation would be quite different if the German political direction were to become identical with the German military direction.

"The minister of religion and education believed that the question must be examined from two perspectives. There had been an attack by the Soviet Russian air force. At noon the express train going from Kőrösmező to Budapest was strafed with machine gun fire. This attack resulted in one death and in three people being wounded. At 1:00 P.M. the Soviet air force attacked Kassa. The post office and the artillery barracks were hit by bombs and, according to the first news, there were many deaths and numerous injuries. In his view we must retaliate immediately with a few planes. He also considered it essential that our borders with Russia be strengthened and that a limited mobilization be ordered. He agreed with the minister of the interior that from the point of view of domestic politics the assessment of this question was indifferent. The domestic political mood should therefore not seriously affect a decision. In his view, however, and from a more elevated perspective, particularly vis-à-vis Romania, he shared the views of the minister of defense. He was convinced that following the disintegration of Soviet Russia and the assignment of Bessarabia to Romania the question of Southern Transylvania would be raised. He joined the prime minister and the minister of defense.

"The minister of finance shared the views of the minister of religion and education and also joined the prime minister and minister of foreign affairs, and the minister of defense. He approved the retaliation and approved the mobilization of about 6,000 men even before the harvest and believed that this was in the nation's interest and had to be done immediately. He felt that it would be objectionable if we Hungarians were the only ones to stay outside of a parade against Bolshevism.

"The minister of agriculture also shared the views of the prime minister, and of the minister of defense who recommended not only a retaliatory move but also a small-scale preparation for war. He would avoid a minor action (sic!).

"The prime minister reflected on the comments of the ministers who had spoken. He stated that the views of the government were united in that the aerial attack had had to be retaliated. Concerning the other question, whether we should announce that we considered ourselves, as of today, to be in a state of war with Soviet Russia, contrary to the views of the minister of the interior, all other members of the government agreed that we should consider ourselves to be in a state of war with Soviet Russia. The minister of the interior did not consider this to be necessary. Subsequent to the entry of Slovakia and Italy into the war he [Bárdossy] considered it impossible from a foreign policy perspective that we could stay outside of a joint action against Bolshevik Soviet Russia. He sketched the antecedents, the reports from our minister in Berlin, the discussions between the deputy chief of the German General Staff, General Halder, and the chief of the Hungarian General Staff, General Henrik Werth, and the most recent communications from the German High Command. It was his opinion that we had to participate in the war against the Soviet Union but that we should do this with the smallest possible forces.

"The government unanimously concluded that it considered it essential that our planes, today, hit back in retaliation against the attack that Soviet planes had made against the moving Kőrösmező train and against the city of Kassa.

"He stated that the minister of the interior did not consider it essential that it be declared that we considered ourselves to be in a state of war with Russia.Contrary to this view, however, it was the decision of the members of the government that in addition to the retaliation for the aerial attack, and at the same time, a proclamation was made stating that because of the repeated attacks of the Soviet air force against Hungarian territory, in violation of international law, unjustified and unprovoked, Hungary considered that a state of war existed with the Soviet Union.

"Dated as above

László Bárdossy, m.p."

Below this there are five comments, without signature, but undoubtedly from the pen of Bárczy de Bárcziháza. They are as follows.

"1. Laky arrived only at the end of the Council of Ministers meeting.

"2. Under Secretary of State Zsindely was at the Margitsziget Spa this afternoon and he was also absent.

"3. Minister of the Interior Ferenc Keresztes-Fischer did not say that he was only temporarily opposed to the war against Russia pending a discussion with the Germans; he was absolutely opposed to it and not because it had not been discussed with the Germans but because our army was not equipped for an offensive and because the war was not in the interests of the country. I have not used the word 'temporarily.' Bárdossy cited the meaning of Keresztes-Fischer's statement incorrectly.

"4. Bárdossy held back my signed and submitted minutes for nine months and forwarded it for signature to the ministers only on March 10, 1942, having modified my original minutes. Thus he made it impossible for them to ask for a correction of the decision announced by Bárdossy immediately after the meeting of the Council of Ministers.

"5. Minister of the Interior Keresztes-Fischer was not the only one opposed to the declaration of war. Bárdossy initially took a position in favor of a declaration of war and then asked Bartha to speak. And when Bartha also asked for an immediate declaration of war, in other words after the prime minister and minister of foreign affairs, and the minister of defense had definitely committed themselves in favor of a declaration of war, did he ask for the opinion of the other ministers. After the minister of the interior spoke, the Minister of Justice László Radocsay strongly supported the views of the minister of the interior and so did Minister Varga. Bánffy also joined the view of the minister of the interior when he spoke later. In his first comments he supported the retaliation for the aerial attacks, the strengthening of the borders and a limited mobilization, but wished to avoid a military action against Russia. To avoid any mistake, he came to me after the session of Council of Ministers and said that this is what he wanted. Bárdossy, seeing that only he, Bartha, Hóman and Reményi-Schneller came out strongly in favor of a declaration of war, omitted Radocsay, Varga and Bánffy's later comment from the minutes. He thus made modifications in the minutes in March 1942 that did not correspond to historic accuracy. It was a falsification of history to omit comments and to make it impossible for ministers to receive the minutes shortly after the meeting of the Council of Ministers."

II. Bárczy de Bárcziháza's version.

Here the list of "those present" agrees with version 1, with the difference that after Zsindely's name we can see that "he was not present" and after Laky's name that "he arrived at the end of the meeting."
The first three paragraphs, other than for three minor differences, agreed with the Bárdossy version and were hence not repeated.

"Prime Minister Bárdossy, 'May I have the opinion of every minister.'

"Minister of the Interior Ferenc Keresztes-Fischer, 'Let's wait. I do not consider this air raid as a serious action. If it comes to that, this will be a reason. It has not been discussed with the Germans, it is too soon today.'

"Minister of Justice László Radocsay shared the views of the minister of the interior, but agreed that the borders should be strengthened.

"Prime Minister Bárdossy, 'We have to do something. This attack will modify the German's stance as well.'

"Minister of Defense Károly Bartha, 'This is the last chance for us to participate on the side of the Germans with honor in the war against the Russians. I could order a mobilization.'

"[Bálint] Hóman, Minister of Religion and Education, 'The cabinet should be informed about what happened.'

"Prime Minister Bárdossy: 'As far as Germany is concerned, i.e. within Germany on a political level, no request or demand has been made. I have attempted to get the secretary of state of the German Reich Ministry of Foreign Affairs, Baron Weizsäcker, to tell me something about the potential of a German-Russian conflict, when he was in

Budapest a few weeks ago in a private capacity. He coolly responded that there was no Russian question. Our minister in Berlin, Döme Sztójay, has urged us right from the beginning that we should actively join the German line of action. Thus both the Hungarian Ministry of Foreign Affairs and our minister in Berlin tried to elucidate the situation. On June 18 the German minister in Budapest said only that it would be advisable to initiate defensive regulations. This was followed by a démarche along military lines. General Halder, the chief of the German General Staff came to Budapest by plane and negotiated with General Henrik Werth, the chief of the Hungarian General Staff. On Sunday, June 22, the German minister in Budapest, von Erdmannsdorff, told me in my capacity as minister of foreign affairs, that since 4:00 A.M. Sunday morning a state of war existed between Germany and Russia. The German minister, Erdmannsdorff, transmitted a letter from Hitler to the regent. In this letter Hitler informed the regent that a state of war had been declared between Germany and Russia and added that he hoped that Hungary would appreciate the steps taken by the German Reich. Nothing else.'"

"General Henrik Werth had just recently received a communication from General Halder, 'Die deutsche Heeresleitung wäre dankbar, wenn Ungarn mittun könnte.' [The German military leadership would be grateful if Hungary could participate]. Werth replied to Halder and told him that he would convey the request to the Hungarian government.'When I reported this to the regent he said that this was a political matter and that it was up to the German government to tell us its opinion.'

"Minister of the Interior Ferenc Keresztes-Fischer, 'The prime minister refers to the public opinion of the country to which a fight against Russian Bolshevism has appeal, but this is of no account when we have to decide to go to war with a Great Power. It is not in Hungary's interest to wage war with Russia. It is possible to send a single plane as a retaliatory gesture. Our army is not strong enough for an offensive. We cannot participate effectively. Internally this may be a gesture but we will get no favorable consideration from the Germans and will have to bear all the consequences of having initiated a war with a Great Power.'

"Prime Minister Bárdossy, 'The Italians will march three motorized brigades and a mounted division across Hungary against the Russians. We must do something immediately. The principle is that we have to hit back.'

"Bálint Hóman, minister of religion and education, 'After the defeat of Russia the question of southern Transylvania will come up. Romania will have to populate Bessarabia with Romanians. I agree with the position of the minister of defense. I am in full support, also because the German military leadership is friendly to Hungary. Therefore we must participate rapidly with 6,000 men now and with more after the harvest. I do not share the opinion of the minister of the interior that we should participate only if the Germans demand it.'

"Minister of Defense Károly Bartha, 'The German military circles tell the Hungarian military circles that we have unfinished business in Slovakia and in Transylvania.'

"Minister of the Interior Ferenc Keresztes-Fischer, 'We must look to the interests of the country. This is an emotional issue. We must not get involved.'

"Minister of Finance Lajos Reményi-Schneller, 'I share Hóman's views.Lets go with 6,000 men before the harvest. We really are in a position where we are the only ones who stay outside of parade against Bolshevism.'

"Minister of Agriculture Baron Dániel Bánffy, 'The Germans don't need us now and don't want us to present a bill later in reference to Southern Transylvania. They will not condemn us if we participate but they will certainly not do us any favors. As far as a low level preparedness is concerned I share the opinion of the ministers who spoke before me but I would avoid even a small-scale action. In this regard I share the opinion of the minister of the interior.'

"Prime Minister László Bárdossy, 'I would not engage in any ground activity at this time.'

"Minister of Defense Károly Bartha, 'Only where we feel that we have the upper hand.'

"Minister of the Interior Ferenc Keresztes-Fischer, 'You must consider where it may lead us if you start an avalanche.'

"Prime Minister László Bárdossy, 'If we do anything we can say that from a military and economic point of view we have done it and that this was the maximum. If later the Germans were to ask that we should participate with greater forces we can say that we cannot go any further.'

"Minister of Agriculture Baron Dániel Bánffy, 'If the Russians were to trounce the Germans Hungary's fate was sealed.' He was against it. He shared the minister of the interior's views.

"General Károly Bartha Minister of Defense, 'Hungary is the only country that is not at war with the Soviets.'

"Prime Minister László Bárdossy, 'I don't believe that there is any significance in the fact that the Germans did not tell us anything. If the air raid on Kassa had not happened I would not have done anything. There was an attack and now we are at a disadvantage. The Slovaks entered the war to gain merit and not in response to German pressure. If we do it now with relatively small forces we will have to make smaller sacrifices.'

"Minister of the Interior Ferenc Keresztes-Fischer, 'I am opposed to any campaign and I oppose mobilization without asking the Germans.'

"Minister of Religion and Education Bálint Hóman, 'We always flaunt our sovereignty, why do we have to ask the Germans?'

"Prime Minister László Bárdossy, 'We have received a military suggestion along military lines. We have asked the German government if this was serious.'

"Minister of the Interior Ferenc Keresztes-Fischer, 'If the German political line becomes identical with the military line it would change the situation.'

"Prime Minister László Bárdossy, 'May I summarize the views of the Council of Ministers? The government is in agreement that we were attacked by airplanes and that our planes should strike back yet today. I declare this to be the unanimous decision of the Council of Ministers. In the other question whether we should declare that a state of war is in existence between Hungary and Soviet Russia, the minister of the interior is opposed, the other ministers are in agreement. I am asking the minister of defense for the third time that we should participate only with limited forces.'

"Minister of Defense Károly Bartha, 'We will use two motorized brigades one mounted brigade and the frontier forces.'

"Prime Minister László Bárdossy, 'I consider it to be out of the question that we can stay out after Slovakia and Italy have entered the fray. Please enter it into the minutes of the meeting that we are to participate with only the minimal possible forces. I am asking the minister of defense to inform the chief of the General Staff that he may throw these limited forces into battle against the Russians facing us if the Russian forces are significantly weaker. In other words, no hussar pranks.'

"Minister of the Interior Ferenc Keresztes-Fischer, 'If we say that there is a state of war, we cannot tie the hands of the chief of the Army Staff. That is a question of implementation.'

"Prime Minister László Bárdossy, 'Shall we then declare a state of war?'

"Minister of Defense Károly Bartha, 'Let us declare the state of war.'

"Minister of the Interior Ferenc Keresztes-Fischer, 'Not I. I am opposed.'

"Minister of Industry József Varga, 'Let us not be hasty, let us sleep on it.'

"Prime Minister László Bárdossy, 'Is retaliation unanimous?'

"The resolution of the Council of Ministers is that, the government unanimously declares that it is essential for immediate retaliation that our planes strike back today in response to the attack carried out today by Russian planes against the moving Kőrösmező train and then against the city of Kassa.

"The minister of the interior does not consider it necessary that we announce today that we are in a state of war with Russia. This view as shared in their comments by the minister of justice, the minister of agriculture, and the minister of industry. The minister without portfolio, Dezső Laky, did not participate in the Council of Ministers meeting. The other members of the government resolved, contrary to this view, that simultaneously with the retaliation for the air raids it be announced that as a consequence of the repeated attacks of the Soviet air force against Hungarian territories in violation of international law, unjustified and unprovoked, Hungary concluded that a state of war had been established between Hungary and the Soviet Union. The minister of finance, the minister of religion and education, and the minister of defense shared the views of the prime minister.

"On the recommendation of the prime minister, the Council of Ministers resolved that Hungary participate in the military action against Russia with minimal forces only.

"Dated as above.

István Bárczy, Secretary, m.p."
Hungary, National Archives, Minutes of the Council of Ministers? K 27 228 dossier

188. The Bárdossy version is as follows:
"Those present were: László Bárdossy, Minister of the Interior Ferenc Keresztes-Fischer, Minister of Finance Lajos Reményi-Schneller, Minister of Agriculture Dániel Bánffy, Minister of Industry Commerce and Transportation József Varga, Minister of Religion and Education Bálint Hóman, Minister of Defense Károly Bartha, Minister of Public Supplies without Portfolio Sándor Győrffy-Bengyel, Under Secretary of State in the Prime Minister's Office Ferenc Zsindely, and István Bárczy de Bárcziháza, keeper of the minutes.

"The Prime Minister announced that calling the extraordinary session of the Council of Ministers was made necessary by the decision of the government of the German Reich, and the royal Italian government, which declared that a state of war existed between the German Reich and the United States and between Italy and the United States.

"After listening to the speech of the Reich Führer and Chancellor, delivered this afternoon and on this matter, he [Bárdossy] considered it immediately essential to discuss the situation with the members of the government and to reach a decision on the action to be taken.

"The prime minister stated that according to the speech of the Reich Führer, probably listened to by the members of the Council of Ministers, the government of the United States had demonstrated a hostile behavior for months and had issued directives against the so-called Axis Powers that were in fact aggressive and belligerent actions.

"Such aggressive actions were taken against German and Italian commercial and naval vessels on the open sea and against the crews of German and Italian commercial vessels detained in American ports. Repeated pronouncements of the president of the United States and of the American secretary of the navy made it clear that these actions were taken on instructions of the government. Accordingly it was the unanimous opinion of German and Italian governments that because of these aggressive acts a state of war had already existed between Germany and Italy on the one side and the United States on the other. The Reich Führer and the Duce noted this and concluded to sever diplomatic relations and to publicly proclaim the state of war.

"There was no question but that this new situation imposed certain obligations on us on the basis of the so-called Tripartite Pact. This was what the undersecretary of state in the Ministry of Foreign Affairs, Weizsäcker alluded to when he told our minister in Berlin, Sztójay, as reported by him in a cable received today, that he hoped that that the Hungarian government would draw the appropriate conclusions from the position taken by the Reich government, in the spirit of the Tripartite Pact.

"The Tripartite Pact in effect directed that if the contracting parties, or any one of them, were attacked by a country with which the attacked party was not at war at the time the pact was signed, the other signatories to the pact had the duty to support the attacked country politically, economically and militarily.

"According to the prime minister we had a choice. We might sever diplomatic relations with the United States. Or, we might go to the maximum and declare that a state of war has been established between Hungary and the United States.

"The prime minister explained that he hoped that the Hungarian government would reach a decision as soon as possible, preferably today. There was no question about our inability to render armed assistance against the United States and therefore it might not be necessary to declare that a state of war existed. The question was whether if we only severed diplomatic relations would this satisfy the expectations of the German Reich government and would we do justice to our obligations under the Tripartite Pact? He would consider it desirable not to wait until the German Reich declared its demands in this regard beyond what Baron Weizsäcker had told Sztójay. Bárdossy therefore recommended that we declare our solidarity with the Axis Powers and this would satisfy the obligations that we assumed under the Tripartite Pact.

"According to the minister of the interior we did not yet know the content of the agreement between Germany, Italy and Japan. If we declared that we wished to join and that we considered ourselves at war with the United States of America would this not also mean that we would have to mobilize our armed forces and be available wherever the military interests of the Great Powers which signed today's agreement might demand. For instance, we must not get into a position where they demand that we enter Serbia to keep order.

"The prime minister responded to the comments of the minister of the interior. He stated that the agreement reached that day by Germany, Italy and Japan, the details of which are not yet known to us, according to Hitler's speech mandates that none of the contracting parties sign a separate peace agreement with the Anglo-Saxon Powers, Great Britain and the United States of America. The agreement did not create a new situation or new obligations for Hungary. We were not partners to this agreement and it was unlikely that we would be invited to participate. Therefore the agreement would have no consequences for us.

"We had to assess our obligations only on the basis of the Tripartite Pact. On the basis of this pact we could not be asked to enter Serbia to keep order and our geographic location made it impossible for us to participate in any military action against the United States or that we be asked to do anything along these lines.

"The minister of defense, in assessing our situation, indicated that we must decide as to what would be more advantageous for us. If it were more advantageous for us to declare a state of war before this was done by the other smaller countries who joined the Tripartite Pact and who signed the Anti-Comintern Pact, he recommended that we should go the maximum right now. Yet, the difference in strength between the armed forces of Hungary and the armed forces of the United States was so great that it would seem grotesque if we were to declare war on the United States, particularly because we didn't even border on an ocean.

"According to the minister of the interior there could be no doubt that Japan was the aggressor who launched the attack.

"On the basis of the above, the prime minister recommended that the following communiqué be issued:

'As it is known, the German Reich government and the royal Italian government have announced in official publications that a state of war was in existence between the German Reich and Italy on one side and the United States of America on the other. Based on the spirit of the Tripartite Pact the royal Hungarian government declared its solidarity with the Axis Powers. The prime minister, holding the portfolio of minister of foreign affairs, had accordingly directed that the minister of the United States of America in Budapest be given his travel documents. Simultaneously, the Hungarian government had ordered its minister in Washington to return home.'

"The prime minister hoped that with the decision expressed in the above communiqué and the steps taken accordingly, we had met our contractual obligations. He saw the advantage of taking this position spontaneously and immediately, but if it should be demanded that we declare a state of war, this might also be deduced from the communiqué.

"The minister of finance approved the proposal of the prime minister. The Council of Ministers unanimously supported the proposal of the prime minister.

"The prime minister was going to report this unanimous decision to His Highness, the regent and, adjourning the meeting of the Council of Ministers, left the Prime Minister's Office to be received in audience by the regent at the Siesta Sanatorium.

"Dated as above

László Bárdossy, m.p.
"István Bárczy, keeper of the minutes, m.p.
"(I have signed it at the end of March 1942. Bárczy m.p.)"

Bárczy de Bárcziháza's version agrees with the above with only insignificant stylistic changes. Only the differences in content are mentioned.

Among those present the name of József Varga did not appear. (In the copy of the Bárdossy version, differently from the June 26 version, there was no mention that Varga was not present.)

After the brief final comment of the minister of the interior, according to Bárczy de Bárcziháza's notes, the following took place,

"The minister of defense reiterated that all depended on what was better for the Germans. If it was better to have a state of war, let us declare one.

"The prime minister, 'We must not ask the Germans. I would not wish to do that.'

"The minister of agriculture, 'This race for the goodwill of the Germans is ridiculous.'"

According to Bárczy de Bárcziháza, the last comment of the Minister of Finance also included the following consideration, "In his view it would be sufficient if the Council of Ministers would decide only to send the American minister home."

The resolution of the Council of Ministers reads, "The Council of Ministers endorses the communiqué proposed by the prime minister that the prime minister characterized as being elastic and expandable. It is the opinion of the Council of Ministers that for the time being it is sufficient to send the American minister home and thereby severing diplomatic relations with the United States of America."

At the end of the minutes there was an undated and unsigned comment that reads, "These are the minutes prepared by Undersecretary of State Bárczy at the meeting of the Council of Ministers that declared the severance of diplomatic relations with America. Not a declaration of war, only the severance of diplomatic relations."

Two comments must be made relative to this appendix. One is that Bárczy de Bárcziháza wanted to make the differences between the two versions of the minutes absolutely clear. The second one is that he talked about a "declaration of war" and not about the existence of a "state of war" which makes it certain that his version, or at least its final form, was written after the end of the Second World War under conditions which were vastly different from the ones in 1941. See Hungary, National Archives, Minutes of the Council of Ministers? K 27 232

189. According to Article 3, a war criminal was one "who tried to prevent the signing of an armistice agreement with force or by using his influence."

According to Article 4, a war criminal was one "who with his leadership activities assisted the Arrow Cross movement in its rebellion to grasp power and preserve its power or who after the Arrow Cross movement had reached a position of power, and without a threat to his life, accepted a leading position in the government, in the administration, or in the armed forces. (A leading position is one of minister, undersecretary of state, lord lieutenant of a county, lord mayor, army commander, division commander or other similar position;)."

190. Bárdossy, *Bárdossy László a népbíróság előtt*, n. 29, p. 36.

191. This is a far from accurate quote but the meaning is correct. See ibid., pp. 48–49 (Deposition of Gábor Vladár).

192. According to Article 5, a war criminal was one, "Who gravely violated international laws regarding the treatment of the population of occupied territories or of prisoners of war, who abusing his position of power committed cruelties toward the population of returned territories or who initiated, committed or was a party to the illegal execution and torture of people."

193. According to the calculations of Enikő Sajti there were ninty-nine death sentences of which seventy-one persons were executed. See Enikő A. Sajti, *Délvidék. 1941–1944* (Budapest: Kossuth Könyvkiadó, 1987), p. 151. This court was set up under ordinance 7650/1941 ME of October 28, 1941. The sentence of the lower court contains the complete text of the pertinent law. See Bárdossy, *Bárdossy László a népbíróság előtt*, p. 308.

194. Accordingly a war criminal was one, "who, in print (reproduced by any method), in a speech before an audience or on the radio, agitated in favor of the a more vigorous conduct of the war."

195. *Új Magyarság*, January 16, 1941.

196. The speech can be found in its entirety in the pamphlet published in Budapest in 1944, containing eighteen undated speeches by László Bárdossy and entitled *Magyar sors, magyar feladat* (Budapest: Egyesült Nemzeti Keresztény Liga, 1944).

197. Hungary, National Archives, Press Archives, K 428, MTI June 25, 1944, 12th edition. The citation, with some inaccuracies, combined some of the various parts of the speech.

198. Accordingly a person was guilty of a crime against the people if, "As a member of a ministry or of the legislature or as a high-ranking public official that person initiated or willfully participated in the enactment of some legislation that seriously violated the interests of the people."

199. The ordinance issued on April 16, 1941 regulated the military service of persons defined as Jews by Act IV of 1939. "Section 1. According to Section 1 of Act IV of 1939, persons defined as Jews who under Act II of 1939 are obligated to military service must fulfill their military obligations as auxiliary troops. Those serving in the auxiliary units must do so without any rank even if they had earlier reached the

rank of officer or non-commissioned officer. Accordingly those serving in the auxiliary units must be considered and treated as having no military rank."

200. The ordinance issued on August 13, 1941, addressed the implementation of Section 18 of Act IV of 1939 and added an appendix to Section 6 of ME Ordinance 1500/1941. Accordingly, "After enactment of this ordinance, a Jew who is removed from his organization as defined by Section 18 of Act IV of 1939, may be paid a commission or other compensation only for such activity that was completed in no more than six months after the Jew has left the organization."

201. The ordinance issued by József Varga on May 16, 1941, does not contain any additional anti-Semitic regulations but serves to explain earlier ordinances of this type. Its title is, "Explanation of ordinance ME7.330/1940 and KKM 100502/1940 concerning the implementation of Section 18 of Act IV, 1941."

202. According to this a person was guilty of a crime against the people who, "Did not try to prevent the performance of activities described in Article 2 of Section 15, even though his legal position might have enabled him to do so."

According to Article 2 of Section 15 a person was guilty of a crime against the people who, "after September 1, 1939, as part of his official duties, went beyond the required implementation of laws and ordinances directed against certain groups of the nation and engaged in such activity as endangered or offended personal freedom or physical well being or promoted the financial ruin of some people."

203. See pp. 59–60.

204. Section 16 of Act XXXIII of 1896 concerning the administration of justice states, "In a criminal case the court where the crime was committed has jurisdiction even though the result of the crime may have occurred elsewhere.

"If the crime was committed in more than jurisdiction or at the border of two or more jurisdictions or if it is uncertain in which area of jurisdiction the crime was committed, the court that takes action first will be considered to have jurisdiction. Taking action first means that a court has rendered a decision or has instituted some action earlier than another court.

"If the site where the crime was committed is known prior to hand-
ing in the indictment, the trial must be held by the court that has jurisdiction over that particular site."

205. According to first paragraph of Section 20, "The crimes
defined by Sections 11, 13, 15 and 17 fall under the jurisdiction of the
People's Court."

206. According to this "Chapter Two of Act XXXIII of 1896
defines jurisdiction. "If crimes alleged to have been committed by the
suspect were performed at different locations, the people's prosecutor
in charge will identify actions and possible evidence and will transfer
these to the people's prosecutor attached to the People's Court having
jurisdiction in the area of the suspect's residence."

207. István Csáky died on January 27, 1941, but Bárdossy was de
jure minister of foreign affairs only after February 4.

208. Deals with the session of the Supreme Defense Council on
April 1, 1941. See pp. 18–20.

209. Zsigmond, ed., *Diplomáciai iratok*, vol 5, pp. 1029–1030.

210. The corect date is April 10.

211. See pp. 20–22.

212. Zsigmond, ed., *Diplomáciai iratok*, vol 5, pp. 1006–1007.

213. Ibid., p. 1009. An imprecise but factually correct citation.

214. Ibid., p. 1027.

215. Ibid., p. 1001. Contains the answer to the telegram printed on
p. 143.

216. Zsigmond, ed., *Diplomáciai iratok*, vol 5, pp. 1057, 1059.
The American statement declared, "Hungary having without justification attacked Yugoslavia a state of war existed between Hungary and
Yugoslavia and that it was necessary to promote the security and preserve the peace of the United States and to protect the lives of citizens
of the United States." See Hungary, National Archives, Szent-Iványi
Manuscript, "Csonka-Magyarország külpolitikája," p. 587.

217. The Soviet-Yugoslav Friendship and Non-Aggression Pact was
signed in Moscow on April 5, 1941, that is one day before the German
attack. Halmosy, ed., *Nemzetközi szerződések 1918–1945*, pp. 518–519.

218. In fact Yugoslavia did not receive a British-French guarantee
such as was given to Poland on March 31, 1939, and to Greece and
Romania on April 13 of that year. The reason for this was that Yugoslav

policies were in favor of getting closer to Germany since 1934 and Yugoslavia did not wish to complicate her relationship with Germany with such a guarantee. It is a different matter that at the same time the Anglo-Saxon Powers encouraged Belgrade to turn against Germany and moreover, the Belgrade turn around of March 27, 1941, clearly showed the hand of the British Secret Service in the background.

219. The April 14 meeting of the Supreme Defense Council.

220. We are not familiar with these minutes.

221. Bartók's telephone call had to arrive earlier because the Council of Ministers meeting began at 10:30 P.M. During the trial it was suggested several times that Bartók also sent a telegram. We are not familiar with such a telegram and Gyula Juhász mentions it only on the basis of the Bárdossy trial material published in 1945. See, Juhász, *A Teleki kormány külpolitikája*, p. 322. It must be assumed that there was only a telephone communication. The sentence of the lower court also mentions a telephone call only.

222. Because the minutes of the April 1 meeting of the Supreme Defense Council have not appeared to this day, no definite position can be taken in this matter. According to the reconstruction of the writer on this subject, Gyula Juhász, such a condition did not appear. See Juhász, *A Teleki kormány külpolitikája*, p. 306.

223. Hungarian troops met practically no resistance. Ibid., p. 325.

224. Zsigmond, ed., *Diplomáciai iratok*, vol 5, pp. 1029–1030.

225. See the deposition of József Bölöny. Bárdossy, *Bárdossy László a népbíróság előtt*, pp. 44–47.

226. For the authentic text of the letter see ibid., p. 60, n. 61. It should be noted that the text appeared in print for the first time in 1959. See Magda Ádám, Gyula Juhász and Lajos Kerekes, eds., *Magyarország és a második világháború. Titkos diplomáciai okmányok a háború előzményeihez és történetéhez* (Budapest: Akadémiai Kiadó, 1959). After the occupation of Budapest the surviving material of Horthy's Cabinet Office was taken to the Soviet Union and was later returned to Hungary. From a total of nine bundles of documents pieces were selected and published in 1962 under the title *Horthy Miklós titkos iratai*. It naturally included the Teleki letters. (In his second letter Teleki resigns, should the suicide miscarry.)

227. Bárdossy used the same arguments every time the issue was raised.

228. Reményi-Schneller was not close to Pál Teleki. He was devoted to the Germans and, according to many, was their paid agent. It must be kept in mind in connection with his deposition that he made it in the shadow of death. He was executed as a war criminal on August 24, 1946.

229. Zsigmond, ed., *Diplomáciai iratok*, vol 5, pp. 1033–1034. The number was coded telegram was 98 and not 68.

230. See endnote 182.

231. There are two sets of minutes from this meeting as well, just as in the case of the meetings of June 26 and December 11.

I. Bárdossy's version.

"The meeting was attended by László Bárdossy, Ferenc Keresztes-Fischer, Lajos Reményi-Schneller, Dániel Bánffy, József Varga, Bálint Hóman, Károly Bartha, Ferenc Zsindely and István Bárczy de Bárcziháza.

"1. [Bárdossy] states that at today's meeting of the Council of Ministers he will recommend that the royal Hungarian government severs diplomatic relations with the Soviet government.

"In support of his recommendation the prime minister stated that on the basis of the completely parallel policies that the royal Hungarian government maintains with the policies of the Axis Powers, as demonstrated by our joining the Tripartite Pact, the fact that the German Reich was in a state of war with the Soviet Union since the 22nd inst. requires that we draw the obvious conclusions.

"The Italian government went well beyond this and considered itself as being at war with the Soviet Union while Hungary would only sever diplomatic relations with the Soviet Union.

"The Soviet government had, in fact, once severed diplomatic relations with Hungary when it announced on February 2, on receiving news that the Hungarian government would join the Anti-Commintern Pact, that it would close its legation in Budapest assuming that the Hungarian government would do likewise in Moscow.

"The Council of Ministers concurs."

II. Bárczy de Bárcziháza's version.

The attendees listed in version I were present at the meeting and so was László Radocsay.

"The prime minister, in his capacity as minister of foreign affairs stated that he would submit a resolution to the Council of Ministers today, that the royal Hungarian government informs the Soviet government that in consequence of the war between Germany and Russia that broke out at 4:00 A.M. on Sunday, June 22, 1941, Hungary severed its diplomatic relations with Soviet Russia.

"The justification for this action was that Hungary followed the policies of the Axis Powers, acted in parallel with their policies and expressed these policies when on Germany's request she was the first one to join the Tripartite Pact.

"The minister of the interior, Keresztes-Fischer interjects, 'not so fast.'

[This rough draft suggests that Bárczy de Bárcziháza jotted down his notes while the version he had prepared in June 1941 followed the customary forms and style. Presumably it was also shorter. Here Bárczy de Bárcziháza put everything down that highlighted Bárdossy's role and responsibility.]

"Prime Minister Bárdossy, 'The more rapid our decision the more valuable it is. In this country, among certain people, there is a race for the favors of Germany. I allude primarily to Imrédy's party. I have also been informed that the Germans' confidential agent András Mecsér will arrive in Berlin today. If there were no race I would not mind being last. This race is not for the German leadership but for the good graces of the German National Socialist Party.'

"'The process would be that I instruct my Permanent Deputy Foreign Minister János Vörnle to summon Sharanov, the Soviet Union's minister in Budapest and inform him that because Hungary has joined the Tripartite Pact it feels compelled to sever diplomatic relations with the Soviet Union as a consequence of the fact that since yesterday morning Germany and Soviet Russia are at war.'

"The Council of Ministers concurs.

"Prime Minister Bárdossy left the Council of Ministers chamber to inform the regent about this resolution of the Council of Ministers, the regent being ill at his country estate of Kenderes.

"Prime Minister Bárdossy returned from the Council of Ministers chamber (sic). 'His Highness the regent concurred with the process recommended by me. I have instructed Minister Vörnle. I am now summoning the German and Italian ministers.'

"The prime minister emphasized that this step was not a declaration of war but only the severance of diplomatic relations. It did not mean that we were at war with the Soviet Union. When asked about the development of the German-Russian war that broke out yesterday, General Vitéz Károly Bartha, minister of defense, stated that since in September 1939 the Germans defeated Poland in three weeks, in May 1940 they defeated the French in the same period of time and in April–May 1941 they only took the same short period of time to defeat Yugoslavia and Greece. He believed that Germany would defeat the Russians in six weeks and that within six weeks the German army would take Moscow.

"Dezső Laky, minister of public supplies without portfolio, arrived late to the meeting of the Council of Ministers. We did not tell him about Point 2 of the minutes because it deals with a different matter."

In the Bárdossy version the date is given as "date as above." Bárczy signed the Bárdossy version on March 20, 1942. Bárczy added an extensive comment to the Bárdossy version.

"I had shown the minutes to Bárdossy three days after the meeting. He took it saying that he wanted to read it carefully, make a copy for the archives of the Ministry of Foreign Affairs and perhaps make some minor stylistic changes. In spite of my repeated requests and Ferenc Keresztes-Fischer's request, Bárdossy refused to submit the minutes to the ministers for their signature or to me for mine. Only when he left his position as prime minister and minister of foreign affairs on March 10, 1942, that is nine months later, did he revise these minutes. The revised minutes should have been given to me to submit them to the ministers for their signature. This is the job of the keeper of the minutes. In effect Bárdossy had one of his confidential aides take the revised minutes in the morning to the five ministries with the request that the ministers sign them instantly. [See Bárdossy's oral deposition in Bárdossy, *Bárdossy László a népbíróság előtt*, pp. 180–181.]

"The ministers signed them without reading them. [This is hardly credible. The importance of the issue would not permit it]. Bárdossy then destroyed the minutes that I had given him on June 27, 1941. I had my notes and I could see that Bárdossy did not say the last two sentences at the June 23, 1941, meeting of the Council of Ministers. [Namely the last two sentences of the first agenda. This also shows how strongly Bárczy de Bárcziháza focuses on this issue in 1945 or even later.] He added these on March 10, 1942. Both sentences were his later additions and because he really did not say them this act constituted a falsification of history. The addition of these two sentences was incomprehensible from a man as intelligent as Bárdossy. [If we consider the importance of the question and the doubtful outcome that could have been foreseen in 1942, it is not at all incomprehensible. The word underscored by us also indicated that Bárczy finalized both versions after Bárdossy's death and added his comments at that time]. Italy signed a Pact of Steel with Germany. Germany supported Italy in 1941 with the war against Yugoslavia after Italy's defeat in Albania and Greece and thus the alteration of the minutes with a reference to Italy was clumsy. [Not so. Bárdossy refers to Italy because Italy was subject to Germany just like Hungary. The two Vienna Awards, the recovery of Subcarpathia and the reattachment of the Délvidék were weighty affairs and there was much to make up for.]

"It was equally clumsy to refer to Litvinov. Because even though Litvinov did sever diplomatic relations it was on the request of the Hungarian government that the Soviet Ambassador Shurits in Paris agreed to see to it that Hungarian-Soviet diplomatic relations be reestablished. Since that time President Kalinin had also spoken. Molotov spoke in 1940 and on June 23, 1941, at 5:00 P.M. he sent Bárdossy a long message via Kristóffy asking that Hungary remain neutral.

"Why did Bárdossy have to add the second sentence to the minutes when he did not say it? At the same time he kept silent about Molotov's message and Kristóffy's telegrams and did not inform the Council of Ministers or the regent. According to Minister of Justice Radocsay, the addition of a sentence that was not uttered, retroactively, to the minutes constituted a falsification of history."

In his repeatedly cited work, Domokos Szent-Iványi states about the June 23 Council of Ministers session that "It is very interestingly highlighted by the comments made by István Bárczy, undersecretary of state in the Prime Minister's Office and the keeper of the minutes, which were not included by the government in the minutes." (See Hungary, National Archives, Szent-Iványi Kézirat, K 63, "Csonka-Magyarország külpolitikája," p. 634.) This wording unmistakably suggests that the Bárczy versions were written in their present format, after the Szent-Iványi manuscript. It makes one wonder why we are not familiar with the handwritten notes of the keeper of the minutes. The available copies were clearly prepared after the Bárdossy trial. During the trial Bárdossy had stated that the minutes contained later and spiteful additions. It seems that Bárdossy's comment is supported by Ákos Major who certainly was not prejudiced in Bárdossy's favor.

232. See pp. 45.

233. The wording of the Anti-Comintern Pact was not anti-Soviet, but in reality it was very much so. It is only thus that the connection can be understood which made the Soviet Union close its legation in Budapest after Hungary's joining the pact was announced. This connection was well understood by the People's Court.

234. The quotation is from the Bárczy version with numerous inaccuracies. See endnote 187.

235. Zsigmond, ed., *Diplomáciai iratok*, vol 5, p. 1228 and Ránki, Pamlényi, Tilkovszky, and Juhász, eds., *Wilhelmstrasse és Magyarország*, pp. 598–599.

236. We have found document 489/biz, 1941. It is not a code telegram but Sztójay's four page report, dated July 2. See Hungary, National Archives, Ministry of Foreign Affairs, Reserved Political Papers, K 64. Item 24, no. 204. The content of the quote can be found on the first page of the letter. Sztójay here truly referred to an earlier report, 84/pol. fon. 1941.

237. Bárdossy consistently explained his activities in this way in every deposition.

238. Zsigmond, ed., *Diplomáciai iratok*, vol 5, p. 1214.

239. We are not familiar with this document.

240. We are not familiar with this deposition.

241. See Bárdossy's oral deposition at the first trial. Bárdossy, *Bárdossy László a népbíróság előtt*, pp. 186–187.

242. Ibid.

243. Many important details are missing from the minutes of the Council of Ministers and therefore the text of the minutes cannot be decisive.

244. This deposition is not among the material of the Bárdossy trial preserved in the Ministry of the Interior.

245. The People's Court was aware of this fact. When it was examining Bárdossy's actions it did not take into account its effects.

246. See Bárdossy, *Bárdossy László a népbíróság előtt*, p. 48 and n. 55.

247. Bárdossy did not do anything like this.

248. Hungary, Parliament, Upper House, *Napló*, vol. 2 (1942), p. 235.

249. Hungary, Parliament, House of Representatives, *Napló*, vol. 10 (1941), p. 495.

250. Ibid., and vol. 11, (1941), p. 7.

251. See endnote 187.

252. See endnote 188.

253. See endnote 188.

254. See endnote 188.

255. Gyula Juhász, *Hungarian Foreign Policy 1919–1945* (Budapest: Akadémiai Kiadó, 1979), pp. 205–206.

256. See pp. 49–51.

257. See p. 50.

258. The Solidarity Declaration proclaimed on December 11 reads,

"As is well-known, the government of the German Reich and the royal Italian government, in their official communiqués issued today, have declared that a state of war exist between the German Reich and Italy on one side and, on the other, the United States of America.

"The royal Hungarian government, in the spirit of the Tripartite Pact, this time also establishes its solidarity with the Axis Powers.

"Accordingly the royal Hungarian prime minister, as acting foreign minister has seen to it that the travel documents are delivered to the Minister of the United States of North America in Budapest.

"At the same time, the royal Hungarian government has recalled its minister in Washington." Quoted in Juhász, *Hungarian Foreign Policy*, p. 205.

259. Ádám, Juhász, and Kerekes, eds. *Magyarország és a második világháború*, pp. 382–383.

260. We don't know where it was found but the lower court sentence contained the entire text. See Bárdossy, *Bárdossy László a népbíróság előtt*, pp. 274–275.

261. Not found in the National Archives.

262. We are not familiar with this telegram.

263. The change in government came about so that Kállay could modify the Hungarian policies that became increasingly pro-German. It

is another matter that Kállay covered up this changeover with eloquent pro-German pronouncements.

264. The citation is not entirely accurate.

265. "We already have the experience," said Kállay on October 12, 1943, "that rash assumption of a position may result in condemnation and in consequences unfavorable to us. Only a child plays with fire and we have to be particularly careful when a tempest is howling around us." See Hungary, Parliament, House of Representatives, *Napló*, vol 17 (1943), p. 227.

266. We are not familiar with this deposition.

267. Ministry of the Interior Archives, The Bárdossy Trial, folio 323 (It is a June entry and not a July one).

268. Ibid., folio 322.

269. Ibid., folio 324. The "Diary" nails this down as Ferenc Fischer's "alleged" two plans.

270. We did not find this among the papers of the trial.

271. We are not familiar with the written deposition.

272. Bárdossy, *Bárdossy László a népbíróság előtt*, pp. 35 and 43.

273. Hungary, Archives of the Ministry of the Interior, The Bárdossy Trial, folio 328. "In connection with the coalition I mentioned that we hear that Bárdossy has accepted the leadership of the united new party," writes Szőllősi in his memorandum. "This would then shape the entire coalition issue so that it would have to be implemented by Szálasi and Bárdossy. I let it be known that I considered it a real possibility that there will be difficulties with Bárdossy. He may not recognize the leading role to be played by the Hungarist Movement and I added that in this regard he, Veesenmayer, may have a great role. I emphasized strongly that this was my personal opinion and that I have not spoken to Szálasi about it. Veesenmayer said that he had not been asked by either side to act as an arbitrator (I didn't ask him that either!) and that he had no intention of assuming such a role because then, if there was any lack of success every responsibility would fall on his head."

274. Ibid., folio 383.

275. Ibid., folio 329.

276. Bárdossy, *Bárdossy László a népbíróság előtt*, p. 41.

277. Hungary, Archives of the Ministry of the Interior, The Bárdossy Trial, folio 330.

278. Ibid., folio 331.

279. Ibid., folio 332.

280. Ibid., folio 335.

281. Ibid., folio 336.

282. Ibid., folio 335.

283. Bárdossy, *Bárdossy László a népbíróság előtt*, p. 43.

284. Hungary, Archives of the Ministry of the Interior, The Bárdossy Trial, folios 337–339.

285. See p. 63 and see Bárdossy, *Bárdossy László a népbíróság előtt*, 1991, p. 36, n. 29.

286. Ibid., p. 37. The quotation is highly arbitrary.

287. Ibid., pp. 36–37.

288. Unknown.

289. Hungary, Archives of the Ministry of the Interior, The Bárdossy Trial, folio 352.

290. Bárdossy, *Bárdossy László a népbíróság előtt*, p. 30.

291. The original is unknown.The sentence quotes the same thing at some length. Ibid., p. 305.

292. The origin of the quotation is unknown.

293. The origin of the quotation is unknown.

294. The origin of the quotation is unknown.

295. In the October 10 deposition this was not mentioned. Ibid., pp. 43–44.

296. Hungary, Archives of the Ministry of the Interior, The Bárdossy Trial, folio 342.

297. Csáklyás (pickman) was the name given to those politicians in the 1930s who opposed the shift toward a dictatorship of the counterrevolutionary system that was associated with the name of Count István Bethlen.

298. Hungary, Archives of the Ministry of the Interior, The Bárdossy Trial, folios 343–345. It should be noted that we deal here with speculation and not with something that has taken place. The planned visit to the prime minister took place on October 12. See Éva Teleki, *Nyilas uralom Magyarországon* (Budapest: Kossuth Könyvkiadó, 1974), pp. 24–25.

299. Hungary, Archives of the Ministry of the Interior, The Bárdossy Trial, folio 346.

300. Ibid., folios 347–348. See Vladár's deposition in Bárdossy, *Bárdossy László a népbíróság előtt*, pp. 48–49.

301. Ibid., folio 384. Published as Ferenc Szálasi, *"Szálasi Naplója": nyilasmozgalom a II. világháború idején*, ed. Elek Karsai (Budapest: Kossuth Könyvkiadó, 1978), p. 429. The October 26 date was also a mistake. The correct date for the diary entry was September 26.

302. See endnote 182.

303. See endnote 189.

304. This deposition is unknown to us.

305. It deals with the proclamation jointly signed by Horthy and Bárdossy on April 10, 1941. See Zsigmond, ed., *Diplomáciai iratok*, vol. 5, pp. 1029–1030. The quotation is somewhat inaccurate because instead of "peacefully" the original has "in peace."

306. Sajti, *A Délvidék* and Károly Vigh, "Bajcsy-Zsilinszky Endre és a 'hideg napok'," *Történelmi Szemle* 11, nos. 1–2 (1968): 81–103.

307. See Sajti, *A Délvidék*, pp. 152–168, and Bárdossy's last word in this volume.

308. The Béla Kun parallel is not proper because the Hungarian Soviet Republic attacked the Czechs and the Romanians to further world revolution and give the Soviet Republic more room to maneuver and not because of nationalist endeavors.

309. Under Section 9 of Act VII of 1945 "As far as the statute of limitations is concerned, Section 108 of the Penal Code applies so that for acts committed after June 21, 1941, and before the signing of the armistice agreement the statute of limitations will start running on the day the armistice was signed (January 20, 1945)."

310. The leaders of the twenty-five year counterrevolutionary era clearly did not regard themselves as the heirs of the Hungarian Soviet Republic in this regard either.

311. The Bruck negotiations began on March 14, 1921. Hungary was represented by Prime Minister Pál Teleki, and Minister of Foreign Affairs Gusztáv Grátz. The Czechoslovak representative was Minister of Foreign Affairs Edvard Beneš. The discussion centered on economic matters and the possibilities of a preferential customs arrangement were considered. The discussions were interrupted by the first monarchist coup attempt. The Marienbad negotiations were held during the same year (June 10–23) and dealt with a Czechoslovak-Hungarian-

Austrian customs union. Because of irreconcilable differences and because the deterioration of the Western Hungary question, the negotiations were abandoned without any results.

312. On August 29, 1926, the 400th anniversary of the Battle of Mohács, Horthy spoke on the old battlefield and made a very complimentary statement about the Yugoslavs.

313. Lajos Walko was minister of foreign affairs from March 17, 1925, to December 9, 1930, and again from August 24, 1931, to October 1, 1932.

314. The reference is to King Alexander of Yugoslavia who was murdered in Marseilles in 1934.

315. In fact, in retaliation many Hungarians were expelled from Yugoslavia.

316. It was one of the duties of the Consular Service to help the Hungarians who went abroad, particularly from Czechoslovakia.

317. Between the two wars the assimilating forces were the crudest and most overt in Romania.

318. This position is highly questionable since there were many manifestations of German revisionism even before 1938.

319. This is really so. The First and Second Vienna Awards were staged by German-Italian arbitration.

320. This is incorrect. Soviet foreign policy would have liked very much to help Czechoslovakia but without Western help this had to be avoided at all costs in order not to confront an increasingly powerful Germany.

321. This was the agreement signed for Germany by Fabricius Wohltat in Bucharest on March 23, 1939. See Halmosy, *Nemzetközi szerződések*, pp. 451–454.

322. This question can and must be raised. Bárdossy completely ignores the fact that the Second World War and the immediately preceding period were devoted to the fight against fascism. It was the great, albeit not striking or isolated mistake of Hungarian foreign policy that it ignored the fact that Germany of that period was fascist. Starting with the fact that Bárdossy had emphasized, namely that the Western Powers could not rise above their own interests, the conclusion should have to be drawn that territorial revisions could not be made a function of unilateral German-Italian arbitration.

323. Presenting public opinion in this way was a highly biased action. It was highly unlikely that the anti-Germans wanted more territorial revisions. It was the Germanophile extreme right wing that attacked the government insisting that territorial revisions would be far more likely if the country would be restructured on the German model and adapt itself even closer to German foreign policy. It is equally fallacious to claim that the decisions moved so many people into the Germanophobe camp. There evidently were some, but the effects were more in the direction of strengthening the Germanophile camp and that this camp became much more vociferous after it became obvious that the return of the territories was in no way due to the Western Powers.

Bárdossy's arguments were even more peculiar because uncovering the real situation would have served in his defense because it was the Germanophile camp that pushed him into the war with the Soviet Union and toward a more complete orientation toward Germany.

324. Bárdossy's words reflected the political thinking of a broad circle of contemporaries. This was a survival of the thought processes which identified world history with European history and which on the basis of the experience of past centuries were firm in their belief that European factors would determine the ultimate outcome of current events. Those who did not think this way and who in the Anglo-Saxon world represented a majority, knew and were very hopeful that regardless how prolonged and bitter the fight might be, the outcome of the war was not in doubt, Germany had to lose. This was the basis of Churchill's thinking. At home, Bárdossy had to be familiar with Teleki's thinking whose thoughts reached well beyond the European horizon. Bárdossy saw Barcza's reports as well, but did not think much of them. Yet the final outcome shows how mistaken the prime minister's views had been.

325. These arguments of Bárdossy are interesting and in themselves negate the statements of the Horthy memoir literature and of contemporary political thinking, according to which the signing of the December 1940 Hungarian-Yugoslav Pact was motivated on the Hungarian side by nothing except anti-German sentiments. What Bárdossy said already in 1945 was proven by György Ránki in 1964 in his book, *Emlékiratok és valóság Magyarország második világháborús szerepéről* (Budapest: Kossuth Könyvkiadó, 1964).

326. Halmosy, *Nemzetközi szerződések*, p. 505. The cited Article 2 reads, "The high contracting parties agree that they will consult with each other in all those questions which, according to their judgment, affect their relationship." This passage was interpreted by Bárdossy, and not for the first time, in the broadest possible way.

327. Truth is that Hitler did not have to make plans for Hungary's occupation. His message of March 27 was answered positively by Horthy the following day. See pp. 15–16.

328. According to Lajos Für's calculations Hungary's casualties in the World War were 1,430,000 if calculated on the basis of the size of the country at that time, or 900,000 on the basis of the Trianon Hungary. See Lajos Für, *Mennyi a sok sírkereszt? Magyarország embervesztesége a második világháborúban* (Budapest: Püski, 1989), pp. 51–54. These numbers contradict Bárdossy's arguments in every way. Partly by the fact that these enormous losses were made up over time and also by the fact that they in no way testified to the "successfulness" of the Bárdossy policies.

329. Yugoslavia's official name until 1929.

330. More accurately, on March 27.

331. More accurately at 5:00 P.M. on the 6th. See Juhász, *A Teleki kormány külpolitikája*, p. 318.

332. Bárdossy forgot that a similar diplomatic request had been sent to him directly. See ibid., p. 320.

333. Bartók's news had to have arrived earlier because at 10:30 P.M. the Council of Ministers was already in session.

334. The Croat separatist movement did represent a considerable force but it was not strong enough to bring about an independent state. This "independent Croatia" became a puppet state that was made possible by German military intervention.

335. On the 17th.

336. The advance party crossed the border at dawn on the 11th, i.e. five days after the German attack. See Juhász. *A Teleki kormány külpolitikája*, pp. 318, 323.

337. The Soviet parallel was appropriate but in a reverse sense. The basis for the Soviet step was in the Secret Additional Protocol to the Soviet-Germanon Non-Aggression Pact, signed on August 23, 1939. Article 2 of the protocol states, "In the event of a territorial and politi-

cal rearrangement of the areas belonging to the Polish state the spheres of influence of Germany and the U.S.S.R. shall be bounded approximately by the line of the Narew, Vistula, and San." See Raymond James Sontag and James Stuart Beddie, *Nazi-Soviet Relations 1939–1941. Documents from the Archives of the German Foreign Office* (Washington: Department of State, 1948), p. 78.

338. On the day that Miklós Horthy entered Komárom, after the First Vienna Award, on November 6, 1938, the prominent poet Mihály Babits published a poem in the *Pesti Napló* with the title, "Áldás a magyarra" (Blessings on the Hungarians). The first stanza of the poem reads:

> Don't say that the country is getting larger
> Our homeland was always the same size
> For a thousand years and will remain so
> It is not a land clobbered together
> Our homeland is one land, a thing alive
> It cannot be disjointed and patched together.

339. The Locarno Treaty was signed on October 16, 1925. It was really a system of agreements wishing to stabilize the European status quo. In Locarno the French-German and Belgian-German borders were guaranteed, but the guarantor powers, Great Britain and Italy were unwilling to guarantee Germany's eastern border. Subsequently France and her allies repeatedly tried to guarantee Germany's eastern borders. This would have been the Eastern Locarno which, however, never materialized. See Halmosy, *Nemzetközi szerződések*, pp. 233–247.

340. Zsigmond, ed., *Diplomáciai iratok*, vol. 5, pp. 1097–1100.

341. Miklós Wesselényi, *Szózat a Magyar és a szláv nemzetiség ügyében* (Kolozsvár: Minerva, 1944).

342. The Baltic States, independent since the end of World War I, were enrolled among the Soviet republics. Lithuania on Aug 3, 1940, Latvia on the 5th and Estonia on the 6th. The basis for this action was the non-aggression pact. According to Article 1 of the secret protocols, "In the event of a territorial and political rearrangement of the Baltic States (Finland, Estonia, Latvia and Lithuania) the northern boundary of Lithuania shall represent the boundary of the spheres of influence of Germany and U.S.S.R. In this connection the interest of Lithuania in the Vilna area are recognized by each party." Sontag and Beddie, eds., *Nazi-Soviet Relations 1939–1941*, p. 78.

343. Eckhardt's editorial "Szovjet-Oroszország és a Ruténföld" was published in *Magyar Nemzet*, October 30 and not on October 15.

344. Not so. The strengthening of the antifascist sentiment proves the opposite. There would have been something to lean on and to support. It is a different matter that the governmental machinery weakened precisely these forces, at times with extreme brutality.

345. In this the governmental terror, the rigid censorship and the-excessive weight of the entire situation played a role. It should suffice to allude to the Christmas 1941 issue of *Népszava*, to the activities of the Historical Memorial Committee and to the liberal press to put this statement into its proper place.

346. A typical example of the sterility of historism.

347. Using the Romanians as an argument was pure speculation. Romania did not have to be encouraged to wage war with the Soviet Union, as Bárdossy knew very well from a variety of contexts, because it was the opinion in Bucharest, that Romanian blood spilled on the eastern front would serve as a basis for territorial revision vis-à-vis the Hungarians and the Soviets. If Hungarian passivity had been such an important consideration in Bucharest, it is extremely unlikely that they would have attacked the Soviet Union before Hungary got involved.

348. In March.

349. It was not necessary to argue with the Germans in June 1941.

350. It is a completely ahistorical argument. The Romanians were well armed and so were the Yugoslavs. The Czechs also had an armed force. The "plunder" was not only hoped for but vigorously demanded. It can be fully proven today, on the basis of French documentation, that every one of the Successor States wished to detach even larger areas of Hungary than what they had received under the terms of the Trianon Peace Treaty. See, Mária Ormos,From Padua to the Trianon 1918–1920 (Boulder, CO: Social Science Monographs, 1990); and Ignác Romsics, *The Dismantling of Historic Hungary: The Peace Treaty of Trianon, 1920* (Boulder, CO: Social Science Monographs, 2002).

351 .A massive exaggeration.Hungary had been an occupied country on several occasions and survived as have other countries under such conditions.

352. Totally unhistorical. There certainly were impulses from Germany to urge entry into the war but the German position was far

from being strong enough so that denial of the request would have led to a civil war.

353. There was no national unanimity.

354. Stilted presentation. The front lines were very clear and it was not everybody's fight against everybody else but of a majority of the Yugoslav people against the fascist intruders.

355. Pál Pritz, *Bárdossy László* (Budapest: Elektra Kiadóház, 2001), p. 88.

356. Communication with the Soviet capital was a given through Ankara.

357. The Council of Ministers decided on June 23rd to sever the diplomatic relations.

358. See endnote 118.

359. The quotation was based on the report from Mihály Jungerth-Arnóthy, Hungarian minister in Moscow, of February 8, 1939. It was accurate as to content but not to format. See Peter Pastor, ed., *A moszkvai magyar követség jelentései 1935–1941* (Budapest: Századvég Kiadó, 1992), pp. 185–189 and Zsigmond, ed., *Diplomáciaiiratok*, vol. 3, *Magyarország külpolitikája 1938–1939*, ed. ÁdámMagda (Budapest, Akadémiai Könyvkiadó, 1970), pp. 443–446.

360. A 21st publication of MTI on April 14, 1941, contains the TASS statement but does not mention the reference to the Subcarpathia.See Hungary, National Archives, Press Archives, K 428, vol. 485.

361. See endnote 187.

362. It was a widely spread error. It was very much part of the confusion within a totalitarian system that the military and political leaderships wanted different things. The contradiction between the true situation and the erroneous picture formed about it was exploited by the political leadership. Compared to the 30s, the situation took a complete turn around. In August 1938 Hitler urged Hungarian participation against Czechoslovakia but the German military leadership supported the Hungarian reluctance. Now it was the German army that took the initiative and Hitler only reaped the reward when he acknowledged Hungary's entry into the war.

363. Bárdossy alludes to Ferenc Keresztes-Fischer.

364. There is much truth in this and almost sixty years later we see these events as being much more inter-related. Yet Bárdossy used this

universal truth to cover up the real responsibility and crime of the Hungarian political leadership which even he admits in some other-points ofthe trial.

365. The attack was begun with approximately 45,000 men.

366. Ránki, Pamlényi, Tilkovszky, and Juhász, eds., *Wilhelmstrasse és Magyarország*, p. 639.

367. Zsigmond, ed., *Diplomáciai iratok*, vol. 5, pp. 732–734. The quotation was not verbatim but was accurate as to content.

368. In a military sense Hungary was truly neutral but by joining the Tripartite Pact on November 20, 1940, it committed itself on the-side of the Axis Powers.

BIBLIOGRAPHY

Ablonczy, Balázs. *Teleki Pál.* Budapest: Elektra Kiadóház, 2000.

Ábrahám, Ferenc and Endre Kussinszky. *Itél a történelem. A Bárdossy-per; a vád, a vallomások és az ítélet* [History Renders Judgment. The Bárdossy Trial; the Indictment, the Trial, and the Sentence]. Budapest: Híradó Könyvtár, 1945.

Ádám, Magda, Gyula Juhász and Lajos Kerekes, eds. *Magyarország és a második világháború. Titkos diplomáciai okmányok a háború előzményeihez és történetéhez* [Hungary and the Second World War. Secret Diplomatic Papers about the Antecedents and History of the War]. Budapest: Akadémiai Kiadó, 1959.

Babits, Mihály. "Áldás a magyarra" [Blessings on the Hungarian]. In *Pesti Napló*, November 6, 1938.

Bajcsy-Zsilinszky, Endre. *Irások tőle és róla* [Papers by Him and about Him]. Edited by Loránt Tilkovszky. Budapest: Kossuth Kiadó, 1986.

Bán, András D. *Illúziók és csalódások. Nagy Britannia és Magyarország 1938–1941* [Illusions and Disappointments. Great Britain and Hungary]. Budapest: Osiris Kiadó, 1998.

Barcza György. *Diplomata emlékeim* [My Diplomat Recollections]. 2 vols. Edited by András D. Bán. Budapest: Európa Kiadó, 1994.

Bárdossy László. *Bárdossy László, a nemzet védelmében* [László Bárdossy in the Defense of the Nation]. Edited by Sándor Esső. Fahrwagen: Duna, 1976.

Bárdossy, László. *Bárdossy László a népbíróság előtt* [László Bárdossy before the People's Court]. Edited and annotated, with an introduction by Pál Pritz. Budapest: Meacenas Kiadó, 1991.

Bárdossy László. *Magyar politika a Mohácsi Vész után* [Hungarian Politics after the Battle Mohács]. Budapest: Egyetemi Nyomda, 1943.

Bárdossy László. "*Magyar sors, magyar feladat*" [Hungarian Fate, Hungarian Duty]. Budapest: Egyesült Nemzeti Keresztény Liga, 1944.

Barker, Elisabeth. *British Policy in South-East Europe in the Second World War*. London: Macmillan, 1976.

Braham, Randolph L. *The Politics of Genocide: the Holocaust in Hungary*. 2 vols. Boulder, CO: Social Science Monographs, 1994.

Czettler, Antal. *A mi kis élet-halál kérdéseink. A Magyar külpolitika a hadba lépéstől a német megszállásig* [Our Small Life-or-Death Problems. Hungarian Foreign Policy from Entry into the War to the German Occupation]. Budapest: Magvető Kiadó, 2000.

Czettler, Antal. *Teleki Pál és a magyar külpolitika 1939–1941* [Pál Teleki and Hungarian Foreign Policy]. Budapest: Magvető Kiadó, 1997.

Dombrády, Loránd. *Hadsereg és politika Magyarországon 1938–1944* [The Military and Politics in Hungary 1938–1944]. Budapest: Kossuth Könyvkiadó, 1986.

Dombrády, Loránd. *Katonapolitika és hadsereg 1938–1944* [Military Politics and the Army]. Budapest: Ister Kiadó, 2000.

Eckhardt, Tibor. "Szovjetoroszország és Ruténföld" [Soviet Russia and Ruthenia]. *Magyar Nemzet*, October 30, 1938.

Fest, Joachim C. *Hitler*. 6th. ed. Frankfurt am Main-Berlin: Ullstein Büch, 1996.

Fülöp, Mihály and Péter Sipos. *Magyarország külpolitikája a XX. században* [Hungary's Foreign Policy in the 20th Century]. Budapest: Aula Kiadó, 1998.

Für, Lajos. *Mennyi a sok sírkereszt? Magyarország embervesztesége a második világháborúban* [How Many Gravestones? The Human Losses of Hungary in World War II]. Budapest: Püski, 1989.

Gergely, Jenő. *Gömbös Gyula. Politikai pályakép* [Gyula Gömbös. A Political Career]. Budapest: Vince Kiadó, 2001.

Gosztonyi, Péter. "Bárdossy Svájcban" [Bárdossy in Switzerland]. *Élet és Irodalom*, January 20, 1989.

Gosztonyi, Péter. "Interjú Gosztonyi Péterrel" [Interview with Peter Gosztonyi]. *168 óra*, July 4, 1989.

Halmosy, Dénes, ed. *Nemzetközi szerződések 1918–1945. A két világháború közötti korszak és a második világháború legfontosabb külpolitikai szerződései* [International Treaties 1918–1945: The Most Important International Treaties of the Interwar Era and of

World War II]. 2nd ed. Budapest: Közgazdasági és Jogi Kiadó, 1983.

Herczegh, Géza. *A szarajevói merénylettől a potsdami konferenciáig* [From the Sarajevo Outrage to the Potsdam Conference]. Budapest: Magyar Szemle Alapítvány, 1999.

Hillgruber, Andreas. *Hitlers Strategie. Politik und Kriegsführung 1940– 1941*. Frankfurt am Main: Bernard & Graefe Verlag für Wehrwesen, 1965.

Hitler, Adolf. *Hitlers Weisungen für die Kriegsführung. Dokumente des Oberkommandos der Wehrmacht*. Frankfurt am Main: Walther Hubatsch, 1962.

Horthy, Miklós. *Horthy Miklós titkos iratai* [The Secret Papers of Miklós Horthy]. Edited by Miklós Szinai and László Szűcs. Budapest: Kossuth Könyvkiadó, 1962.

Horthy, Miklós. *Emlékirataim* [My Memoirs]. Budapest: Európa Kiadó, 1990.

Horthy, Miklós. *Horthy Miklós dokumentumok tükrében* [Miklós Horthy as Reflected in Documents]. Edited by Éva H. Haraszti. Budapest: Balassi Kiadó, 1993.

Hóry, András. *Bukaresttől Varsóig* [From Bucharest to Warsaw]. Edited by Pál Pritz, Budapest: Gondolat Kiadó, 1987.

Hungary. Archives of the Ministry of the Interior. The Bárdossy Trial.

Hungary. National Archives. Ministry of Foreign Affairs, Reserved Political Papers. K 64.

Hungary. National Archives. Press Archives. K 428.

Hungary. National Archives, Szent-Iványi Kézirat [Szent-Iványi Manuscript]. "Csonka-Magyarország külpolitikája 1919 júniusától 1944. március 19-ig" [The Foreign Policy of Hungary from June 1919 to March 19, 1944]. K 63.

Hungary. Parliament. House of Representatives. *Napló* [Journal]. Budapest: Athenaeum, 1939–1942.

Hungary. Parliament. Upper House. *Napló* [Journal]. Budapest: Athenaeum, 1939–1942.

Illyés, Gyula. *Naplójegyzetek* [Diary Notes]. Vol. 1, 1929–1945. Edited by Gyuláné Illyés. Budapest: Szépirodalmi Könyvkiadó, 1986.

Jaszovszky, László. *Bűnös volt-e Bárdossy László*. Budapest: Püski, 1996.

Juhász, Gyula. *Hungarian Foreign Policy 1919–1945*. Budapest: Akadémiai Kiadó, 1979.

Juhász, Gyula. *A Teleki kormány külpolitikája 1939–1941* [Foreign Policy of the Teleki Government]. Budapest, Kossuth Könyvkiadó, 1964.

Karsai, Elek. *Itél a nép* [The People Judge]. Budapest: Kossuth Könyvkiadó, 1977.

Kádár, Gyula. *A Ludovikától Sopronkőhidáig* [From the Ludovika to Sopronkőhida]. Budapest: Magvető Kiadó,1978. 2 vols.

Kállay, Miklós. *Magyarország miniszterelnöke voltam 1942–1944* [I Was Hungary's Prime Minister]. Budapest: Európa Kiadó,1991.

Kun, József. "A m. kir. Honvédség fővezérségéhez beosztott német tábornok naplója" [War Diary of the German General Assigned to the High Command of the Royal Hungarian Army]. *Századok* 99, no. 6 (1965): 1231–1246.

L. Nagy, Zsuzsa. *Bethlen liberális ellenzéke. A liberális polgári pártok 1919–1931* [Bethlen's Liberal Opposition. The Liberal Bourgeois Parties 1919–1931]. Budapest: Akadémiai Kiadó, 1980.

Lukács John. *The Hitler in History*. New York: Vintage Books, 1997.

Lukács, Tibor Zs. "Magyarország és az 1933-as négyhatalmi paktum" [Hungary and the Four-Power Pact of 1933]. PhD diss., Eötvös Loránd University, 2000.

Macartney, C. A. *October Fifteenth. A History of Modern Hungary 1927–1945*. 2 vols. Edinburgh: Edinburgh University Press, 1956–1957.

Major, Ákos. *Népbíráskodás, forradalmi törvényesség. Egy népbíró visszaemlékezései* [People's Courts, Revolutionary Legality. Memoirs of a Judge of the People's Court]. Edited by Tibor Zinner. Budapest: Minerva Kiadó, 1988.

Martin, Bernd. *Friedensinitiativen und Machtpolitik im Zweiten Weltkrieg 1939–1942*. Düsseldorf: Droste Verlag, 1976.

Nagy, Vince. *Októbertől októberig* [From October to October]. Budapest: Európa Kiadó, 1991.

Náray, Antal. *Náray Antal visszaemlékezése 1945* [Memoirs of Antal Náray, 1945]. Edited by Sándor Szakály. Budapest: Zrínyi Kiadó, 1988.

Ormos, Mária. *From Padua to the Trianon 1918–1920*. Boulder, CO: Social Science Monographs, 1990.

Ormos, Mária. *Egy magyar médiavezér: Kozma Miklós* [A Hungarian Media Leader: Miklós Kozma]. Budapest: PolgArt Kiadó, 2000.

Ormos, Mária. *Hitler.* 2nd edition. Budapest: Polgár Kiadó, 1997.

Pastor, Peter, ed. *A moszkvai magyar követség jelentései 1935–1941* [Reports of the Hungarian Legation in Moscow 1935–1941]. Budapest: Századvég Kiadó, 1992.

Perjés, Géza. "Bárdossy László és pere" [László Bárdossy and His Trial]. *Hadtörténelmi Közlemények* 113, no. 4 (2000): 771–840.

Póth, Piroska. "Rákosi Mátyás előadása Moszkvában 1945 júniusában" [Mátyás Rákosi's lecture in Moscow in June 1945]. *Múltunk* 44, no. 4, (1999): 199–223.

Pritz, Pál. *Bárdossy László.* Budapest: Elektra Kiadóház, 2001.

Pritz, Pál. "A kieli találkozó (forráskritikai tanulmány)" [The Meeting at Kiel (Internal Criticism of a Primary Source)]. In Pál Pritz, *Magyar diplomácia a két háború között* [Interwar Hungarian Diplomacy] Budapest: Magyar Történelmi Társulat, 1995.

Ránki, György. *Emlékiaratok és a valóság Magyarország második világháborús szerepéről* [Memoirs and Truth about Hungary's Role in World War II]. Budapest: Kossuth Könyvkiadó, 1964.

Ránki, György, ed. *Hitler 98 tárgyalása* [Hitler's 98 Negotiations]. Budapest: Magvető Kiadó, 1993.

Ránki, György, Ervin Pamlényi, Loránt Tilkovszky, and Gyula Juhász, eds. *Wilhelmstrasse és Magyarország. Német diplomáciai iratok Magyarországról 1933–1944* [Wilhelmstrasse and Hungary. German Diplomatic Papers About Hungary]. Budapest: Kossuth Könyvkiadó, 1968.

Romsics, Ignác. *The Dismantling of Historic Hungary: The Peace Treaty of Trianon, 1920.* Boulder, CO: Social Science Monographs, 2002.

Romsics, Ignác. *István Bethlen: A Great Conservative Statesman of Hungary, 1874–1946.* Boulder, CO: Social Science Monographs, 1993.

Romsics, Ignác. *Helyünk és sorsunk a Duna-medencében* [Our Place and Fate in the Danube Basin]. Budapest: Osiris Kiadó, 1996.

Sajti, Enikő A. *Délvidék. 1941–1944* [Historic Southern Hungary]. Budapest: Kossuth Könyvkiadó, 1987.

Sakmyster, Thomas. *Hungary's Admiral on Herseback. Miklós Horthy, 1918–1944.* Boulder, CO: Social Science Monographs, 1994.

Serédi, Jusztinian. *Serédi Jusztinian hercegprímás feljegyzései 1941–1944* [Jottings of Cardinal-Primate Justinian Serédi 1941–1944]. Edited by Sándor Orbán and István Vida. Budapest: Zrinyi Kiadó, 1990.

Sontag, Raymond James, and James Stuart Beddie. *Nazi-Soviet Relations 1939–1941. Documents from the Archives of the German Foreign Office*. Washington: Department of State, 1948.

Szálasi, Ferenc. *"Szálasi naplója": a nyilasmozgalom a II. világháború idején* ["Szálasi's Diary": The Arrow Cross Movement at the Time of World War II]. Edited by Elek Karsai. Budapest: Kossuth Könyvkiadó, 1978.

Szegedy-Maszák, Aladár. *Az ember ősszel visszanéz. Egy volt magyar diplomata emlékirataiból* [Looking Back in the Autumn. Selections from the Recollections of a Former Hungarian Diplomat]. Edited by László Csorba. Budapest: Európa Kiadó, 1996.

Teleki, Éva. *Nyilas uralom Magyarországon* [The Arrow Cross Rule in Hungary]. Budapest: Kossuth Könyvkiadó, 1974.

Tilkovszky, Loránt. *Nemzetiségi politika Magyarországon a 20. században* [Nationality Policies in Hungary in the Twentieth Century]. Debrecen: Csokonai Kiadó, 1998.

Ullein-Reviczky, Antal. *Német háború—orosz béke* [German War-Russian Peace] Budapest: Európa Kiadó, 1993.

Vigh, Károly. "Bajcsy-Zsilinszky Endre és a 'hideg napok'" [Endre Bajcsy-Zsilinszky and the "Cold Days"]. *Történelmi Szemle* 11, nos. 1–2 (1968): 81–103.

Weizsäcker, Ernst von. *Die Weizsäcker-Papiere, 1933–1950*. Berlin: Propyläen, 1974.

Wesselényi, Miklós. *Szózat a Magyar és a szláv nemzetiség ügyében* [Declaration in the Case of the Hungarian and Slav Nations]. Kolozsvár: Minerva, 1944.

Zinner, Tibor, and Péter Róna. *Szálasiék bilincsben* [The Szálasi Gang in Shackles]. 2 vols. Budapest: Lapkiadó Vállalat, 1986.

Zsigmond, László, ed. *Diplomáciai iratok Magyarország külpolitikájához 1936–1945* [Diplomatic Papers of Hungarian Foreign Policy 1936–1945], vol. 3, *Magyarország külpolitikája 1938–1939* [Hungarian Foreign Policy 1938–1939]. Edited by Magda Ádám. Budapest: Akadémiai Kiadó, 1970.

Zsigmond, László, ed. *Diplomáciai iratok Magyarország külpolitikájá-*

hoz 1936–1945 [Diplomatic Papers of Hungarian Foreign Policy 1936–1945], vol. 5, *Magyarország külpolitikája a nyugati hadjárattól a Szovjetunió megtámadásáig 1940–1941* [Hungarian Foreign Policy from the Western Campaign to the Attack on the Soviet Union]. Edited by Gyula Juhász. Budapest: Akadémiai Kiadó, 1982.

MAP

Hungary's Boundaries 1914–1945

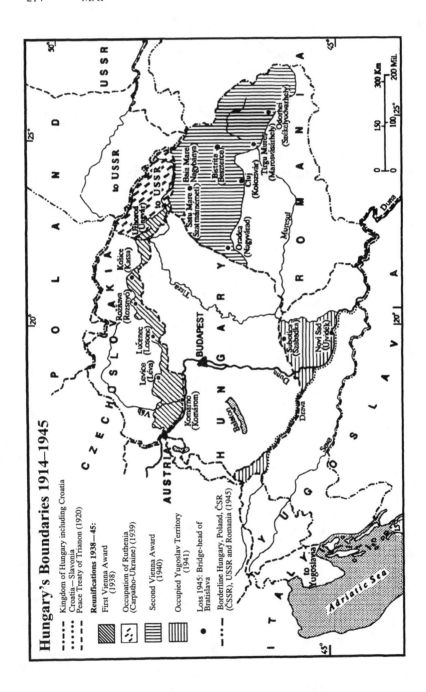

Hungary's Boundaries 1914–1945

- - - - - - Kingdom of Hungary including Croatia
· · · · · · Croatia—Slavonia
- · - · - Peace Treaty of Trianon (1920)

Reunifications 1938—45:

First Vienna Award
(1938)

Occupation of Ruthenia
(Carpatho-Ukraine) (1939)

Second Vienna Award
(1940)

Occupied Yugoslav Territory
(1941)

· Loss 1945: Bridge-head of
Bratislava

- · - · - Borderline Hungary, Poland, ČSR
(ČSSR), USSR and Romania (1945)

INDEX

ABOUT THE AUTHOR

PÁL PRITZ is professor of history at Eötvös Loránd University in Budapest. His specialty is diplomatic history. He is the author of a number of monographs and essays published in Hungarian.

BOOKS PUBLISHED BY THE CENTER FOR HUNGARIAN STUDIES AND PUBLICATIONS

CHSP Hungarian Authors Series:

No. 1.   *False Tsars*. Gyula Szvák. 2000.

No. 2.   *Book of the Sun*. Marcell Jankovics. 2001.

No. 3.   *The Dismantling of Historic Hungary: The Peace Treaty of Trianon, 1920*. Ignác Romsics. 2002.

CHSP Hungarian Studies Series:

No. 1.   *Emperor Francis Joseph, King of the Hungarians*. András Gerő. 2001.

No. 2.   *Global Monetary Regime and National Central Banking. The Case of Hungary, 1921–1929*. György Péteri. 2002.

No. 3.   *Hungarian-Italian Relations in the Shadow of Hitler's Germany, 1933–1940*. György Réti. 2003.

No. 4.   *The War Crimes Trial of Hungarian Prime Minister László Bárdossy*. Pál Pritz. 2004.